HENRY MOORE

Adina Kamien-Kazhdan

The Israel Museum, Jerusalem

The Israel Museum, Jerusalem

Focus on the Collection: Henry Moore
Summer 2004 – Winter 2005
Rena (Fisch) and Robert Lewin Gallery,
Hildegard and Simon Rothschild Foundation
(Switzerland) Gallery,
Nathan Cummings 20th Century Art Building

Exhibition curator: Adina Kamien-Kazhdan
Exhibition design: Rivka Myers and Shirly Yahalomi

Catalogue design: Tirtsa Barri
Photographs: © The Israel Museum, Jerusalem,
by Avshalom Avital
© The Henry Moore Foundation (pp. 19, 20 [right], 21, 22)
© Tel Aviv Museum of Art, by Avraham Hay (p. 57)

Color separations, printing, and binding:
Keter Enterprises Ltd., Jerusalem

All works by Henry Moore © The Henry Moore
Foundation, Much Hadham, Hertfordshire, England

Catalogue no. 493
ISBN 965 278 304 8

The exhibition and publication were made possible
by a donation in honor of the memory of Benjamin Miller

On the cover:
Three Piece Sculpture: Vertebrae (detail)
Cat. no. 73, p. 36; see photograph
on pp. 46–47 in the Hebrew section

All works are from the Israel Museum collection unless
otherwise indicated

All measurements are given as height preceding width
preceding depth

Illustrations in the Hebrew section are numbered
according to the Catalogue of Works (p. 30)

CGM, HMF, and LH refer to catalogue raisonné numbers;
see References, p. 85 (Hebrew section). These numbers
are given in the Catalogue of Works, following the
Museum's registration number

Director's Foreword   5

Acknowledgments   6

Introduction   7

Moore in Jerusalem   10

Unraveling Moore's Enigma   13

Family Groups   16

Reclining Figures   19

Seated Figures   21

Upright Figures   23

Heads in Transformation   24

Shelter Drawings   26

On Observation and Imagination: 28
Moore's Albums

Catalogue of Works in the Collection   30

References   85 (in the Hebrew section)

Director's Foreword

Since the Israel Museum's founding in 1965, its collections in the field of modern art have grown remarkably, thanks to the generosity of many donors. As these holdings have expanded, we have been blessed with the opportunity to amass important groups of works by single artists, with the result that the Museum now has exceptional concentrations of the oeuvre of such artists as Auguste Rodin, Pablo Picasso, Jean Arp, Jean Dubuffet, and Jacob Epstein.

The *Focus on the Collection* series, inaugurated by Senior Curator of Modern Art Stephanie Rachum, highlights the Museum's holdings of individual artists, as an ensemble and in singular depth. Because these works generally cover a range of mediums and periods, the series aims for unifying presentations, which emphasize each artist's creative development, sources of inspiration, and significance for modern art. Exhibitions in the series are mounted on an annual basis, each focusing on a major artist while highlighting the Museum's evolving strengths.

The sixth in the Modern Art Department's *Focus on the Collection* series is dedicated to Henry Moore, and the present publication offers a comprehensive look at the Museum's holdings of works by this groundbreaking artist. The Israel Museum owes the richness of its Moore collection to many generous donors but first and foremost to Charlotte Bergman, who over the years gifted many works by the artist to the Museum, and, upon her death in July 2002, bequeathed us her entire art collection, including some fifty examples of Moore's achievement. We are also deeply grateful to the sponsor of the exhibition and catalogue for her generous anonymous donation in honor of the memory of Benjamin Miller and acknowledge the scholarship and professionalism of Associate Curator of Modern Art Adina Kamien-Kazhdan, in the preparation of the exhibition and this publication.

James S. Snyder
Anne and Jerome Fisher Director

Acknowledgments

This artistic venture was realized through the collaboration of many individuals. My deepest gratitude to the sponsor of the exhibition and catalogue for her intense interest and generous support of the Focus on the Collection series in honor of the memory of Benjamin Miller. I would also like to thank the Henry Moore Foundation, Much Hadham, and particularly Martin Davis and Michael Phipps, for generously sharing their expertise and archival material.

My appreciation goes to Stephanie Rachum, David Rockefeller Senior Curator of Modern Art, for her ongoing support of this project. I am grateful to catalogue designer Tirtsa Barri and exhibition designers Rivka Myers and Shirly Yahalomi for their creative contributions. Special thanks to rigorous and insightful editor Revital Mazover. I would like to thank Yael Golan of the Publications Department and department head Nirit Zur. Yigal Zalmona, Suzanne Landau, Tallay Ornan, Tami Michaeli, and Anna Barber, members of the Editorial Committee, offered important comments and suggestions. Of invaluable assistance in the preparation of this project were volunteers Bernice Wigder, Yael Eshel, Juliana Ochs, Abigail Zausmer, Shai Davis, Dassi Sigel, and Keren Williams. Thanks to Michael Maggen, Marina Rassovsky, Ruchi Baharad, Irit Lev, and particularly Ludmila Hodorkovsky for their artful conservation work. Timor Cohen, Rory Hooper, and Michael Barcik beautifully prepared the prints and drawings for exhibition. Dalia Angel faithfully supervised the budget of this project, and Tal Elispor assisted with exhibition loans. I would like to acknowledge the efforts of project coordinator Raphael Radovan; the head of the Museum's audio-visual systems, Menachem Amin; and the its Technical Services Department – Moris Lasry, Artur Avakov, Alex Markov, Raanan Perry, Yaniv Cohen, Ari Porat, and Yuval Benjamin, headed by Pesach Ruder. I am indebted to Avshalom Avital, who produced splendid photographs of Moore's works; Amalya Keshet, head of the Visual Resources Department; and Einat Arif-Galanti and Ziva Haller for arranging copyright matters and other assistance.

Finally, I would like to recognize the lenders to the exhibition for sharing their works of art, enabling others to discover the multiple facets of Henry Moore's oeuvre.

Adina Kamien-Kazhdan
Associate Curator
The Stella Fischbach Department of Modern Art

Introduction

One of the twentieth century's most important sculptors, Henry Moore enjoyed staggering success in his lifetime. Focusing on the human figure, Moore demonstrates great humanism and expresses profound ideas and emotions through organic form. He sculpted with intense discipline, using form in what he called "its full spatial completeness."[1] Drawing on diverse cultures, his work resonates with the art of the past. His full-bodied, earthbound female figures suggest the contours of mountains, valleys, cliffs, and caves; embodying a "prehuman or subhuman vitalism,"[2] they reflect the artist's fascination with nature and its mysteries.

Born in 1898, Henry Spencer Moore was raised in the small industrial town of Castleford, Yorkshire. At age eleven, while in Sunday school, Moore learned about Michelangelo and decided to become a sculptor himself. The following year, he won a scholarship to the local secondary school and began studying drawing and pottery. After graduation, Moore taught elementary school. A year later, in 1917, he left for London to join the Civil Service Rifles; trained as a machine-gunner, he was sent to France. Gassed in the Battle of Cambrai, he returned to England to convalesce.

In 1920 Moore became the first student in the Leeds School of Art's new sculpture department. Until now, his exposure to original works of art had been minimal. In Leeds, however, he enjoyed access to the art collection of the vice-chancellor of Leeds University, which included works by Cézanne, Gauguin, Matisse, and Kandinsky as well as African pieces. In 1921 Moore chanced upon Roger Fry's *Vision and Design* (1920), a book whose celebration of non-western sculpture shaped the artist's early work.

That year, Moore moved to London to study sculpture at the Royal College of Art, where he had received a scholarship. During weekly visits to the British Museum, he sketched Paleolithic fertility goddesses, Cycladic and Egyptian figures, Assyrian reliefs, African and Oceanic wood carvings, and pre-Columbian and North American objects. Modernism and its preoccupation with non-western art freed him from the subjects and aesthetic of classical and Renaissance art and academic tradition.[3] Moore befriended the controversial sculptor Jacob Epstein, who bought some of his pieces and shared his collection of Egyptian and primitive art. Like Britain's pioneers of direct carving – Epstein, Henri Gaudier-Brzeska, and Eric Gill – Moore believed passionately in "truth to materials" and in the carver's symbiotic relationship with tool and material. Almost all his sculptures of the 1920s and 1930s were inspired by pre-Columbian stone carving.

Moore made his first trip to Paris in 1923, where he was deeply impressed by the work of Cézanne, especially the *Grandes Baigneuses*. In 1924, Moore was appointed sculpture instructor at the Royal College. Awarded a travel scholarship, he spent half of 1925 visiting museums and churches in France and Italy, greatly admiring the frescos of Giotto and Masaccio and the late work of Michelangelo. Back in Britain, Moore found it difficult to escape their influence and maintain his basis in non-western art. He began studying bones at the Natural History Museum and English stone at the Geological Museum. Hence the interplay of natural forms and the human figure throughout his mature work.

In 1928 Moore held his first solo exhibition, at the Warren Gallery in London. On Epstein's recommendation, Moore landed his first public commission, *West Wind* (1928–29), a relief sculpture for the façade of the London Underground Railway headquarters. Influential art critic Herbert Read became

---

1   James, *Moore on Sculpture*, p. 62.
2   Pevsner, "Thoughts on Moore," in Kosinsky, *Sculpting the 20th Century*, p. 22.
3   Ibid.

his friend and supporter. In 1929 Moore married Irina Radetsky, a student of painting at the Royal College, whom he sketched repeatedly. He also began his most important sculpture of the decade, *Reclining Figure*, carved in brown Hornton stone and inspired by depictions of the Toltec-Mayan warrior-altar Chacmool. In 1930, he joined the avant-garde 7 and 5 Society and exhibited in the British Pavilion at the Venice Biennale. Moore left the Royal College in 1931 to head the new sculpture department at the Chelsea School of Art, where he taught until the outbreak of war in 1939.

Moore's sculpture of the 1930s reflects contemporary developments in Paris, particularly the work of Picasso, Hans Arp, and Alberto Giacometti. Biomorphic abstractions are pierced with holes, and anatomy is distorted or freely rearranged, although the human element is always present. Visiting Paris in 1933, Moore met the sculptors Giacometti, Jacques Lipchitz, and Ossip Zadkine. He then joined Unit One, a group of British avant-garde painters, sculptors, and architects. Living in Hampstead, an artists' colony in North London, Moore collaborated with neighbors Barbara Hepworth and Ben Nicholson.

Around 1935, Moore began making small terracotta or plaster maquettes to be realized as larger-scale sculptures. In the late 1930s, he abandoned a doctrinaire belief in direct carving, preferring bronze casting. Even in this medium, rather than building up his model in clay or soft plaster, he usually carved it in hardened plaster, thus remaining essentially a carver yet working in a more malleable material than stone or wood. The versatility of bronze and its inherent modeling and enlarging procedures, liberated the artist from his early modernism.[4] Bronze's durability also enabled him to explore his conviction that "A hole can itself have as much shape-meaning as a solid mass."[5]

In 1940, Moore began his famous series of Shelter Drawings, showing Londoners taking refuge from the Blitz on Underground station platforms. These drawings led to his appointment as an Official War Artist. After Moore's studio was damaged in a bombing, he moved to Hoglands, a former farmhouse at Perry Green, in Hertfordshire, north of London. Upon completing the Shelter Drawings in 1941, Moore visited the Wheldale Colliery in his native Castleford, where he sketched miners at work. His art during and after the war reflected his growing social consciousness, which prompted a reassessment of his abstract experiments of the 1930s and the introduction of a more accessible figuration.[6]

Newly considered more mainstream than radical modernist, Moore was commissioned to create *Madonna and Child* (1943–44) for St. Matthew's Church, Northampton, and *Family Group* (1954–55) in Harlow New Town, both of which came to symbolize family values in a postwar Britain eager to rebuild and rejoice in its survival.[7] Endorsed by the British Council, he became England's preeminent artist. His personal life also flourished with the birth of his and Irina's only child, Mary, in 1946. Mary's arrival revitalized Moore's depictions of mother and child, and his many drawings of Irina nursing the baby reflect his pleasure in family life.

In 1946, New York's Museum of Modern Art mounted a major Moore retrospective, and in 1948 his global career was further launched when he won the International Prize for Sculpture at the Venice Biennale. One of the artist's most prestigious public commissions was the massive, marble *Reclining Figure* (1958) outside the UNESCO building in Paris.

The bronze *Reclining Figure* of 1951, commissioned by the Arts Council for the Festival of Britain, was a landmark in Moore's development. Previously the holes in his sculptures were features in

---

4   Kosinsky, *Sculpting the 20th Century*, p. 23.
5   Wilkinson, *Moore: Writings and Conversations*, p. 196.
6   Cohen, "Who's Afraid of Moore?" p. 264.
7   Stallabrass, "Mother and Child"; Garlake, *New Art, New World*.

themselves, but here space and form were inseparable.[8] His work became less frontal and more three-dimensional. The reclining figure and the mother and child remained his dominant motifs, while many of his sculptures were inspired by natural forms such as driftwood, bones, shells, pebbles, and flint stones, which Moore collected in his studio.

During the 1960s and 1970s, financial success allowed Moore to work on a grander scale. Between 1959 and 1964, he created a series of two- and three-piece reclining figures, culminating in the largest, the bronze *Reclining Figure* (1963–65) commissioned by Lincoln Center, in New York. The artist felt that these gigantic sculptures belonged in nature, seen against the expansive sky.

Moore devoted his last fifteen years increasingly to drawing. He had made his first prints in 1931 and illustrated a French translation of Goethe's *Prometheus* in 1950, but printmaking became a significant part of his oeuvre only with such illustrated portfolios as *Elephant Skull* (1969), *Stonehenge* (1973), *Auden Poems, Moore Lithographs* (1974), and *Sheep Portfolios* (1972 and 1974).

Throughout the second half of his life, Moore was a cultural icon and celebrity. The 1970s saw many major exhibitions of his work, the most monumental in 1972 at the Forte di Belvedere, overlooking Florence. In 1977, the Henry Moore Foundation was established at Much Hadham, and the following year he presented thirty-six sculptures to London's Tate Gallery. Immensely prolific, Moore completed almost a thousand works before his death in 1986. Including his bronzes, which each exist in several casts, his creative output reaches 6,000. These works fill museums and plazas around the world.[9]

Moore's enormous fame incensed critics and artists. The *New Aspects of British Sculpture* exhibition at the 1952 Venice Biennale represented a new generation of British sculptors dubbed the "Geometry of Fear" group, including Kenneth Armitage, Lynn Chadwick, Eduardo Paolozzi, Reg Butler, Robert Adams, and Bernard Meadows. Employing industrial skills and sinewy materials, their jagged, disturbing images encapsulated despair, defiance, and angst as well as a conscious departure from Moore's massive, rounded forms. In 1960, Anthony Caro, who had been Moore's assistant, asserted that he and other upcoming sculptors abhorred "the idea of a father-figure" and that "when you try to think clearly about Henry Moore you are deafened by the applause."[10] Yet Caro acknowledged that Moore had given the younger generation self-confidence and made an important contribution to the conception of public art. In the 1970s, avant-garde critics Rosalind Krauss and Clement Greenberg abandoned Moore, branding his work populist and conservative.[11]

Moore lacked formal and thematic followers, probably because "he developed his personal language so fully that anyone else who began to speak it was trapped in mimicry."[12] Young sculptors therefore defined themselves in opposition to him. In the 1960s, Bruce Nauman created three related series of works dealing with this Oedipal conflict, including his witty *Seated Storage Capsule for H. M.* (1966). "Moore had been the dominant presence in British art for years," Nauman explained. "I figured the younger sculptors would need him someday, so I came up with the idea for a storage capsule."[13] Nevertheless, Moore's impact on modern British sculptors such as Caro, Anish Kapoor, Richard Deacon, and Tony Cragg is evident in their innovative experiments with form and void, respectful manipulation of materials,

---

8   Hedgecoe, *Moore*, p. 188.
9   "From a leftist perspective, the international export of Moore became emblematic of a kind of new colonialism. . . . More serious than the charges of overeditioning and inflation of scale is the charge of repetitiveness." Cohen, "Who's Afraid of Moore?" pp. 265–66.
10   Caro, "Master Sculptor," p. 21.
11   Ibid., pp. 21–23.
12   Kosinsky, *Sculpting the 20th Century*, p. 266.
13   Van Bruggen, *Nauman*, p. 110.

dialogue with nature, and interaction with their audience.[14]

Though Moore perceived himself as driven by an inexplicable creative force, his writings and recorded conversations offer sensitive, incisive reflections on his sculpture and on art in general. Moore demanded that sculpture have intrinsic energy: "If a work of sculpture has its own life and form, it will be alive and expansive, seeming larger than the stone or wood from which it is carved. It should always give the impression . . . of having grown organically, created by pressure from within."[15] Many of his creations indeed generate this energy, revealing the sculptor's great integrity and imagination.

The Israel Museum's collection includes seventy-nine works by Moore the sculptor, draughtsman, and printmaker. This exhibition and catalogue highlight his central themes, including reclining, seated, and upright figures, heads, and family groups, as well as his albums and drawings of wartime shelters. The opening essay attempts to decipher Moore's wrapped and tied objects, exploring his notion of struggle. As for his drawings, prints, maquettes, and large-scale bronze sculptures, all aspire to penetrate the surface of life and portray fundamental emotions.

---

14   Kosinsky, *Sculpting the 20th Century*, pp. 28–29.
15   James, *Moore on Sculpture*, p. 58.

Moore in Jerusalem
A Tribute to Charlotte Bergman

The uniqueness of the Israel Museum's Henry Moore collection results from the multiple inter-connections between the Museum, the artist, and his principal supporters and collectors. The Museum owes the richness of its Moore collection to many generous donors, first and foremost Charlotte Bergman. Upon her death in July 2002, Mrs. Bergman bequeathed her entire art collection to the Museum, including close to fifty drawings and sculptures by Moore. This exhibition and catalogue celebrate her friendship with Moore and honor her memory.

Moore's association with the Israel Museum began in the formative years of its forerunner, The Jewish National Museum Bezalel. Already in 1944, with the cooperation of the British Council in Jerusalem, Prof. Mordechai Narkiss, director and curator of Bezalel, incorporated five drawings by Moore into an exhibition of *English Water Colours and Drawings, Sixteenth to Twentieth Century*. This exhibit demonstrated Narkiss's determination to keep art alive in Palestine even during World War II, when loans from abroad were almost impossible. Twelve years later, Bezalel devoted an entire exhibition to Moore, displaying four bronzes and thirty-one photographs and reproductions of sculptures and drawings. The British Council arranged the show with the assistance of William Wilson, British consul general in Jerusalem. Wilson subsequently asked the artist to send Narkiss an inscribed copy of a book on Moore's art. In a moving letter from his sickbed, Narkiss writes in February 1957 that the volume contributed to his recovery: "It is a pity there are not enough Henry Moores in the world in order to restore my health completely."

In 1965, Teddy Kollek, then chairman of the Israel Museum board of directors, and Karl Katz, chief curator of Bezalel, invited Moore to the inauguration of the Israel Museum in Jerusalem, though this visit did not materialize. Four months later, an indoor pavilion in the Billy Rose Art Garden was dedicated to more than forty of his sculptures and drawings – all on loan from Mrs. Bergman, one of the Museum's founders and honorary fellows.

As early as 1934, even before Moore gained fame, Charlotte and Louis Bergman began acquiring his works. Though the Bergmans lived in the United States since the outbreak of World War II, they enjoyed a close relationship with Moore, stopping off to visit him in England during their frequent trips to Europe. The works the couple amassed over thirty-five years, purchased directly from the artist, represent a cross-section of his drawings, maquettes, and medium-scale sculptures. The Bergmans' drawing collection in particular was among the finest in private hands.

In a correspondence with Moore that spanned four decades, Mrs. Bergman often enthused about his works. "Most of 'my' Moores are home and I arranged a complete Moore room which looks fabulous!" she wrote in 1964. "Hope you see it soon one day." Moore in turn reported on his projects, exhibitions, and daily life. Mrs. Bergman accumulated an extensive library on the artist, collected related clippings, and encouraged friends to acquire his works. In 1962, she introduced him to Donald Brewer, director of the Art Center in La Jolla, California, which led to a display of one hundred works by Moore there in 1963.

The first Moore sculpture Mrs. Bergman donated to Israel was the large-scale *Draped Seated Woman* (p. 55),* unveiled at the Givat Ram campus of the Hebrew University in Jerusalem in November 1962.[1] *The Jerusalem Post* reported that the sculpture "was presented by an art lover and collector in the U.S. who wishes to remain anonymous, in memory of the late Louis Bergman, of London and New York, a man who was devoted to art and to the aim of making it accessible to the younger generation." Mrs. Bergman believed that "young people should be exposed to good art,

even if they don't like it. And the young people in Israel should get the best in the world."[2] Bergman moved from New York to Jerusalem in the 1960s and built her home on the grounds of the Museum. Until age ninety-eight, she lived amidst her art collection, which included important works by Braque, Dufy, Rouault, Maillol, and Picasso. Moore's maquettes and drawings graced her bedroom (p. 13).

Other patrons and friends of Moore have also been major supporters of the Israel Museum. The Henry Moore Sculpture Center at the Art Gallery of Ontario – the world's largest public repository of his work – was established largely by Sam and Ayala Zacks. Ayala Zacks has enriched the Israel Museum with *Woman* (p. 50), the most important Moore sculpture in the Zacks Collection.

In 1966, the Museum exhibited sixty-eight of Moore's finest works. Organized by the British Council in London, the show later moved to the Tel Aviv Museum of Art. Dr. Willem Sandberg, advisor to the Israel Museum, wrote in the catalogue in the free-verse style all his own:

> the strong simplicity
> of his large forms
> open and closed at the time
> always in intimate relations with nature
> reclining shapes like mountains
> human limbs apart like pieces of rock
> uprising warnings like lifted forefingers
> express a humanity
> rare in our time.

Moore came to Israel for the exhibit. At the Museum, he photographed his sculptures in the Billy Rose Art Garden (p. 11) and held a workshop in the Youth Wing. A wonderful photograph (p. 14) shows the artist with a group of children,

---

*   All pages indicated refer to illustrations in the Hebrew section of this publication

1   Bergman agreed with Moore that a basalt base be carved in Israel according to the sculptor's instructions.

2   Bergman, quoted in Hebrew University press release.

shaping a piece of clay. He later wrote Sandberg: "I am very pleased now that I came – I had no idea before coming what it was like at all. I enjoyed being with you in Jerusalem very much indeed. . . . I have just had some of the colour photographs I took returned from the photographers, and the brightness and sunshine is unbelievable."

Between 1965 and 1972, three outstanding, large-scale sculptures by Moore became part of the Billy Rose Art Garden. The first, *Upright Motive No. 7* (p. 63), was at first lent by the Marlborough Gallery London in 1965. In 1969, this loan became a gift thanks to Moore and the British Friends of the Art Museums of Israel, led by Lord Arnold Goodman and Doris Morrison. In 1967, the second piece, *Reclining Figure: External Form* (p. 38), was donated by Celeste and Joel Starrels of Chicago. (P. 15 shows Isamu Noguchi, designer of the garden, leaning on this sculpture.)

The third sculpture, *Three Piece Sculpture: Vertebrae* (pp. 46–47), came through the good offices of Sir Philip Hendy, the Museum's second advisor. Writing to Moore in 1968, Hendy stated that his chief acquisition project was "to get three good, large Henry Moores for the sculpture garden. All in all, it's the best site of its kind (museum) that I know. The hills and olive trees are marvelous; so are the rocks and the light." The artist promised to help however he could.[3] In 1972, Moore and the British Friends donated *Vertebrae*, a monumental work cast by Hermann Noack in Berlin.

The placement of *Vertebrae* was a difficult matter. Moore advised Hendy to experiment with polystyrene models in order to find the best location for the work. Hendy wrote: "The site for the triplets[4] is central to the whole garden, which will seem to radiate from it. . . . Teddy Kollek came out from his Town Hall, and was much impressed." Moore saw photographs of the mock-up positioned in the garden and wrote Hendy: "It looks to me a splendid position you have chosen for it, and perfect in scale." The artist planned to come to Israel with his wife, Irina, and daughter, Mary, for the unveiling of the sculpture on December 1, 1972. Stormy seas delayed the sculpture's arrival, however, so the Moores canceled their trip. By the time the bronze arrived from the foundry, Hendy had returned to Oxford. So James Sweeney, the Museum's third advisor, finalized the placement of *Vertebrae*, moving it up the incline to be seen against the sky. (P. 15 shows Sweeney with one of the sculpture's three units.)[5]

In 1973, Moore gifted the Israel Museum with *Relief No. 1* (p. 45) and was made a Museum patron.[6] That year saw two other important donations of works by the artist: *Working Model for Three Way Piece No. 2: Archer* (p. 48); and *Elephant Skull Album* (p. 79), which was exhibited in the fall of 1973. The current exhibition – the first devoted to Moore in thirty-one years – brings together all the Museum's holdings of the artist's work: sculptures, maquettes, drawings, and prints. It demonstrates the extraordinary sixty-year relationship between Moore, his patrons, and the Israel Museum.

---

3   During Hendy's visit with Moore that year, the artist and his wife donated a painting by Ceri Richards, *La Cathedrale Engloutie*, to the Museum.

4   Referring to the three-unit *Vertebrae*.

5   While Hendy and Sandberg had situated the dummy in the center of the garden, Sweeney and Noack thought *Vertebrae* deserved a higher pedestal in order to stand out against the sky. Noguchi proposed a separate area in the garden for the sculpture. Moore supported Hendy's placement, with a raised pedestal, and did not want the piece "tucked away in a corner." Finally, in April 1973, *Vertebrae* was moved up the incline.

6   In October 1972, Golda Meir had asked Moore to contribute to a portfolio of "original works by the most distinguished artists of our time," marking the twenty-fifth anniversary of the State of Israel. According to the rules governing the new Henry Moore Foundation, however, he could no longer part with a complete series of prints. In 1983, the artist received an honorary doctorate from Tel Aviv University. Moore also supported the Painters and Sculptors League of the Kibbutz Artzi Federation and met with Israeli artists visiting England.

Unraveling Moore's Enigma

Mystery plays a large and enlivening part in our lives: not knowing but wanting to know, wondering and guessing, questioning and exploring. We are perpetually intrigued and fascinated by the unknown.

Henry Moore, 1974[1]

In 1942 Moore created his most famous pictorial composition,[2] *Crowd Looking at a Tied-up Object* (p. 17). The drawing depicts a group of people in an expansive, dream-like space looking up at a "veiled" or "white draped object."[3] Though the sky is dark, the time of day is indeterminate. Near the crowd are three stone formations recalling the artist's own reclining figures. The scene, and particularly the wrapped and bound object of observation, is extremely enigmatic. Alan Wilkinson traces the image to a photograph in Leo Frobenius's book on tribal art, *Kulturgeschichte Afrikas* (1933), in which Nupe tribesmen from northern Nigeria stand before two large, veiled, cultic dance costumes (p. 17).[4] Though Moore owned this book, the question remains: What is this crowd doing in a wasteland, and what is its object of fascination? To unravel the mystery, we must investigate Moore's images of wrapped and tied objects.

Crowd Looking at a Tied-up Object likely deals with Moore's World War II experience, the picture's barren landscape hinting at a deserted battlefield. Robert Melville asserts that the drawing "is obviously connected with his desire to resume his sculptural activities, which were suspended when he was engaged as a War Artist, and is conceived in terms of an enigmatic promise."[5] Since Moore could not cast his sculptures during the war, here he wraps and ties one of them, symbolically keeping it moist. The crowd awaits this masterwork.

Moore himself attributed his tied-up objects to his studies at the Royal College of Art, during which he kept clay moist by tying it in a damp cloth.[6] As a mature sculptor, Moore often covered his work, and in 1938, visiting his Hampstead studio with Roland Penrose, Max Ernst commented "on the impressive way in which the work stood around the studio, draped mysteriously in white sheets which had to be lifted from each piece by the sculptor and unveiled according to his discretion."[7] Ernst must have recalled Man Ray's Surrealist *Enigma of Isidore Ducasse* (1920), composed of a sewing machine wrapped in burlap and string. Moore may well have been acquainted with *Enigma*, which evokes similar mystery and expectations of unveiling.[8]

Moore "quoted" his *Crowd Looking at a Tied-up Object* in another drawing, *Girl Reading to a Woman and Child*, created in 1946 (p. 19). At first glance this is a domestic scene, as described in the title. However, the view seen through the window and framed by the curtains is Moore's own *Crowd*. The pairing of the enigmatic rite outdoors with an indoor scene focusing on female activities and the interaction of mother and child may well mean that the wrapped and tied object of observation also deals with the mother-child theme. Indoors mother and child embrace, while outdoors they constitute a hidden and bound monument of fascination. The artist's preoccupation with the mother-child relationship is thus mystified and magnified.

1   Moore, "Spatial and Pictorial Drawing."

2   Moore explained: "By pictorial drawing I mean setting the subject in space." Ibid.

3   Moore, notes on *Study for Crowd Looking at a Tied-up Object*, HMF 2045.

4   Wilkinson, *Drawings*, p. 42. Sir Kenneth Clark likewise reads the form as "a sort of fetish, the *objet de culte* of a primitive community." Clark, *Moore Drawings*, p. 120.

5   Melville, *Moore: Sculpture and Drawings*, p. 26. Melville continues: "The wrapping evidently hides a new sculpture by Henry Moore although the sculptor himself only knows that it is vertical and of a colossal size. One could now easily be convinced that the wrappings hide a version of one of the *Upright Motives* of 1955–56, the tallest and grandest of which is called *Glenkiln Cross*." Ibid., p. 27.

6   Wilkinson, *Drawings*, pp. 41–42.

7   Penrose, *Scrap Book*, p. 102. Susan Compton raises the possibility that the wrapped object in Moore's work originated in Ernst's remark. Compton, *Moore*, p. 254.

8   Similar awe attends a related drawing, *Figures in an Art Gallery* (1943, HMF 2161), in which spectators contemplate a Moore sculpture.

Two spectacular drawings in the Israel Museum's collection, bequeathed by Charlotte Bergman, shed more light on Moore's *Crowd Looking at a Tied-up Object* and allow us to partially unravel its enigma. *Wrapped Madonna and Child: Night Time* (p. 18) and *Wrapped Madonna and Child: Day Time* (p. 16), both created in 1950, also depict a wrapped and tied object.[9] While in both drawings the viewer can vaguely make out the form of a woman and a smaller figure – the Child – it is the titles of the works that spell out the subject matter. These titles, however, are just as enigmatic as the images. Why would Madonna and Child be wrapped and tied, and why at both times of day?

Regarding his sculpture *Madonna and Child (Northampton)* of 1943–44, Moore wrote: "The Madonna and Child should have an austerity and a nobility, and some touch of grandeur (even hieratic aloofness) which is missing in the everyday Mother and Child idea."[10] The white shroud in *Wrapped Madonna* definitely imbues the image with austerity and grandeur. The binding of mother and child also reflects a desire for physical and emotional oneness. As in the *Northampton* carving, the infant is safe in his mother's arms. Together, the daytime and nighttime drawings create a complete, twenty-four-hour experience and grant Moore's wish that his sculpture be viewed in the open air by day and night, under all conditions. As in *Crowd Looking at a Tied-up Object*, the artist sets the subject in space. Here the darkness and light focus us on the iconic image yet create a "landscape" around the bound figures. The layers of crayon, ink, gouache, and wash form a textural background that "break[s] the tyranny of the flat plane of the paper and open[s] up the suggestion of space."[11]

The visual source of *Wrapped Madonna and Child* is Moore's own sculpture *Standing Figure*, a maquette of which is also in the Bergman bequest (1950, p. 20). At first glance, the sculpture differs completely. The double-headed figure is gaunt and angular, "rising in agitated verticals."[12] In casting *Standing Figure* in bronze, however, Moore created a plaster mold tied together with ropes or elastic. A photograph of this bound plaster (p. 20), taken by the artist in his studio, is the exact image seen in *Wrapped Madonna and Child*.[13] In these drawings, the plaster becomes the cloth-like veiling, and the two-headed sculpture the Madonna and Child. We can now decipher the shield-like shape under the Child's head as one of the triangular shoulder blades in *Standing Figure*. The void in the center of the drawing likewise corresponds to the hollow of the sculpture's chest. Moore was inspired by the sight of the bound plaster and transformed the technical state into haunting and dramatic drawings.[14]

In Moore's photographs of the large *Standing Figure* situated in the landscape (p. 21), the double-headed figure stands heroic and monumental. The artist described it as "staring out into space. . . . It's as though the back head is helping the front head to look in that direction. You double up as it were." Furthermore, "It is placed on a lonely moor in Scotland and the bleak nature of the landscape brings out the skeletonic, stark and solitary quality of the work." The poetic connection between sculpture and nature led Moore to refer to this piece as "Sculpture in Landscape – Standing Man."[15] The desolate surroundings and dramatic atmosphere captured in these photographs resemble those in *Crowd Looking at a Tied-up Object*.[16]

---

9   Moore created other drawings entitled *Wrapped Madonna and Child or Tied-up Object* in 1950 and 1951, which are closely related to those in the Israel Museum collection (HMF 2712, 2713, 2716).

10   James, *Moore on Sculpture*, p. 220.

11   Moore, quoted in *Auden Poems*.

12   Wilkinson, *Moore Collection*, p. 113.

13   I am extremely grateful to Martin Davis, information manager at the Henry Moore Foundation, for his valuable assistance to my research.

14   Similarly, the bound plaster negative of *Double Standing Figure* (1950, LH 291) must have moved Moore to draw *Two Wrapped Standing Figures* (1951, HMF 2717).

15   Wilkinson, *Writings and Conversations*, p. 275.

Other themes in Moore's drawings deepen our understanding of string or rope in his oeuvre. In 1942, the same year as *Crowd Looking at a Tied-up Object*, he began drawing women winding yarn. Typically, one woman holds wool wrapped around her hands — held open at arm's length — while another winds it into a ball. The motif reappears in 1948 and 1949 (*Two Women Winding Wool*, p. 22).[17] These works belong to a group devoted to massive female figures reading or knitting in domestic interiors. Moore's interest in women's handiwork dates back to a 1927 portrait of his mother sewing.[18] Yarn, winding, tying, and string thus symbolize womanly or motherly activity. Moore's postwar depiction of mother and child, family, and the reclining figure "provided reassurance in their permanence and stability — affirming the survival of humanity and a union of man and nature."[19] Drawings such as *Two Women Winding Wool* celebrate community and family continuity.

Female domesticity evolves and becomes more profound in Moore's drawings of the *Three Fates*.[20] In Greek mythology, the Fates spin and cut the thread of life. In a 1950 drawing (p. 23), we see the three Fates: on the right, Lachesis — the Apportioner, holding the distaff and representing birth; on the left, Klotho — the Spinner, symbolizing life; and in the center, Atropos — the Inflexible, with open shears ready to sever the lifeline.[21] These birth spirits were believed to visit a newborn and determine his or her destiny, signified by the thread they spin.[22] In *Wrapped Madonna and Child*, mother and child are bound together by this thread of life, a figurative umbilical cord.

Moore's wrapped and tied images also reflect the sculptor's concern with what he called "the hidden struggle."[23] The artist wrote that great art must contain conflict, or a disturbing, mysterious element: This struggle is the subject of his wrapped and tied images. In 1966, more than twenty years after drawing *Crowd Looking at a Tied-up Object*, Moore stated that the work "has a close affinity in theme to my interpretation of the Auden poems — the mystery of what is under the shroud is somewhat akin to the mystery in poetry. It is this element of the unknown that fascinates me in caves and the holes in the sides of hills — you don't know what is there until you look and explore them. This mystery excites the imagination. . . ."[24] He told Sir Kenneth Clark, who owned the drawing, "that he saw a tied-up piece of stone being transported by a lorry, and this made him feel how mysterious such an object can be, half revealing its form by the tension of the cords, and half arousing our curiosity as to its real shape."[25]

Moore's wrapping and tying suggest multiple meanings. The artist encouraged exploration of his work but not his psyche. He refused to read past the first chapter of Erich Neumann's Jungian analysis of his art,[26] fearing enslavement to proving the analyst right or wrong. The same ambivalence is evident in Moore's recognition that "From early on I have had an obsession with the Mother and Child theme,"[27] while consciously steering clear of

---

16 Another 1942 drawing, *Standing Figures* (HMF 2079), shows that Moore had conceived the double-headed figure long before sculpting *Standing Figure* in 1950. In *Auden Poems*, this drawing is reproduced directly after *Crowd Looking at a Tied-up Object*. Both have similar contours, though created many years apart. Moore etched *Crowd Looking at a Tied-up Object* in 1966 (CGM 79) for the *Meditations on the Effigy* portfolio, marking his seventieth birthday. In this memento of the 1942 drawing, the wrapped and tied object resembles a cross, as in Moore's *Upright Motive No. 1: Glenkiln Cross* (1955–56, LH 377), so called because it was first situated — like *Standing Figure* — at the Glenkiln Farm Estate (see n. 5).

17 HMF 2083, 2084, 2495, 2496, 2497, 2498, 2528, 2529, 2530.

18 Wilkinson, *Drawings*, no. 27.

19 Feldman Bennet, "Drawings," p. 16.

20 *The Three Fates* are depicted in 1948 (HMF 2163, 2497 [though called *Women Winding Wool*]) and in the *Prométhée Sketchbook* of 1949–50 (HMF 2554), in what may be a study for the drawing in the Israel Museum collection.

21 The dark background may allude to Night, mother of the Fates.

22 Rose, *Greek Mythology*, p. 24.

23 James, *Moore on Sculpture*, p. 91.

24 Moore, introduction to *Auden Poems*.

25 Clark, *Moore Drawings*, p. 120.

26 Neumann, *Archetypal World*.

27 Wilkinson, *Writings and Conversations*, p. 213.

28 Hedgecoe, *Moore*, p. 151.

exploring this obsession: "I decided I did not want to be psycho-analyzed, nor understand what makes me tick."[28] Nevertheless, the unraveling of Moore's *Wrapped Madonna and Child* reveals much about his intensely private world. *Standing Figure*'s bound plaster transforms into a mysterious symbolic image, which expresses his longing for symbiosis. Here he affirms that the double-headed "Standing Man" – perhaps the artist himself – combines mother and child, whose sacred relationship alleviates life's tenuousness. Thus the engulfing shroud reveals more than it hides.

Family Groups

Henry Moore was the seventh of eight children. His mother, Mary, "a woman of exceptional character, energy and determination,"[1] played a central role in her youngest son's life. To Moore she was

> absolutely feminine, womanly, motherly. . . .
> I suppose I've got a mother complex. . . . She
> was to me the absolute stability, the whole thing
> in life that one knew was there for one's
> protection. . . . So it's not surprising that the kind
> of women I've done in sculpture are mature
> women rather than young.[2]

Mary Moore suffered from terrible rheumatism. Moore recalled: "She would often say to me in winter, when I came back from school: 'Henry, boy, come and rub my back.' Then I would massage her back with liniment." This experience inspired his 1957 sculpture of a seated mature woman. "I found," he said, "that I was unconsciously giving to its back the long-forgotten shape of the one I had so often rubbed as a boy."[3] Peter Fuller links "the security and happiness of Moore's childhood environment and . . . his adult sculptural vision."[4] Similarly, the artist's mother-and-child pieces often correspond with events in his personal life – the births of his nephew and niece, his marriage to Irina, and the arrivals of daughter Mary and grandson Gus.[5]

For Moore, mother and child constituted a "fundamental obsession."[6] Throughout the 1920s, he created at least one such sculpture practically every year. These primitivist direct carvings in stone depict a monumental mother cradling her nursing baby, an infant seated upon its mother's

---

1   Berthoud, *Life of Moore*, p. 21.
2   Moore, *Observer*, p. 30.
3   Roditi, *Dialogues*, pp. 191–92.
4   Fuller, "Mother-spaces," 13.
5   Garrould, "Moore: Drawings," p. 21.
6   James, *Moore on Sculpture*, p. 220.

head, or a baby suckling from isolated breasts. Retaining the character and shape of the stone block, the undifferentiated mother-child symbiosis transmits emotional unity. This theme also casts the artist as "mother," birthing sculpture from stone.

From 1932 until World War II, Moore's work underwent a process of abstraction. Mother and child became large mass and small form, respectively, symbolizing preverbal infancy and affording psychological insight into the mother-child relationship. Several of these pieces reveal Moore's interest in Surrealism and Constructivism. In 1938, after viewing mathematical string configurations at the London Science Museum, the artist strung crossbeams between mother and child, emphasizing their dyadic bond.

In 1943 Moore was commissioned to carve a Madonna and Child for St. Matthew's Church in Northampton. Intimidated by the great tradition of religious art, he hesitated to accept the commission, promising only drawings and small, clay models. A bronze maquette cast from one such model (p. 25) portrays a very earthly Madonna affectionately interacting with her child. Her skirt reaches just mid-thigh, and her weight is expressed by the curvature of the stool upon which she sits.[7]

In his Madonna and Child drawings, Moore ponders the mother-child dynamic. On p. 26 (right), the child playfully balancing on his mother's lap and holding an apple represents the holy Child, though this study shares the spirit of the 1956 bronze *Mother and Child No. 1: Reaching for Apple* (p. 24), in which the mother's skirt resembles a tree trunk, alluding to Mother Earth.[8] On p. 26 (left), a sublime mother tenderly holds her child's hand. Despite its title, *Two Women and Children* (p. 28) likely features the Madonna and Child together with St. Anne and the young John the Baptist. The pencil sketch at the top recalls Renaissance drawings of the Assumption of the Virgin. The frontal position of the child in the Madonna's lap

and the throne-like chair in the drawings on p. 27, and the architectural niche in the work on p. 30 (right), create a venerable image. Moore's experimentation with contrasting styles (p. 27, right) acknowledges his difficulty in expressing spirituality.[9] The final stone Madonna and Child projects "an austerity and a nobility, and some touch of grandeur . . . a quiet dignity and gentleness," the artist commented. "I have tried to give a sense of complete easiness and repose, as though the Madonna could stay in that position for ever."[10] These depictions of Madonna and Child lay the foundation for Moore's family groups.

In 1943–44, when educator Henry Morris sought a sculpture for the grounds of a proposed village college in Impington, Cambridgeshire, Moore produced a notebook of family-group drawings. He later wrote, "The Family Group in all its differing forms sprang from my absorbing [Morris's] idea of the village college – that it should be an institution which could provide for the family unit at all its stages."[11] Following the drawings, Moore made about fourteen sketch models in terracotta, later cast in bronze. Although the commission was delayed and finally withdrawn for lack of funds, a cast of *Family Group* (1948–49) was installed at Barclay School, Stevenage, in 1950.[12] In an elaborate study for the sculpture (p. 29), linked arms and joined knees evoke family unity, and Moore's two-way sectional-line method transmits the three-dimensionality of the final bronze.

Like his Madonna and Child series, Moore's family-group drawings emerged during World War II's restructuring of the family. In many homes, enlistment and injury removed men from domestic

---

7   I thank Sam Sylvester for pointing out the down-to-earth quality of this Madonna.

8   The apple, which the child holds or reaches for, must be bitten into rather than sucked, suggesting infantile oral sadism. See Schneider, "Mother and Child," 263, n. 8.

9   Garrould, *Moore: Complete Drawings*, vol. 3, p. 192.

10   James, *Moore on Sculpture*, p. 223.

11   *Moore: War and Utility*, p. 21.

12   Ibid.

life. After the war, renewed traditionalism, greater security, and higher standards of living increased marriages and births significantly. Moore's work provided the requisite model family.[13]

Of his 1942 drawings of coal miners, the artist stated, "I discovered the male figure and the qualities of the figure in action."[14] These miners prefigured the fathers in Moore's family studies, though the harsh, masculine setting of the former starkly contrasts with the tranquility of the latter. Other roots of these studies can be seen in a drawing on p. 30 (left), whose upper right displays a very regal Madonna and Child. Below, parents protectively frame their children. Mother is majestic in red and blue, colors originally reserved for the Madonna. Occasionally Moore's noble mothers stand, as in his interesting composition of nine family groups (p. 31, right), which defines relationships through positions and postures. Yet mother and baby are never separated.

In *Family Group* (1943–44, p. 31), a man tenderly touches his wife and their older child, who stands between his father's legs holding a book. Though Moore drew women reading, mothers reading to children, and mothers and children being read to, reading often defines the attachment between father and older child. The artist's own father, Raymond Spencer Moore, a miner who worked his way up to qualify as pit under-manager, was intelligent and well read. Determined that none of his sons "work down in the pit," he insisted that all his children receive a good education.

In a beautiful drawing (ca. 1947, p. 32), Moore depicts his only child, Mary, holding a book. This work is part of a series of life drawings of Mary, after the bath, sleeping, playing, or nursing from her mother. *Studies of the Artist's Child* is more close-up and detailed than many of his sketches, reflecting the intimacy between the artist and his daughter. Moore acknowledged that her birth "re-invoked in my sculpture my Mother and Child theme" and that these drawings "try to understand

more about the mother and child relationship." The three vital and richly colored studies of Mary demonstrate his view that "drawings done from love seem different in kind from purely observational drawings because one is emotionally involved."[15]

The Moores' young daughter also inspired *Rocking Chairs* (ca. 1949), a series of drawings and small bronzes extending the mother-child motif.[16] The Museum's collection includes three delightful studies from this series. In *Five Studies for Rocking Chairs* (p. 37), Moore experiments with positions, balance, and chair curvature as the mother playfully tosses the child aloft. Read as a sequence, the five drawings approximate an action photograph, conveying movement and liveliness. The two *Studies for Sculpture* (pp. 34–35) are compartmentalized drawings within drawings. Each section depicts one of Moore's major themes: rocking chairs, family groups, and reclining and upright figures. Against a dense wax- and colored-crayon background, the artist produces a highly organized picture rather than mere sculptural ideas.

A further development of the mother and child theme appears in Moore's *Internal/External Form* series of the 1950s and 60s (p. 36). Inspired by malanggan carvings from New Ireland (wooden sculptures created for burial rituals, which include an interplay between inner and outer forms), the series contains some of his few postwar sculptures based on non-western art.[17] Moore envisaged an "embryo being protected by an outer form, a mother and child idea, or the stamen in a flower, that is, something young and growing being protected by an outer shell." This motif was an extension of the *Helmet Head* series (p. 68), also focusing on a larger form protecting or enclosing a

---

13 Stallabrass, "Mother and Child," pp. 15, 17.
14 James, *Moore on Sculpture*, p. 216.
15 Wilkinson, *Writings and Conversations*, pp. 66, 307.
16 Read, *Moore: Life and Work*, p. 174.
17 Turner, *Dictionary*, s.v. "Henry Moore."

smaller, delicate one. For Moore, the relationship between the forms and the dependency of the smaller upon the larger express "two basic human experiences: to be a child and to be a parent."[18] The intense feeling of engulfment conveyed in this work relates to the early symbiotic period in which the child experiences himself as inseparable from the mother.

Moore's images of mother and child, Madonna and Child, and family groups reflect domestic tranquility and idealize the relationship between parent and child. In almost all works, Moore depicts intimate, warm physical and emotional attachments.[19] Whether naturalistic or abstract, they convey emotion and kinship through gestures rather than facial expressions. In his choice of materials and relationships between forms, the artist strives to transmit the infant-mother bond as experienced from within. His drawings and sculptures transcend individual experience and explore the primal, universal questions of life, growth, creativity, and love. Within a caring family unit, Moore portrays "happiness based on human affection."[20]

---

18 James, *Moore on Sculpture*, p. 247.
19 Only Moore's *Mother and Child* of 1952 (LH 315) depicts antagonism between mother and child. Here the suckling child seems about to devour the mother's breast, illustrating Melanie Klein's psychoanalytic theories regarding oral sadism among infants. See Read, *Moore: Life and Work*, p. 176.
20 Clark, *Moore Drawings*, p. 255.

Reclining Figures

Henry Moore considered the reclining figure "an absolute obsession." While he sculpted the human figure upright and seated as well, the reclining figure offered "the most freedom, compositionally and spatially."[1] The horizontal pose creates a wide, stable base that obviates pedestals and frees the artist to experiment with composition. The stability of this posture also conveys permanence and repose, which were critical to Moore.

Particularly in his reclining figures, Moore strove for warmth, vitality, and feeling for organic form. Nature was a major inspiration. His tunnel-like holes recall stones weathered by wind and water (see p. 38).[2] The horizontal pose parallels the convergence of land and sky, and the nude female alludes to Mother Earth as giver of life. Idealized rather than individualized, Moore's reclining women are full-bodied and grounded. Their posture evokes representations of Mexico's Toltec-Mayan Chacmool (900–1050 C.E.) – a Toltec warrior-altar with an offering bowl on his stomach. The sculptor admired these sublime, reclining figures, which reminded him of mountains, boulders, and sea-worn pebbles.[3]

The organic nature of Moore's reclining figures also emerged from the rise of functionalism in the 1930s, As architecture eliminated decorative non-essentials, he initiated sculpture that was independent yet closely connected to buildings and their surroundings. Moore's *Recumbent Figure* (1938, maquette p. 40), created for architect Serge Chermayeff's terrace in Sussex, linked the horizontal modern structure and the landscape: "My figure looked out across a great sweep of Downs, and her gaze gathered in the horizon."[4]

The Museum's collection of maquettes and enlarged reclining figures reveals Moore's sculptural

---

1 James, *Moore on Sculpture*, pp. 264–65.
2 Sylvester, *Moore*, p. 5.
3 Wilkinson, *Writings and Conversations*, p. 97.
4 James, *Moore on Sculpture*, p. 99.

shifts. The figures gradually open up. In one group of works, the poses dictate the holes in form. Elsewhere, non-naturalistic, expressive hollows connect both sides of the sculpture, heightening its three-dimensionality. In the 1960s, Moore turned to semi-abstraction and truncation of the human form. Throughout this process, he enlists space as an active participant in the creation of the work, transforming negative space into positive, or "pregnant," voids.

Draped Reclining Figure (1952–53, maquette p. 40) launches Moore's opening out of space, portraying a relatively naturalistic woman whose mass is almost completely maintained. Resembling classical Greek sculpture, this bronze is the first of several important draped works of the 1950s,[5] all building on the importance of fabric in Moore's Shelter Drawings of 1940–41 (pp. 26–27). In the sculpture, the drapery's many small crinkles and folds emphasize tension. The material pulls tightly across the woman's shoulders but slackens between her thighs. Though the figure is gentle and flowing, her alert pose conjures up the reclining Chacmool, his upper torso similarly supported by his arms. Other sculptures and drawings from the late 1930s to the 1950s are more stylized. With torso twisted out of line, weight supported by an elbow, and knees spread wide, sculptures such as the angular *Reclining Figure No. 2* (1953, p. 41) reflect Moore's belief that "nothing living is purely symmetrical."[6] These asymmetrical works offer endless viewpoints.

In one group of reclining figures (p. 42), the only cavities are the natural spaces between the figure's parted thighs or between the arms and chest. In others, the female body becomes a more imaginative web of holes and tunnels. These apertures highlight Moore's fascination with caves and the female form, both arousing his sense of mystery.[7] A striking opening in the rib cage of several reclining figures (e.g., *Recumbent Figure*, p. 40) accentuates pointed breasts. Some figures, such as on p. 43 (bottom), raise an arm to support the head, exposing another space. On p. 39, the

woman's organs are cradled within her boat-like body, and a curious space opens up by the head. A cleavage in the top figure on p. 43 creates a double-headed image – perhaps a child lying next to his mother, or two people joined in copulation.[8] Moore endows his reclining women with minimal facial characteristics, occasionally piercing small holes for eyes, which mimic the sculpture's perforated nipples (p. 43, bottom).

As stated, Moore's later reclining figures exhibit a greater degree of abstraction. They are, in his words, "less dominated by representational considerations," and employ "forms and their relationships quite freely."[9] *Reclining Figure: External Form* (1953–54, p. 38) is exemplary. Here, the figure originally within the cave-like form is gone, leaving a hollow shell. Next the artist divided the female form into two or three, arriving at figures composed of separate masses[10] and allowing for "many more three-dimensional variations than if it had just been a monolithic piece."[11] The space between sections is vital and revelatory. In *Studies for Sculpture: Two and Three Pieces Reclining Figures* (1967, p. 44), *Relief No. 1* (1959, p. 45), *Three Piece Reclining Figure* (1961), and *Three Piece Sculpture: Vertebrae* (1968–69, pp. 46–47), Moore playfully rearranges the figure in numerous ways.

In the small maquette *Three Piece Reclining Figure* (p. 44), the nude is severed into head and upper torso, abdomen, and legs. Moore transforms these body parts into cliffs and rocky formations, and the jagged metal adds to the sculpture's primordial quality. In contrast, the heroic *Vertebrae* is

---

5   These works follow Moore's first visit to Greece, in 1951. See Wilkinson, *Moore Collection*, p. 120.

6   Wilkinson, *Writings and Conversations*, p. 198.

7   See the opening quote of "Unraveling Moore's Enigma," p. 13.

8   Compton, *Moore*, p. 224.

9   James, *Moore on Sculpture*, p. 258.

10 Though his first multifigures were executed in 1934, Moore returned to the theme twenty-five years later in a magnificent series of two- and three-piece reclining figures.

11 Hedgecoe, *Moore*, p. 338.

12 Wilkinson, *Writings and Conversations*, p. 198.

composed of smooth, polished forms, lending the bronze a tactile sheen. Dominating a hill in the Israel Museum's Billy Rose Art Garden, the work's three units are unified only by the viewer's gaze. The reclining figure is no longer obvious, and elements of the female form are overshadowed by three adjacent, seemingly interlocking vertebrae. Moore's interest in bones, also manifest in *Working Model for Three Way Piece No. 2: Archer* (1964, p. 48), derives from his aspiration that his work embody an inner vitality. To him, bone is the source of movement and energy, "the inner structure of all living form."[12] *Vertebrae* transforms itself from every viewpoint, containing tremendous energy. The form presses outward, bursting skyward with immense strength.

Seated Figures

Written in cooperation with Yael Eshel

Henry Moore's drawings and sculptures of isolated, seated women convey great confidence and power. These subjects are independent, no longer linked to depictions of mother and child or Madonna and Child. Influenced by prehistoric, ancient Near Eastern, and Aegean art, Moore's women are timeless yet contemporary, neither goddesses nor mythological figures but "superior, modern beings, guardians of a university, a museum or a public square."[1]

Moore greatly admired Mesopotamian art, especially Sumerian sculpture, for its "richness of feeling for life and its wonder and mystery, welded to direct plastic statement born of a real creative urge. It has a bigness and simplicity with no decorative trimmings."[2] These artists reserved the seated pose for gods and kings, who were worshipped by standing figures.[3] While seated subjects were either male or female, Moore employs this pose almost exclusively for women.

The setting of the seated figure contributes greatly to the impact of Moore's work. Some sit on throne-like chairs (*Five Seated Figures*, 1934, p. 51), which frame the figure and emphasize its monumental weightiness. Others are regally erect despite their backless base (*Woman*, 1957–58, p. 50; *Maquette for Seated Woman: Thin Neck*, 1960, p. 52). Several are positioned on insubstantial, bench-like constructions providing minimal support (*Seated Figure*, 1949, p. 52; *Seated Girl*, 1956, p. 53). Moore's *Draped Seated Woman* (1957–58, p. 55) half-reclines on dark, basalt boulders on the Hebrew University of Jerusalem's Edmond J. Safra Campus. The green patina of the bronze contrasts with the black stone yet

1   Grohmann, *Art of Moore*, p. 229.

2   Wilkinson, *Writings and Conversations*, p. 101.

3   Winter, "Iconography," 255; Winter, "Royal Images," 12–42. We thank Dr. Tallay Ornan, Rodney E. Soher Curator of Western Asiatic Antiquities at the Israel Museum, for her expertise.

integrates the sculpture into its natural surroundings. One hand rests on a boulder, while the other supports the woman's colossal body. For Moore, hands convey not only physical support but emotion.[4] Those in *Seated Figure* are clasped together, resting prayer-like on the woman's knees.

The relationship between subject and support is fundamental to Moore's seated figures. The interdependency of the two underlies *Ashdoda*, a Philistine figurine of the Iron Age (twelfth century B.C.E.) in the Museum's collection. On p. 9, Moore is shown holding a replica of this figurine given to him following his visit to the Israel Museum in 1966. He remarked how Henry Moore–like the figurine was. Woman and chair are united, as in Moore's *Female Figure* of 1928 (p. 53), in which the subject's pelvis is extended into a seat supported by her parted legs. Such sculptures probably derived from Aegean seated female figurines of the late Mycenean III period, whose mother-goddess theme[5] profoundly inspired Moore's work.

In contrast to this transformation of woman, *Seated Nude* (1929, p. 54) is one of Moore's many naturalistic figure studies created after graduating from the Royal College of Art in 1924. The monumental nude glances sideways, while her body is positioned frontally. Additional contours around the profiled face hint at multiple viewpoints and, together with the scale of the figure, suggest Picasso's heavy-limbed, monumental female nudes of the 1920s.[6] Yet the delicate necklace adorning Moore's nude undercuts her full figure. In *Draped Seated Woman* (p. 55), the artist intensifies the scale, focusing on the drapery and minimizing facial features. Lest dust and rain accumulate in the drapery folds, a drainage tunnel was installed between the legs.[7] The multiple, small folds reflect classical Greek sculpture, unlike the schematic, horizontal bands of cloth in the bare-chested *Seated Figure* (p. 52).

A small head atop a large, voluptuous body typifies Moore's seated women. "For me," the artist explained, "the head is the most important part of a piece of sculpture. It gives to the rest a scale, . . . a certain human poise, and meaning."[8] The small head focuses viewers on the body. In *Woman* and *Seated Woman: Thin Neck* (p. 52), Moore intensifies this effect by truncating arms and legs: *Thin Neck* features rounded shoulders and legs ending in a squared stub; *Woman*'s rough, sharp-edged shoulders contrast with rounded, smooth leg stumps. Feminine features are emphasized in *Woman*, as in depictions of prehistoric fertility goddesses. The body's large, circular forms are echoed in the round markings on the breasts and stomach. The incised naval may represent a life growing inside the womb, and the breasts appear to be engorged with milk. This sculpture recalls Moore's drawings of the Paleolithic *Venus from Grimaldi*, her fecundity similarly accentuated by the truncation of arms and legs.[9]

Moore's fondness for the elemental simplicity of sharp-edged Cycladic idols and his interest in bone and flint led to his *Knife-Edge* sculptures of the 1960s. In *Seated Woman: Thin Neck*, part of this series, "the thin neck and head, by contrast with the width and bulk of the body, give more monumentality to the work."[10] Combining rounded and rough surfaces, the seated figure retains the qualities of a sculpture hewn in stone. This coalescence of delicacy and strength, independence and vulnerability, completeness and fragmentation distinguishes Moore's seated women and offers a complex, comprehensive investigation of femininity.

---

4   Wilkinson, *Writings and Conversations*, p. 220.
5   Meshorer, *Archaeology*, p. 60.
6   Wilkinson, *Drawings*, p. 81.
7   Wilkinson, *Moore Remembered*, p. 179.
8   Wilkinson, *Writings and Conversations*, p. 219.
9   Wilkinson, *Moore Remembered*, p. 183.
10   Wilkinson, *Writings and Conversations*, p. 290.

Upright Figures

The upright figure – whether full-, half-, or three-quarter-length – is vital to Henry Moore's work and changes radically throughout his career. These figures range from solemn to playful. The Israel Museum's collection reveals shifts and contrasts between angular and rounded, hard and soft, skeletal and corpulent.

Figure with Clasped Hands (1929, p. 57), from the Tel Aviv Museum of Art, is one of Moore's finest carvings of the 1920s. The squareness of this half-figure reflects the key influence of Toltec and Aztec art as well as the sculptor's wish to maintain the shape of the travertine marble block. By turning the mask-like face to one side, he rejects symmetry and cubistically combines frontal and profile views. The woman's gathered hair is schematized as a stone projection in back. As in other early carvings, Moore sculpts practically no neck, fearful perhaps of weakening the stone. The only breathing spaces in this monolithic work are those between the body and arms. Clasped under the breasts, the hands recall such sculptures as the Sumerian Gudea[1] but also emphasize the figure's femininity.

Half-Figure (ca. 1932, p. 59) demonstrates Moore's radical transition to a sculptural language allied with the biomorphic forms of the Surrealists. The artist participated in the international Surrealist exhibition at the Burlington Galleries in London in 1936 but never committed to the movement. The work of Arp, Picasso, Miró, and Tanguy was a liberating influence, however, infusing Moore's sculpture with the notion of metamorphosis. *Half-Figure* actually depicts a three-quarter female figure, from head to mid-thigh.[2] The artist toys with anatomy: The head is almost undifferentiated from the neck, the breasts are misaligned, and the backside is twisted frontward. The delicate incisions in the bronze contribute to its playfulness. Round, simplified eyes stand in for all facial features, and a narrow crevice down the woman's shoulder humorously represents her hair. She touches her breast and thigh with lightly incised fingers, and pierced nipples and belly button animate the surface.

In *Figure* (ca. 1935, p. 58), Moore's biomorphism reaches new heights as smoothly flowing, rounded forms and perforations abstractly represent the artist's subject. Viewing the sculpture from each side of the central hole reveals great differences both in general contour and in the descriptive yet decorative incisions. Moore burrows through the woman's torso, while in the drawing Four Figures (1941, p. 60) dark, mysterious shading hints at woman's cavernous nature.

The 1950s saw radical innovation in a series of skeletal vertical figures. In *Maquette for Standing Figure* (p. 20, left), and in *Standing Figure No. 1* and *Standing Figure No. 3* (both on p. 62), an opened-out, linear approach yields fleshless "animated wishbones."[3] In stark contrast to classical, full-bodied women such as in the drawing *Standing Women* (1948, p. 56), these sinuous figures reflect Moore's interest in the work of Brancusi and Giacometti as well as his assimilation of the freedom and distortion of Picasso's body imagery during this period.[4]

In *Maquette for Standing Figure* (p. 20), the human frame has been sliced open and emptied. Nodular joints at the hips and knees link the skeletal strips of metal representing arms and legs. Flattened, triangular protrusions at shoulder height suggest shoulder blades or small shields, and two antenna-like necks and heads spring up out of them. The enlarged bronze cast premiered at lakeside Battersea Park, London, where the gaunt, vertical figure contrasted with the tranquil, flat sheet of water.[5] Moore traced this work to a photograph

---

1 Wilkinson, *Moore Collection*, p. 101.
2 This sculpture closely resembles Moore's 1931 *Half-Figure* (LH 98), carved in alabaster.
3 Russell, *Moore*, p. 143.
4 Wilkinson, *Moore Collection*, p. 113.
5 James, *Moore on Sculpture*, p. 108.

of African tribesmen standing motionless in the marshes, about to skewer fish.[6] The sculptor had originally envisioned four figures in a row on a joint base but eventually settled on two molds of one figure.[7]

Standing Figure No. 1 is more naturalistic, though it shares the former sculpture's leanness and bony knees and waist. The figure is of undetermined gender, although the small waist and protruding chest may indicate femininity. Raised arms infuse the work with tension and an energetic tautness. *Standing Figure No. 3*, semi-clothed with a recessed chest, communicates a clenching loneliness and expectancy.

Moore's development of the vertical figure culminated in his 1955–56 *Upright Motive* series, originally planned for the courtyard of a new Olivetti building in Milan (p. 63). Moore sculpted thirteen maquettes for a vertical work envisioned as a counterfoil to the horizontal building. The upright motives no longer allude to the body, and the totem-like forms comprise a fascinating variety of organic shapes balanced one upon the other. When the artist sought to enlarge certain maquettes, "three of them grouped themselves together, and in my mind, assumed the aspect of a crucifixion scene."[8] Together with *Upright Motive No. 2* and *Upright Motive No. 7* (p. 63), *Upright Motive No. 1: Glenkiln Cross* (LH 377) represents the crucified Christ between the two thieves. Viewed individually, without this symbolism, these phallic works project ever-evolving organic growth.

---

6 Wilkinson, *Moore Collection*, p. 113.

7 See pp. 13–16 for further interpretation of this and related works.

8 Wilkinson, *Writings and Conversations*, p. 285.

Heads in Transformation

Written in cooperation with Juliana Ochs

Minimally detailed and often dwarfed by a large body, Henry Moore's sculpted heads may appear insignificant or neglected by the artist. "This is a mistake," insists Sir Kenneth Clark. "He is, if anything, too much interested in [them]."[1] Moore's exploration of human and animal heads spanned more than five decades. The Museum's collection contains a range of these drawings and sculptures, which transmit great intensity and completeness.

Moore isolates and observes the human head in two 1932 drawings. The grid-like *Sixteen Heads* (p. 66) surveys the head from various angles. While its faces are similar and perhaps belong to the same woman, fluid lines attest to a dynamic interpretation of the model. *Studies of Heads* (p. 64) is arranged irregularly and displays a wider variety of media. Large and dramatically shadowed, the central heads command attention, while smaller, fainter heads surround and echo them. Each work is at once a free sketch and an organized drawing.

Between 1937 and 1940, Moore imaginatively experimented with sculptures incorporating string. This series was inspired by malanggan carvings from New Ireland in the British Museum's collection (which Moore called "bird in a cage" carvings) and by the London Science Museum's mathematical models.[2] Moore's stringed heads are bowl-like, with bulbous necks and drilled eyes. Cast in terracotta, *Stringed Head* (1958, p. 67) feels earthy, but cast in bronze (1986, p. 67) with a gold patina, the head is modernistic, reflecting the sculptor's early interest in machine art. In both versions, the lightness of the string contrasts with the density of the sculpture. Eight parallel, horizontal strings cut across the concave head, heightening awareness of the sculptural space[3] while maintaining openness.

---

1 Clark, *Moore Drawings*, p. 221.

2 Grohmann, *Art of Moore*, p. 103.

3 Sylvester, *Moore*, p. 105.

This interaction between internal and external space dominates Moore's "helmet head" drawings and sculptures, begun in 1939.[4] Composed of a shell and a delicate inner form, these helmet heads embody "the mystery of not entirely knowing the form inside . . . it's rather like armor which protects – the outer shell protecting the softer inside."[5] In 1950 Moore sculpted several such heads, preceded by preparatory drawings. For example, he drew five helmet shells (p. 68, right), emphasizing their dark, cavernous spaces. In a vividly colored variation (p. 68, left), the sinuous internal forms shielded or imprisoned by the helmet are only partially visible. And on p. 69, the artist stresses the helmet's humanity by including ears and two holes representing eyes.

The perplexing internal shapes represent the soft brain tissue, or thoughts and ideas. "In the immediate aftermath of the Second World War," these helmet heads "produced an eerie and sinister effect on the viewer, for they seem to encapsulate the uneasy mood of those years."[6] The helmet heads spawned and perhaps served as a male equivalent of the more feminine *Internal/External Forms* Moore would develop ten years later. Both series relate to Winnicott's theories of creativity as an interior-exterior process in which the preconscious mediates between the unconscious store of memory, fantasy, and energy and the conscious transformation of these elements into art.[7]

Concurrent with his helmet heads, Moore created a lifelike, miniature *Small Head* (1953, p. 65), defined in greater detail than many of the artist's larger figures. Possibly inspired by his studies for the queen in the group sculpture *King and Queen* (1952–53, LH 350), *Small Head* reveals a similar pathos. The pained expression and detailed modeling of eyes, nose, mouth, and chin reflect the artist's admiration for the psychological articulacy of Rodin's sculpture. Moore lends this bronze a textured quality, incising and chafing the woman's deep, sorrowful eyes and emphasizing her protruding cheekbones and sunken cheeks.

Head-like forms project from *Wall Relief: Three Forms* (1955, p. 70), part of a series of wall reliefs developed out of Moore's *Time/Life Screen* (1952–53, LH 344). The artist worked in soft plaster to model and then carve three forms, exploiting what he called "the projection and recession of form."[8] Globular shapes and deep, eye-like recessions characterize the embedded heads. Embellished with decorative veining, the relief recalls Moore's 1952 series of bronze *Leaf Figures*.[9]

Animal Form (1959, p. 71) was extracted from *Three Motives against a Wall No. 1* (1958). Related to *Goat Head* (1952), *Animal Form* may have been inspired by bones of farm animals unearthed in Moore's garden. Unlike the repose common to his work, this twisted, expressionistic rendering of the animal body exudes motion and energy.[10]

The head captivated Moore's imagination and allowed him to express pathos, explore the intricacy of enclosure and openness, and convey the mystery of internal and external forms. It provided him with a contained form whose complexity encompassed the entire human body and psyche. Decorative or naturalistic, brooding or playful, Moore's heads were vessels for his thoughts about human form and sculptural space.

---

4   Interestingly, in 1932, a year before Moore visited Jacques Lipchitz in Paris, Lipchitz created several works entitled *Sketch for Head*, which resemble the shell of Moore's *Helmet Head* sculptures. Thanks to Suzanne Landau, the Israel Museum's Chief Curator of the Arts, for this comparison.

5   Gilmour, *Graphics*, p. 43.

6   Compton, *Moore*, p. 227. Indeed Will Grohmann suggests that war paraphernalia, namely steel helmets and gas masks, may have influenced Moore here. Grohmann, *Art of Moore*, p. 106.

7   Deri, "Vicissitudes," in Schneider, "Mother and Child," 263, n. 6.

8   James, *Moore on Sculpture*, p. 275.

9   Read, *Moore: Life and Work*, p. 181.

10   Appropriately, for six years the Zoological Society of London presented casts of *Animal Form* as awards – until they became too expensive. Berthoud, *Life of Moore*, pp. 309–10.

Shelter Drawings

Written in cooperation with Juliana Ochs

Amidst the brutality of World War II, Henry Moore tenderly depicted fragile individuals and families seeking solace and refuge. "Without the war, which directed one's direction to life itself," he reflected, "I think I would have been a far less sensitive and responsible person. The war brought out and encouraged the humanist side in one's work."[1]

Moore was living and working in Kingston, near Dover, when war was declared on September 3, 1939. Pending a German invasion of England, his village became a restricted war zone, and he and his wife moved back to London. On September 7, 1940, the Blitz began. Subjected to full-scale day and night aerial bombings, thousands of Londoners transformed the London Underground into an improvised bomb shelter. Like the creation of the shelters themselves, Moore's interest in them was spontaneous and instinctive. One evening during the initial air raids, he saw rows of people huddled together under blankets on the cold station floor. These scenes evoked the reclining figures and encased human forms that had dominated his earlier sculpture:

> I had never seen so many rows of reclining figures and even the holes out of which the trains were coming seemed to me to be like the holes in my sculpture. And there were intimate little touches. Children fast asleep, with trains roaring past only a couple yards away. People who were obviously strangers to one another forming tight little intimate groups. They were cut off from what was happening up above, but they were aware of it. There was tension in the air. They were a bit like the chorus in a Greek drama telling us about the violence we don't actually witness.[2]

Over the next two months, Moore returned almost nightly to different Underground stations in London, where private life was rendered public and surreal. His observations filled several sketchbooks. Initially an unplanned response to scenes that intrigued him, these sketches caught the attention of Sir Kenneth Clark, chairman of the War Artists' Advisory Committee, and led to his appointment as an Official War Artist. After Moore completed his *First Shelter Sketchbook*, the committee urged a sequel and commissioned large-scale drawings, many of which were exhibited at the National Gallery in London during the war. The Israel Museum's collection includes four of Moore's Shelter Drawings, representing the range of styles through which the artist captured human experience during World War II.

In *Shelter Scene* (1941, p. 73), the station's curved, cave-like walls extend into a dark, spiraling tunnel. Moore details the tunnel contours and heavy brick but portrays the human forms – standing, sitting, and reclining – as indistinct silhouettes, an anonymous, mute wartime mass. The shelter emerges as tense and turbulent but also as a silent, passive refuge. Monochromatic grays and blue-grays color the murky, womb-like tunnel. As in many of his Shelter Drawings, the artist combines up to five media – pencil, chalk, crayon, pen and ink, and wash – to produce a wonderful richness and subtle depth even in monochromatic compositions. To delineate the tunnel walls and figures, Moore employs a wax-resist technique, layering a dark watercolor wash over a white wax crayon. The resulting vivid white accentuates the darkness.

In *Shelter Drawing* (1941, p. 74) and *Shelter Scene: Two Reclining Figures* (1941, p. 72), Moore focuses on the gentle passivity of those sleeping in the Underground. The viewer seems to look down on these foreshortened figures, creating the illusion of depth. The artist exposes only their arms and blurred faces, yet their tension is palpable. Unlike his leisurely reclining figures, repose here conveys

---

1   Compton, *Moore*, p. 32.

2   *Moore: Shelter Sketchbook*, p. 9.

no relaxation. The naturalistic *Shelter Drawing*[3] pairs similar women, one tranquil and the other in agony. The woman on the left raises clenched hands towards her eyes as if blocking out a nightmare. In *Two Reclining Figures*, Moore expresses his subjects' turmoil via deformity and dislocation. This foreshortened drawing is full of ambiguity. Despite its title, vestiges of a third head hint at an additional figure between the two. Or is the head of the figure on the left bizarrely cleaved? The gender of that figure is also indeterminate. While most of Moore's subjects were women, here the square, skeletal jaw and high brow suggest a male. As for the striking redhead on the right, her egg-shaped head appears detached from her body, and her gaunt facial features are almost inhuman. The configuration of the bodies is also strangely distorted: Whose arm reaches across the blanket?

The agitated faces in *Shelter Drawing* and *Two Reclining Figures* contrast with the immobility and passivity of the sleeping bodies. In both drawings, Moore protectively envelopes his subjects in blankets and coats, a shelter within a shelter. In *Two Reclining Figures*, a blanket done in gray wash and blue and green wax crayon rises over the figures like an ocean swell. In *Shelter Drawing*, golden and blue crayon form the blankets and coat, a makeshift cover. Fine pen and ink arches reinforce the boundedness of *Two Reclining Figures*' sleepers. The carefully molded folds and layers of fabric later became a formal element in Moore's sculpture, as in his postwar *Draped Seated Woman* (p. 55).

The bound figures recall Moore's "transformation" drawings of the 1930s, which "humanize" such natural objects as pebbles and shells.[4] His Shelter Drawings reverse the process: "Buried" in heavy blankets, the sleeping bodies turn into inert cocoons.

Though Moore focused on the subterranean shelter, he also depicted scenes of bombed London buildings. *Women and Children in Bombed-out Building* (1940–41, p. 75) is one of several such sketches that make up his *Third Shelter Sketchbook*.[5] The hurried sketches suggest the documentary style of a War Artist. Reminiscent of his earlier sculptural studies, four clusters of figures are arranged collage-like against brick wreckage, forming a community.

Several months into the Blitz, the government outfitted the shelters with bunks and canteens, and organization replaced spontaneity.[6] Without the chaotic "drama and strangeness" of crowded platforms and burrowing families, Moore lost interest, and his shelter drawing ended. Ironically, though engaged by the tunnel's turmoil, the artist emphasized the immobility of sleep, underscoring the tense wartime coexistence of comfort and horror, life and death.

---

3   *Shelter Drawing* is based on *Study for Shelter Drawing* (HMF 1667), from Moore's Second Shelter Sketchbook. *Shelter Drawing* is also related to HMF 1661, a study of sleeping positions, which is inscribed, "Sleeping positions – hands and arms thrown about, mouths open, complete abandon."

4   Studies of natural forms, such as *Ideas for Sculpture: Transformation of Bones* (HMF 965), appear in one of Moore's sketchbooks from the early 1930s. Within these drawings, he explores the human form. Compton, *Moore*, p. 28.

5   A disbanded sketchbook of 1940–41 has been dubbed the Third Shelter Sketchbook. See Garrould, *Moore: Complete Drawings*, vol. 3, p. 70.

6   *Moore: Shelter Sketchbook*, p. 12.

On Observation and Imagination
Moore's Albums

The Israel Museum boasts works from three of Henry Moore's major print portfolios: *Prométhée* (1950), *Elephant Skull Album* (1969–70), and *Auden Poems, Moore Lithographs* (1973). These lithographs and etchings demonstrate Moore's sensitivity and versatility as a graphic artist as well as his broad understanding of techniques and materials. His sculptural expertise in three-dimensional perspective transcended the flatness of the two-dimensional page, animating his prints and drawings.

Prométhée

Moore created fifteen lithographs to illustrate *Prométhée*, André Gide's French translation of Goethe's poem. The first book to contain the artist's original graphics, *Prométhée* drew on his *Prométhée Sketchbook* (1949–50). The book's opening print, *Head of Prometheus* (p. 76), portrays the courageous Greek god as melancholy, with sad eyes, pursed lips, and a vulnerable demeanor. Erich Neumann writes of Moore's Prometheus:

> Whereas the feminine, in good and evil alike,
> exercises a fate-like power in Moore's work, the
> masculine always remains stuck at the
> "adolescent" stage and never gets beyond the
> phase of bondage to the Great Mother. We are
> thinking here … of the youthful *Head of
> Prometheus*, whom no one would credit either
> with having made humanity or with the theft of
> fire.[1]

Nonetheless, Moore shows the head from below, imbuing his subject with heroic triumph. Like a visionary, Prometheus gazes ahead and upward. The artist's sectional lines create a sculptural sense of three-dimensionality and suggest armor, at once protective and penetrable.[2] Prometheus's eye sockets are an empty white and gray. Elsewhere in this portrait, however, the artist adds yellow to the light gray and blue-gray, injecting force and depth.

In another illustration, *Pandora and the Imprisoned Statues* (p. 77), most of the biomorphic figures are encased in a brick-like cladding, anticipating the sculptor's *Internal/External Forms* (see p. 36)[3] and intimating his identification with Prometheus, mankind's first "sculptor."

Elephant Skull Album

The model for this spectacular album was a massive elephant skull presented to Moore by his friends Juliette and Sir Julian Huxley, who had been on safari in Kenya in the early 1960s. Kept in one of his studios, the skull gradually became – in Moore's words – "the most impressive item in my 'library' of natural forms."[4] The artist's wife, Irina, proposed a series of etchings of the skull for the Genevan print publisher Gérald Cramer. Moore began etching directly on the copper plate and soon grew enamored of the skull's complexity:

> By bringing the skull very close to me and
> drawing various details I found so many contrasts
> of form and shape that I could begin to see in it
> great deserts and rocky landscapes, big caves in
> the side of hills, great pieces of architecture,
> columns and dungeons, and so this series of
> etchings is really a mixture of observation and
> imagination.[5]

Thirty-two etchings explore the skull's outline, tunnels, and cavities. The etchings' countless forms reflect Moore's fascination with empty spaces, mystery, and the human figure. To achieve the depth and complexity found in these works, he varied the pressure and angle of the etching needle and then the length of time the etched plate remained in acid. Subtle effects resulted: "a line etched for a minute or so can have the most

---

1   Neumann, *Archetypal World*, pp. 117–19. I would like to thank Shai
    Davis for his assistance in preparing this essay.
2   Moore's *Openwork Head and Shoulders* (LH 287) and *Openwork Head
    No. 2* (LH 289), completed in 1950 along with the lithographs for
    Goethe's *Prometheus*, share its cage-like structure and eery stare.
    See Compton, *Moore*, pp. 228–29.
3   Cramer et al., *Moore: Graphic Work*, vol. 1, p. 6.
4   Moore, *Elephant Skull*, pl. XXIII.
5   Cramer et al., *Moore: Graphic Work*, vol. 1, p. 5.

delicate wispiness, as was used to capture the papery thinness of bone."[6] The artist also plays with dark and light to convey shades and depths not only in the skull but in the background and negative spaces. Plate I (p. 79) features a lightly sketched background that emphasizes the boldness of the skull. Background lines energize rather than distract. The frontal orientation places the viewer eye to eye with the elephant. Its great tusks nearly slope off the page, offset by the delicate bone on the left. The eye sockets recall Moore's reclining figures. In plate VIII (p. 79), the dark background hatching deepens and intensifies the bone. The artist's trademark "box lines" simulate three-dimensionality, and the central, bulbous negative space hints at a female form. According to Moore's commentary on the adjacent leaf, he read the image as the arm of a reclining figure. Creating this text was a new challenge for the artist, and he wisely lets his work speak mostly for itself.

Auden Poems, Moore Lithographs

Moore's final album consisted of a series of lithographs illustrating poetry by W. H. Auden. Though Moore had known his fellow Yorkshireman since the 1930s and was excited about the project, he found it difficult to juxtapose Auden's poems with his own images. Finally, he decided "not so much to illustrate as to complement or even contrast."[7] Moore found working on a book "very different from doing a single drawing or print, or even a series of them without any text. One has always to think in terms of the book as a whole, and of the images not only in themselves but in relation to the text and as they will appear in their sequence in relation to each other."[8]

Cavern (p. 78) reflects the album's uniqueness. The weighty darkness evokes a sense of mystery. Reminiscent of Seurat's drawings, the image is difficult to decipher. Against a backdrop of half-hidden trees, one discerns the curve of the lower half of a reclining figure. Moore creates an atmospheric image inviting multiple associations.

Rather than viewing the paper as a limitation, the sculptor harnesses its surface. With brush, pencil, and etching needle, he builds an illusion.

---

6 Gilmour, *Graphics*, p. 13.
7 Cramer et al., *Moore: Graphic Work*, vol. I, p. 6.
8 Ibid.

Catalogue of Works in the Collection*

1 *Female Figure*, 1928
Plaster, 12 x 6 x 4.5 cm
Gift of Hilda Goldberg,
Jerusalem, in memory of her
husband, Hilary Goldberg
B77.299; LH 130a
(p. 53 left)

2 *Seated Nude*, 1929
Pen and ink, brush and ink,
chalk, wash, 430 x 320 mm
Signed lower right: "Moore 29"
Gift of Charlotte Bergman,
Jerusalem, to AFIM**
B85.525; HMF 704
(p. 54)

3 *Sixteen Heads*, ca. 1932
Pencil, chalk, wash, pen and ink,
381 x 318 mm
Signed lower right: "Moore 30"
HMF 935
(p. 66)

4 *Studies of Heads*, 1932
Crayon, chalk, wash, pen and ink,
413 x 330 mm
Signed lower right: "Moore 32"
HMF 934
(p. 64)

5 *Fifteen Standing Figures*, 1933
Pen and ink, wash,
368 x 273 mm
Signed lower right: "Moore 33"
Gift of Charlotte Bergman,
Jerusalem, to AFIM
B92.1103; HMF 1018

6 *Five Seated Figures*, 1934
Pen and ink, wash, 380 x 275 mm
Signed lower right: "Moore 34"
Gift of Charlotte Bergman,
Jerusalem, to AFIM
B85.526; HMF 1080
(p. 51)

7 *Figure*, ca. 1935
Bronze (edition of ca. 8),
14.6 x 5.5 x 4.5 cm
LH 157
(p. 58 right)

8 *Recumbent Figure*, 1938
Bronze (edition of 9),
8.3 x 12.7 x 7 cm
LH 184
(p. 40 right)

9 *Reclining Figure*, 1938
Polished bronze (edition of 9),
6.7 x 12.7 x 4 cm
LH 193
(p. 43 top)

10 *Women and Children in Bombed-out Building*, 1940–41
Pencil, wax crayon, wash,
216 x 172 mm
Signed lower right: "Moore 41"
HMF 1753
(p. 75)

11 *Four Figures*, 1941
Wax crayon, chalk, watercolor,
wash, pen and ink, 279 x 387 mm
Signed lower left: "Moore 41"
HMF 1548
(p. 60)

12 *Shelter Scene*, 1941
Pencil, wax crayon, colored
crayon, chalk, wash, pen and ink,
159 x 203 mm
Signed lower right: "Moore 41"
HMF 1803
(p. 73)

13 *Shelter Drawing*, 1941
Pencil, wax crayon, wash, pen
and ink, 336 x 563 mm
Signed lower right: "Moore 41"
Gift of Lord and Lady Clark,
Saltwood, through the
British Friends of the Art
Museums of Israel
B70.294; HMF 1850
(p. 74)

14 *Shelter Scene: Two Reclining Figures*, 1941
Pencil, wax crayon, wash,
305 x 330 mm
Signed lower right: "Moore 41"
HMF 1841
(p. 72)

15 *Draped Reclining Figures*, 1942
Pencil, wax crayon, charcoal
(rubbed), watercolor wash, pen
and ink, 225 x 117 mm
Signed lower right: "Moore 42"
HMF 2042
(p. 49)

16 *Madonna and Child*, 1943
Pencil, wax crayon, colored
crayon, watercolor wash, pen and
ink, 250 x 175 mm
Signed lower right: "Moore 43"
Gift of Charlotte Bergman,
Jerusalem, to AFIM
B85.523; HMF 2179
(p. 26 left)

17 *Madonna and Child Studies*, 1943
Pencil, wax crayon, colored
crayon, watercolor wash, pen and
ink, 175 x 159 mm
Signed lower right: "Moore 43"
HMF 2178
(p. 26 right)

---

* Unless otherwise indicated, works are
on loan from the Charlotte Bergman
Estate

** American Friends of the Israel
Museum has been abbreviated as
AFIM

18 *Madonna and Child Studies*, 1943
Pencil, wax crayon, colored
crayon, watercolor, pen and ink,
215 x 175 mm
Signed lower right: "Moore 43"
Gift of Charlotte Bergman,
Jerusalem, to AFIM
B85.524; HMF 2182
(p. 27 left)

19 *Madonna and Child Studies*, 1943
Pencil, wax crayon, colored
crayon, watercolor wash, pen and
ink, 200 x 165 mm
Signed lower right: "Moore 43"
Gift of Charlotte Bergman,
Jerusalem, to AFIM
B85.522; HMF 2180
(p. 27 right)

20 *Madonna and Child Studies*, 1943
Pencil, wax crayon, colored
crayon, watercolor, pen and ink,
222 x 172 mm
Signed lower right: "Moore 43"
HMF 2177
(p. 30 right)

21 *Mother and Child Studies*, 1943
Pencil, wax crayon, watercolor
wash, pen and ink, 168 x 216 mm
Signed lower right: "Moore 43"
HMF 2186

22 *Two Women and Children*,
1943–44
Pencil, wax crayon, colored
crayon, watercolor wash,
229 x 191 mm
Signed lower right: "Moore 44"
HMF 2201
(p. 28)

23 *Family Groups and Madonna and
Child*, ca. 1943–44
Pencil, wax crayon, colored
crayon, watercolor wash, pen and
ink, 229 x 165 mm
Signed lower left: "Moore 44"
HMF 2202
(p. 30 left)

24 *Family Group*, ca. 1943–44
Pencil, wax crayon, colored
crayon, watercolor wash, pen and
ink, 165 x 178 mm
Signed lower right: "Moore 45"
HMF 2329
(p. 31 left)

25 *Studies for Family Groups*,
ca. 1943–44
Pencil, wax crayon, colored
crayon, watercolor wash, pen and
ink, 210 x 164 mm
Signed lower right: "Moore 44"
Gift of Charlotte Bergman,
Jerusalem, to AFIM
B80.2891; HMF 2222

26 *Reclining Figure*, 1945
Bronze (edition of 7),
7.2 x 19.8 x 6.4 cm
LH 256
(p. 39)

27 *Reclining Figure (Maquette for
Elmwood Figure)*, 1945
Bronze (edition of 7),
8.7 x 17 x 7.5 cm
LH 249
(p. 42 top)

28 *Reclining Figure*, 1945
Bronze (edition of 7),
8 x 15 x 7 cm
LH 263
(p. 42 bottom)

29 *Reclining Figure*, 1946–47
Bronze (edition of ca. 8),
8.2 x 16.8 x 8.5 cm
LH 266
(p. 43 bottom)

30 *Studies of the Artist's Child*,
ca. 1947
Pencil, wax crayon, colored
crayon, watercolor wash, pen and
ink, 288.8 x 241.3 mm
Signed lower left: "Moore 47"
HMF 2399
(p. 32)

31 *Standing Women*, 1948
Pencil, wax crayon, pen and ink,
gouache, 711 x 546 mm
Signed lower left: "Moore 48"
HMF 2482
(p. 56)

32a *Five Studies for Rocking Chairs*,
ca. 1949
Pencil, colored crayon, charcoal
wash, pen and ink, 289 x 237 mm
Gift of Charlotte Bergman,
Jerusalem, to AFIM
B79.951; HMF 2433
(p. 37)

32b Verso
Pencil, ink, crayon, watercolor

33 *Family Groups*, ca. 1949
Pencil, wax crayon, colored
crayon, watercolor wash, pen and
ink, 293 x 242 mm
Signed lower left: "Moore 49"
Gift of Charlotte Bergman,
Jerusalem, to AFIM
B92.1101; HMF 2470
(p. 31 right)

34 *Seated Figure*, 1949
Bronze (edition of 7),
24 x 11 x 10.5 cm
Signed on base: "Moore"
LH 272
(p. 52 left)

35 *Standing, Seated and Reclining
Figures*, ca. 1949
Pencil, wax crayon, colored
crayon, watercolor wash, pen and
ink, 230 x 290 mm
Signed lower right: "Moore 49"
Gift of Charlotte Bergman,
Jerusalem, to AFIM
B79.950; HMF 2459
(p. 61)

36 *Family Group*, 1950
Lithograph (numbered 43/50),
289 x 238 mm
Signed lower right: "Moore 50"
Gift of Cynthia Polsky,
New York, to AFIM
B73.1044; CGM 12

37 *Wrapped Madonna and Child:
Day Time*, 1950
Pencil, wax crayon, colored
crayon, pen and ink, gouache,
343 x 242 mm
HMF 2715
(p. 16)

38 *Wrapped Madonna and Child:
Night Time*, 1950
Pencil, wax crayon, watercolor
wash, pen and ink, 342 x 242 mm
HMF 2714
(p. 18)

39 *Three Fates*, 1950
Chalk, colored crayon, watercolor
wash, gouache, 584 x 762 mm
Signed (later) lower right:
"Moore 50"
HMF 2618
(p. 23)

40 *Maquette for Standing Figure*, 1950
Bronze (edition of 7),
26.8 x 6.4 x 4.5 cm
LH 290a
(p. 20 left)

41a *Helmet Heads*, 1950
Gouache and charcoal,
292 x 244 mm
Signed lower right:
"Moore, 10-12-50"
Gift of Charlotte Bergman,
Jerusalem, to AFIM
B92.1102; HMF 2641
(p. 68 right)

41b Verso
Gouache, crayon, pastel
(p. 68 left)

42 *Head of Prometheus*, 1950
Lithograph (numbered 34/50),
317 x 235 mm
Print from Johann Wolfgang von
Goethe, *Prométhée*, translated by
André Gide, published by Nicaise,
Paris, 1950
Gift of Lois Handler, Agoura
Hills, California, to AFIM
B95.0844; CGM 22
(p. 76)

43 *Pandora and the Imprisoned
Statues*, 1950
Lithograph, 314 x 222 cm
Illustration in Johann Wolfgang
von Goethe, *Prométhée*,
translated by André Gide,
published by Nicaise, Paris, 1951
Folio, 68 pp., with 14 original
color lithographs, edition of 183,
390 x 297 mm
The Vera and Arturo Schwarz
Collection of Dada and Surrealist
Art in the Israel Museum
M00 76/SPE; CGM 31
(p. 77)

44a *Studies for Sculpture*, 1950–51
Wax crayon, colored crayon,
watercolor wash, pen and ink,
290 x 235 mm
Signed lower left: "Moore"
HMF 2637
(p. 36)

44b Verso
Pencil

45a *Studies for Sculpture*, 1950–51
Pencil, wax crayon, watercolor
wash, pen and ink, gouache,
290 x 235 mm
Signed lower right: "Moore 50"
HMF 2638
(p. 35)

45b Verso
Pencil, ink, watercolor
(p. 69)

46 *Maquette for Upright Internal/
External Form*, 1951
Bronze (edition of 7),
21.2 x 8.4 x 6 cm
LH 294
(p. 36)

47 *Two Seated Figures I*, 1951
Etching (numbered 22/50),
73 x 124 mm
Signed lower right: "Moore"
On long-term loan from the
Fritz Naphtali Foundation
B70.70; CGM 35

48 *Standing Figure No. 1*, 1952
Bronze (edition of 9),
23.8 x 6 x 5.5 cm
LH 317
(p. 62 right)

49 *Standing Figure No. 3*, 1952
Bronze (edition of 10),
20.5 x 4.2 x 3.8 cm
LH 319
(p. 62 left)

50 *Mother and Child*, 1952
Carbon line, 328 x 278 mm
Signed lower right: "Moore 52"
Gift of Charlotte Bergman,
Jerusalem, to AFIM
B79.157; HMF 2738
(p. 33)

51 *Maquette for Draped Reclining
Figure (Reclining Woman)*, 1952
Bronze with brown, marble base
(edition of 10), 19 x 10 x 16 cm
Bequest of Loula Lasker,
New York, through the America-
Israel Cultural Foundation
B61.1039; LH 335
(p. 40 left)

52 *Reclining Figure No. 2*, 1953
Bronze (edition of 7),
41 x 96 x 40 cm
Gift of Charlotte Bergman,
Jerusalem, to AFIM
B73.1166; LH 329
(p. 41)

53 *Small Head*, 1953
Bronze (edition of 10),
7 x 4.7 x 5.4 cm
Bequest of Loula Lasker,
New York, through the America-
Israel Cultural Foundation
B61.1040; LH 356
(p. 65)

54 *Reclining Figure: External Form*,
1953–54
Bronze (edition of 6),
105 x 215 x 85 cm
Gift of Celeste and Joel Starrels,
Chicago
B67.791; LH 299
(p. 38)

55 *Wall Relief: Three Forms*, 1955
Bronze (edition of 12),
18.4 x 32.6 x 3.2 cm
Signed lower right: "Moore"
LH 374
(p. 70)

56 *Upright Motive No. 7*, 1955–56
Bronze (edition of 5),
332 x 69 cm
Gift of the British Friends of the
Art Museums of Israel
B69.199; LH 386
(p. 63)

57 *Mother and Child No. 1: Reaching
for Apple*, 1956
Bronze (edition of 10),
72 x 45 x 50 cm
Gift of Andrea Bronfman and
Kappy Flanders, Montreal,
in honor of their parents, Doris
and Hyam Morrison
B95.0137; LH 406
(p. 24)

58 *Seated Girl*, 1956
Bronze (edition of 9),
21 x 18.5 x 12 cm
Sam Spiegel Collection
B97.0511; LH 420
(p. 53 left)

59 *Studies for Sculpture on Blue-Grey
Background*, 1957
Lithograph (numbered 38/60),
432 x 349 mm
Signed lower right: "Moore"
Gift of Norman Davis, Seattle,
through the America-Israel
Cultural Foundation
B66.684; CGM 39

60 *Woman (Seated Torso, Parze)*,
1957–58
Bronze (edition of 8),
142.2 x 91.4 x 78.7 cm
Signed and numbered on base:
"Moore 1/4"
Sam and Ayala Zacks Collection
L-B04.002; LH 439
(p. 50)

61 *Frontispiece to Henry Moore,
Heads, Figures and Ideas*,
published by George Rainbow
Ltd., London and Greenwich, 1958
Pencil on paper, 238 x 287 mm
The Vera and Henry Mottek
Collection
On permanent loan from the
Administrator General of the
State of Israel
L-B97.094

62 *Stringed Head*, 1958
Fired terracotta and string,
7.8 x 5.8 x 2.5 cm
LH 186g
(p. 67 right)

63 *Relief No. 1*, 1959
Bronze (edition of 6),
224 x 12.5 x 48 cm
Gift of the artist
B73.1173; LH 450
(p. 45)

64 *Maquette for Seated Woman:
Thin Neck*, 1960
Bronze (edition of 11),
26.8 x 12 x 12 cm
LH 471
(p. 52 right)

65 *Three Piece Reclining Figure:
Maquette No. 1*, 1961
Bronze (edition of 9),
11.4 x 20.4 x 9 cm
LH 499
(p. 44 bottom)

66 *Seventeen Reclining Figures*, 1963
Lithograph (numbered 40/50),
585 x 800 mm
From *Album International*,
published by Éditions Alpic
Geneve
Signed lower right: "Moore 63"
Acquired through funds donated
by Walter Bick, Ontario
B74.689; CGM 46

67 *Working Model for Three Way Piece
No. 2: Archer*, 1964
Bronze (numbered 6/7),
91.5 x 91.5 x 53.4 cm
Signed: "Moore 6/7"
Gift of Isidore M. Cohen,
New York, to AFIM
B73.105; LH 534
(p. 48)

68 *Hommage à Rodin*, 1966
In *Hommage à Rodin portfolio*,
1967
Lithograph, 295 x 235 mm,
artist's proof
Signed lower right: "Moore"
Gift of Prof. Ionel Jianou, Paris
B68.446; CGM 59

69 *Eight Reclining Figures in Yellow
Red and Blue*, 1966
Color lithograph (artist's proof),
550 x 375 mm
Signed lower right: "Moore"
The Vera and Henry Mottek
Collection
On permanent loan from the
Administrator General of the
State of Israel
L-B97.092; CGM 58

70 *Black Seated Figure on Orange
Ground*, 1966
Color lithograph (artist's proof),
550 x 377 mm
Signed lower right: "Moore"
The Vera and Henry Mottek
Collection
On permanent loan from the
Administrator General of the
State of Israel
L-B97.091; CGM 80

71 *Studies for Sculpture: Two and
Three Pieces Reclining Figures*
From *Gérald Cramer: Trente ans
d'activité*, containing 15 prints by
various artists, 1967
Etching and dry point (numbered
110/125), 308 x 232 mm
Signed lower right: "Moore"
Gift of Gérald Cramer, Geneva
B72.1268; CGM 95
(p. 44 top)

72 *Studies for Head and Shoulders
Sculpture*, 1967
Etching (numbered 18/50,
second state), 308 x 238 mm
Signed lower right: "Moore"
On long-term loan from the Fritz
Naphtali Foundation
B71.70; CGM 94

73 *Three Piece Sculpture: Vertebrae*,
1968–69
Bronze (edition of 3),
base 710 x 355 cm
Gift of the artist and of the
British Friends of the Art
Museums of Israel
B72.1277; LH 580
(pp. 46–47)

74 *Elephant Skull*, Plate I, 1969
Etching, 254 x 200 mm
From *Elephant Skull Album*,
32 original etchings by Henry
Moore, published by Gérald
Cramer, Geneva, 1970
Acquired through funds donated
by the Hon. Philip Klutznik,
Chicago
B72.1256; CGM 114
(p. 79 top)

75 *Elephant Skull*, Plate VIII, 1969
Etching (numbered 84/100),
235 x 308 mm
From *Elephant Skull Album*
Gift of Adam Mekler, Pasadena,
to AFIM
B98.0651; CGM 121
(p. 79 bottom)

76 *Cavern*, 1973
Lithograph, 321 x 267 mm
Print from "The Three
Companions," in *Auden Poems,
Moore Lithographs (1974)*,
published by Petersburg Press
Ltd, London, 1974
Signed lower right: "Moore"
Gift of Sylvia Gadd, Long Branch,
New Jersey, to afim
B88.14; CGM 248
(p. 78)

77 *Reclining Figure: Idea for
Sculpture*, 1981
Ballpoint pen, felt-tipped pen,
wax crayon, watercolor wash,
chinagraph on T. H. Saunders
watercolor paper, 140 x 275 mm
Signed lower right: "Moore"
Gift of Ken Melamed,
New York, to AFIM, in memory of
Sarah R. Beningson
B00.1102; HMF 81 [317]

78 *Female Torso*, 1984
Bronze (numbered 4/9),
17.2 x 5.7 x 6 cm
The Vera and Arturo Schwarz
Collection of Dada and Surrealist
Art in the Israel Museum
B98.0545; LH 913
(p. 58 left)

79 *Stringed Head*, 1986
Bronze and string
(numbered 2/5), 11.4 x 5 x 5 cm
LH 186g
(p. 67 left)

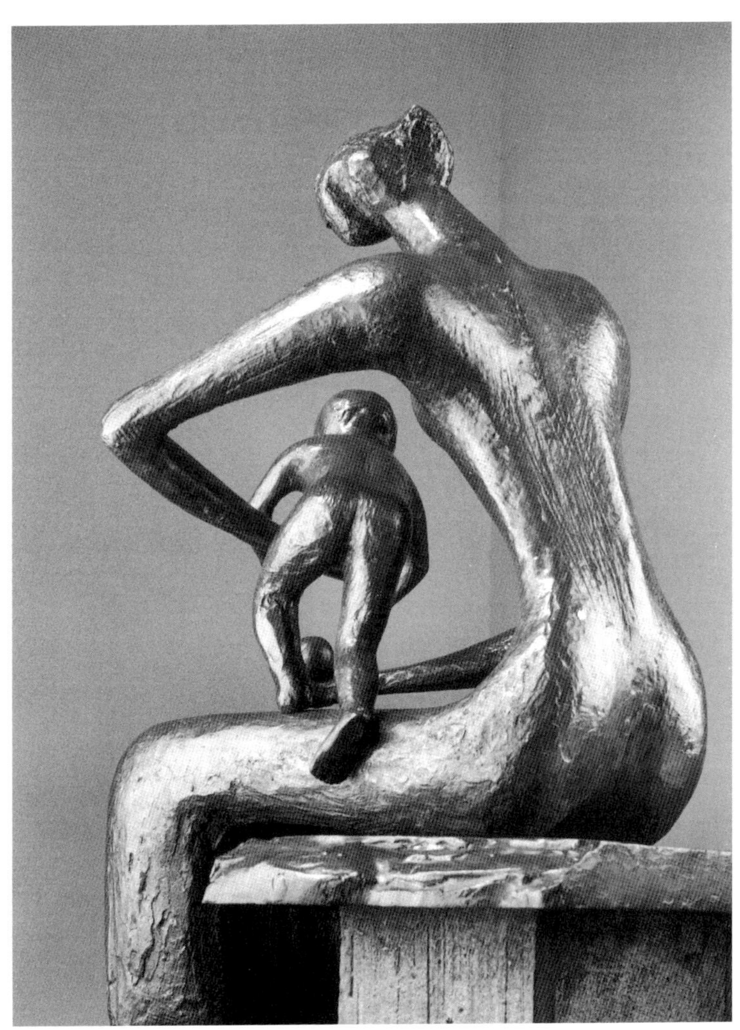

אם וילד מס' 1: מושיט יד לתפוח, 1956 (ראה עמוד 24)
Mother and Child No. 1: Reaching for Apple, 1956 (see p. 24)

הנרי מור

עדינה קמיאן-קשדן

מוזיאון ישראל, ירושלים

מוזיאון ישראל, ירושלים

מבט על האוסף: הנרי מור
קיץ תשס"ד - חורף תשס"ה
אולם רנה (פיש) ורוברט לוין
ואולם קרן הילדגרד וסימון רוטשילד (שווייץ),
הבניין לאמנות המאה ה־20 ע"ש נתן קמינגס

אוצרת התערוכה: עדינה קמיאן-קשדן
עיצוב התערוכה: רבקה מאירס ושירלי יהלומי

עיצוב הקטלוג: תרצה ברי
תרגום: תמי מיכאלי, עמ' 7-22; ענת שולץ,
עמ' 25-62; דליה קרפלוס-פויכטוונגר, עמ' 65-80
עריכה: רויטל מזובר
צילום: © מוזיאון ישראל, ירושלים,
על־ידי אבשלום אביטל
© קרן הנרי מור (עמ' 19, 20 מימין, 21, 22)
© מוזיאון תל אביב לאמנות,
על־ידי אברהם חי (עמ' 57)

הפרדת צבעים, הדפסה וכריכה:
מפעלי דפוס כתר בע"מ, ירושלים

כל עבודותיו של הנרי מור © קרן הנרי מור,
מאץ' האדהם, הרטפורדשיר, אנגליה

קטלוג מס' 493
מסת"ב 8 304 278 965

התערוכה והקטלוג התממשו בזכות
תרומה לכבוד זכרו של בנג'מין מילר

על העטיפה:
פסל בשלושה חלקים: חוליות (פרט)
עמ' 83, מס' 73; תצלום בעמ' 7-46

כל העבודות מאוסף מוזיאון ישראל, אלא אם צוין אחרת

במידות העבודות הגובה קודם לרוחב

מספר העבודה הוא מספרה
ברשימת העבודות באוסף (עמ' 80)

הצירופים HMF;CGM;‏ LH הם קיצורים לקטלוגים המקיפים
של האמן (פירוט בעמ' 85); ברשימת העבודות הם
מובאים אחרי מספר הרישום במוזיאון

דבר המנכ"ל 5

תודות 6

הקדמה 7

מור בירושלים: 11
בהוקרה לשרלוט ברגמן

פענוח התעלומה של הנרי מור 17

קבוצות משפחה 25

הדמויות השוכבות 39

הדמויות היושבות 51

הדמויות הניצבות 57

ראשים משתנים 65

רישומים מן המקלט 73

על צפייה ודמיון: האלבומים של מור 77

רשימת העבודות באוסף 80

רשימת הקיצורים וביבליוגרפיה 85

5

דבר המנכ"ל

מאז ייסודו של מוזיאון ישראל בשנת 1965 גדלו אוספי האמנות המודרנית שלו עד מאוד הודות לנדיבותם של תורמים רבים, והם כוללים עתה ריכוזי יצירות חשובות מאת אמנים יחידים, כגון אוגוסט רודן, פבלו פיקאסו, ז'אן ארפ, ז'אן דובופה, וג'ייקוב אפשטיין.

סדרת התערוכות "מבט על האוסף", שיזמה האוצרת הבכירה לאמנות מודרנית, סטפני רחום, נועדה להציג לפני הציבור את נכסי המוזיאון ולהעמיק את ההתבוננות ביצירתם של אמנים יחידים. על־פי־רוב נעשו היצירות במגוון טכניקות ועל פני תקופות שונות, ובהצגתן יחד מנסה הסדרה להדגיש את התפתחותו היצירתית של כל אמן, את מקורות ההשראה שלו ואת תרומתו לאמנות המודרנית. במסגרת זו הסדרה מתמקדת בכל שנה באמן חשוב אחר, וכך גם מדגישה את ההתחדשות ואת הדינמיות שבאוסף המוזיאון.

זאת התערוכה השישית בסדרה "מבט על האוסף"; היא מוקדשת להנרי מור ומציעה, כמו גם הקטלוג הנלווה לה, מבט מקיף וחדשני על האוסף הרחב של יצירות אמן חלוצי זה. עושרו של האוסף נזקף לזכותם של תורמים נדיבים רבים, והראשונה בהם היא שרלוט ברגמן, אשר תרמה למוזיאון ישראל יצירות של מור עוד בחייה. עם מותה ביולי 2002, ציוותה גברת ברגמן למוזיאון את האוסף שלה כולו, והוא כולל גם כ־50 יצירות של מור – רבות מהן ציוני־דרך חשובים בעבודתו.

תודות מקרב־הלב לנותנת החסות לתערוכה ולקטלוג על תרומתה הנדיבה לכבוד זכרו של בנג'מין מילר. תודה מיוחדת לעדינה קמיאן-קשדן, אוצרת־משנה לאמנות מודרנית, על מחקרה המעמיק אשר הכשיר את הקרקע לפרויקט כולו.

ג'יימס סניידר
מנכ"ל ע"ש אן וג'רום פישר

תודות

פרויקט חשוב זה התממש בזכות שיתוף פעולה בין גורמים רבים, ולכולם אני מודה מקרב־לב. אני מודה לאנשי קרן הנרי מור שבהרטפורדשיר, ובייחוד למרטין דייויס ולמיכאל פיפס – על שחלקו עמי את מומחיותם ולא נלאו מלנבור בארכיון ולספק לי חומר נדיר להעשרת הספר והתערוכה.

הערכתי נתונה לסטפני רחום, אוצרת בכירה לאמנות מודרנית ע"ש דויד רוקפלר, על תמיכתה המתמשכת בפרויקט. אני אסירת תודה למעצבת הקטלוג תרצה ברי ולמעצבות התערוכה רבקה מאירס ושירלי יהלומי על תרומתן היצירתית לקטלוג ולתערוכה. תודה למתרגמות תמי מיכאלי, דליה קרפלוס־פויכטונגר וענת שולץ על עבודתן היסודית. תודה מיוחדת לעורכת המעמיקה והרגישה רויטל מזובר. תודה ליעל גולן ממחלקת הפרסומים ולמנהלת המחלקה, נירית צור. יגאל צלמונה, סוזן לנדאו, טלי אורנן, תמי מיכאלי ואנה בארבר, חברי ועדת המערכת, העירו הערות בשום שכל, והן היו לי לעזר רב. בהכנת הקטלוג סייעו בידי מתנדבי המחלקה בתקופות שונות – ברניס ויגדר, יעל אשל, ג'וליאנה אוקס, אביגיל זאוסמר, שי דיווים, דסי סיגל וקרן וויליאמס – ואני מודה לכולם מעומק לבי על עזרתם רבת־הערך. אני מודה למיכאל מגן, למרינה רסובסקי, לרוחי בהרד, לעירית לב ובמיוחד ללודמילה חודורקובסקי על עבודת השימור העדינה; לתימור כהן, לרורי הופר ולמיכאל ברצ'יק, אשר הכינו בטוב טעם את העבודות על נייר לתצוגה. דליה אנג'ל פיקחה נאמנה על תקציב הפרויקט, וטל אליספור סייעה בארגון ההשאלות לתערוכה. תודה לרפאל רדובן, מתאם הפרויקטים; לראש המערך האור־קולי, מנחם אמין; ולמחלקת השירותים הטכניים של המוזיאון – מוריס לסרי, ארתור אבקוב, אלכס מרקוב, רענן פרי, יניב כהן, ארי פורת ויובל בנז'מין, בניהולו של פסח רודר. תודה לצלם אבשלום אביטל, שהפליא לצלם את עבודותיו של הנרי מור; לעינת עריף־גלנטי ולזיוה הלר ממחלקת שירותי הצילום ולעמליה קשת, ראש המחלקה, על טיפולן בזכויות היוצרים ועל סיועון לצלם.

לסיום, שלמי תודה שלוחים למשאילי העבודות לתערוכה; בזכותם יכול הציבור כולו לגלות את הפנים הרבות ביצירתו של הנרי מור.

עדינה קמיאן־קשדן
אוצרת־משנה
המחלקה לאמנות מודרנית ע"ש סטלה פישבך

הנרי מור, מחשובי הפסלים במאה ה־20, זכה להצלחה מסחררת בעודו בחייו. יצירתו הממזגת בין גוף האדם ובין הצורות האורגניות שבטבע מבטאת הומניזם גדול, רעיונות ורגשות עמוקים. הוא פיסל מתוך משמעת חזקה והשתמש בצורה במלוא "שלמותה המרחבית" כלשונו.[1] בעבודתו, השואבת מתרבויות שונות, מהדהדת אמנות העבר. דמויות הנשים המלאות והארציות שלו מזכירות מתארי הרים, גאיות, צוקים ומערות, מגלמות "חיית קדם־אנושית או תת־אנושית"[2] ומשקפות את היפעלותו מן הטבע ומן המסתורין החבוי בו.

הוא נולד ב־1898 בשם הנרי ספנסר מור, וגדל בעיירת הפועלים קאסלפורד שביורקשיר, אנגליה. כשהיה בן 11 הכיר את אמנותו של מיכאלאנג'לו במסגרת לימודיו בבית־ספר־של־יום־ראשון, ובעקבות זה גמלה בלבו ההחלטה להיעשות פסל. שנה לאחר מכן זכה למלגת לימודים בבית־הספר המקומי, והחל ללמוד רישום וקדרות. עם סיום לימודיו, לימד בבית־ספר יסודי, וכעבור שנה, ב־1917, עבר ללונדון, הצטרף לחיל הרובאים, הוכשר כמקלען ונשלח לצרפת. בקרב קמבריי הורעל במתקפת גזים, וחזר לאנגליה להחלים.

ב־1920 היה מור התלמיד הראשון במחלקה החדשה לפיסול שבבית־הספר לאמנות בלידס. עד אז כמעט שלא נחשף כלל ליצירות אמנות מקוריות. בלידס התאפשר לו לפקוד בכל עת שרצה את אוסף האמנות של סגן נשיא האוניברסיטה, שכלל יצירות מאת סזאן, גוגן, מאטיס וקנדינסקי וכן חפצי אמנות אפריקניים. ב־1921 התגלגל לידיו ספרו של רוג'ר פריי *ראייה ועיצוב* (Vision and Design), שפרסם ברבים את הפיסול הלא־מערבי, והשפיע מאוד על יצירתו המוקדמת של מור.

באותה שנה קיבל הנרי מור מלגת לימודים מבית־הספר המלכותי לאמנות בלונדון והחל ללמוד שם. בביקוריו השבועיים במוזיאון הבריטי רשם צלמיות פריון פלאוליתיות, דמויות ציקלדיות ומצריות, תבליטים אשוריים, חפצי עץ מגולפים מאפריקה ומאוקיאניה וחפצים קדם־קולומביאניים צפון־אמריקניים. עניינו של המודרניזם באמנות הלא־מערבית פטר אותו מן הצורך לעסוק בנושאי האמנות הקלסית ואמנות הרנסנס ובאסתטיקה שלהן ושחרר אותו מכבלי המסורת האקדמית.[3] הוא התיידד עם הפסל השני במחלוקת, ג'ייקוב אפשטיין, וזה קנה כמה מיצירותיו וחלק עמו את אוסף האמנות המצרית והפרימיטיווית שלו. כמו

חלוצי הגילוף הישיר הבריטים אפשטיין, אנרי גודייה־ ברזסקה ואריק גיל, דגל מור ב"נאמנות לחומר" וביחסים הסימביוטיים שבין האמן־הגלף לבין כלי עבודתו וחומריו. כמעט כל הפסלים שיצר בשנות ה־20 וה־30 שאבו את השראתם מפסלי אבן מגולפים קדם־קולומביאניים.

ביקורו הראשון של מור בפריז היה בשנת 1923, שם התרשם עמוקות מעבודתו של סזאן, ובעיקר מן ה"מתרחצות הגדולות". ב־1924 קיבל מינוי של מורה לפיסול בבית־הספר המלכותי. מלגת מסע שזכה בה אפשרה לו לבלות את המחצית הראשונה של 1925 במוזיאונים ובכנסיות ברחבי צרפת ואיטליה, והוא נעשה למעריץ נלהב של תמשיחי־הקיר מאת ג'וטו ומזאצ'ו ושל עבודתו המאוחרת של מיכאלאנג'לו. משוב לבריטניה, התקשה מור להיפטר מהשפעתם ולדבוק באמנות הלא־ מערבית. הוא החל אז ללמוד ולבחון עצמות במוזיאון הטבע ואבנים מקומיות במוזיאון הגאולוגי, וללימוד זה מיוחסות השפעות־הגומלין בין הצורות הטבעיות לגוף האנושי שביצירתו הבוגרת.

ב־1928 הציג מור את תערוכת־היחיד הראשונה שלו בגלריה וורן בלונדון. ההזמנה הציבורית הראשונה שקיבל, בהמלצת ידידו אפשטיין, היתה תבליט לחזית מטה הרכבת התחתית שנקרא "רוח מערבית" ונוצר בשנים 1928-29. באותה עת נעשה מבקר האמנות רב־ ההשפעה, הרברט ריד, לחברו ולתומכו. ב־1929 התחתן מור עם אירינה רדצקי, סטודנטית לציור בבית־הספר המלכותי, שאותה הרבה לצייר. בעת ההיא החל גם לפסל את פסלו הנודע ביותר באותו עשור, "דמות שוכבת", באבן הורנטון חומה ובהשראת פסלי צ'אקמואל ממקסיקו. ב־1930 הצטרף אל אגודת האוונגרד "7 ו־5" והציג בביתן הבריטי בביאנלה של ונציה. ב־1931 עזב את בית־הספר המלכותי ועבר לנהל את מחלקת הפיסול בבית־הספר לאמנות בצ'לסי, שם לימד עד פרוץ מלחמת העולם השנייה ב־1939.

פיסולו של מור משנות ה־30 משקף את ההתפתחויות שהתחוללו באותם ימים בפריז ואת השפעתם של פיקאסו, הנס ארפ ואלברטו ג'אקומטי. עבודותיו התאפיינו

James, *Moore on Sculpture*, p. 62   1

Pevsner, "Thoughts on Moore," in Kosinsky, *Sculpting the 20th Century*, p. 22   2

שם.   3

בצורות ביומורפיות מופשטות ומנוקבות ובאנטומיה מעוותת או מאורגנת בחופשיות, אם כי היסוד האנושי מעולם לא נעלם מהן. בביקורו בפריז ב-1933 פגש מור את הפסלים ג'אקומטי, ז'אק ליפשיץ ואוסיף צדקין, והצטרף אל "יחידה 1", קבוצת אמני אוונגרד בריטים שהחברים בה היו ציירים, פסלים ואדריכלים. באותה תקופה גר בהמסטד, מושבת אמנים בצפון לונדון, ושם עבד בשיתוף פעולה עם ברברה הפוורת ובן ניקולסון.

ב-1935 החל מור ליצור דגמים קטנים עשויים טרקוטה או גבס של הפסלים הגדולים שהתעתד לפסל. בסוף שנות ה-30 הוא נטש את דוקטרינת הגילוף הישיר והעדיף את היציקה בברונזה. ואולם, גם בטכניקה זו, הוא לא עיצב תחילה את הפסל בחומר או בגבס רך, אלא גילף על-פי-רוב את הגבס המוקשה והמשיך אפוא להיות גלף במהותו, אם כי בחומר רך יותר מאבן או מעץ. טכניקת היציקה בברונזה והאפשרות להגדיל את היצירה ולשכפל אותה בסיועם של עוזרים שחררו את האמן מן המודרניזם המוקדם שלו.[4] עמידותו של החומר גם אפשרה לו לבסס את תפיסתו ש"החור עשוי לשאת לפחות אותה משמעות שנושאת המסה כולה".[5]

ב-1940 החל מור לעבוד על סדרתו המפורסמת *רישומים מן המקלט*, שתיארה את פליטי הבליץ על רציפי הרכבת התחתית בלונדון. רישומים אלו הובילו למינויו לאמן מלחמה רשמי. אחרי שהסטודיו שלו נפגע מהפגזה, הוא עבר להתגורר בחווה בפרי גרין שבהרטפורדשיר, צפונית ללונדון. כשסיים לעבוד על סדרת הרישומים, ביקר במכרה הפחם שבעיירת הולדתו קאסלפורד, וצייר שם כורים בעבודתם. אמנותו בזמן המלחמה ולאחריה שיקפה מודעות חברתית הולכת וגדלה, וזו הולידה בעקבותיה הערכה מחדש של ניסיונותיו המופשטים משנות ה-30 ופנייה לסגנון פיגורטיווי ונגיש יותר.[6] עתה, משנחשב יותר לאמן הזרם המרכזי ופחות למודרניסט מהפכן, נבחר מור ליצור את "המדונה והילד" (1943-44) בכנסיית סנט מתיו שבנורתהמפטון ואת "קבוצת משפחה" (1954-55) בהארלו ניו-טאון – שתי יצירות שהפכו סמל לערכי המשפחה בבריטניה שאחרי המלחמה, אשר השתוקקה להיבנות מחדש ולחגוג את הישרדותה.[7] נתמך על-ידי המועצה הבריטית, הוא נעשה לאמן הבולט ביותר באנגליה. היתה זו תקופת פריחה גם בחייו האישיים, עם הולדת בתו היחידה, מרי, ב-1946. הגעתה לעולם הזרימה דם חדש בתיאוריו את האם והילד, והרישומים הרבים של אירינה המינית את התינוקת מלמדים על העונג שהפיק מחיי המשפחה.

ב-1946 חצתה ההכרה במור את גבולות בריטניה, כשהוצגה במוזיאון לאמנות מודרנית בניו-יורק תערוכה רטרוספקטיווית גדולה מיצירותיו, וב-1948 זכה בפרס הבינלאומי לפיסול בביאנלה של ונציה. אחת מהזמנות העבודה היוקרתיות ביותר שקיבל היתה "דמות שוכבת": מור פיסל אותה בשיש טרוורטין, וב-1958 הציב אותה ליד בניין אונסק"ו בפריז.

"דמות שוכבת" (1951) מברונזה, שהזמינה המועצה הבריטית לרגל פסטיבל בריטניה, היתה אבן-דרך בהתפתחותו של מור. אם בעבר היו החורים שבפסליו למאפיין בלבד, הרי שעתה לא היה עוד אפשר להפריד בין הפתחים ובין הצורה.[8] עבודתו נעשתה חזיתית פחות ותלת-ממדית יותר. הדמות השוכבת והאם והילד נשארו המוטיבים השליטים ביצירתו, ורבים מפסליו שאבו את השראתם מצורות של הטבע כגון עצים סחופים, עצמות, צדפים, חלוקי נחל ואבני צור, שאסף אל סדנת העבודה שלו.

שנות ה-60 וה-70 הביאו בכנפיהן הצלחה כלכלית, וזו אפשרה למור לעבוד בממדים גדולים יותר. מ-1959 עד 1964 הוא יצר סדרה של דמויות שוכבות שהורכבו משניים ומשלושה חלקים, ושיאה היה "דמות שוכבת" (1963-65) מברונזה שהזמין מרכז לינקולן בניו-יורק. מור ביקש להציב פסלים גדולי-ממדים אלה בטבע, על רקע השמים הפרוסים מעל.

ב-15 שנותיו האחרונות הקדיש מור את עצמו יותר ויותר לרישומים. ב-1931 יצר את הדפסיו הראשונים וב-1950 אייר את *פרומתאוס* מאת גתה, ועם יצירת אלבום *גולגולת הפיל* (1969), *סטונהנג'* (1973), *שירי אודן / הדפסי-אבן מאת מור* (1974) ו*אלבום הכבשים* (1972 ו-1974) נעשה ההדפס לחלק חשוב במכלול יצירתו.

במחצית השנייה של חייו היה מור לידוען ולדמות בולטת בשדה התרבות. בשנות ה-70 הוצגו תערוכות גדולות מיצירתו, שהמרשימה בהן היתה ב-1972 בפורטה די-בלוודרה הצופה על פירנצה. ב-1977 נוסדה קרן הנרי מור, ובשנה שלאחר מכן הציג 36 פסלים בגלריה טייט הלונדונית. עד מותו ב-1986 יצר אמן פורה זה כמעט

Kosinsky, *Sculpting the 20th Century*, p. 23   4
Wilkinson, *Moore: Writings and Conversations*, p. 196   5
Cohen, "Who's Afraid of Moore?" p. 264   6
Stallabrass, "Mother and Child"; Garlake, *New Art, New World*   7
Hedgecoe, *Moore*, p. 188   8

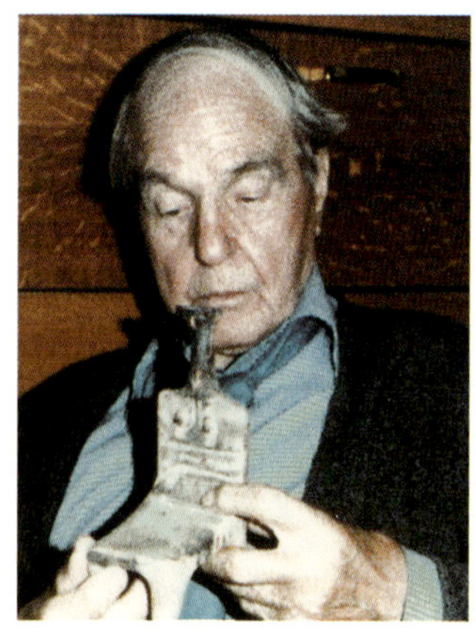

מור מחזיק העתק של הצלמית הפלשתית "אשדודה"
לאחר ביקורו במוזיאון ישראל

Moore holding a replica of the Israel
Museum's Philistine figurine *Ashdoda*

אלף עבודות. סך כל יצירתו האמנותית – לרבות פסלי
הברונזה, שמכל אחד מהם נוצרה מהדורה ובה יציקות
כמעט זהות – מונה 6000 יצירות. עבודות אלה ממלאות
מוזיאונים וכיכרות ברחבי העולם.[9]

ואולם, תהילתו העצומה של מור עוררה את חמתם של
מבקרים ואמנים. בתערוכה "היבטים חדשים בפיסול
בריטי" שנערכה ב־1952 בביאנלה של ונציה השתתף דור
חדש של פסלים בריטים, שהתקבצו תחת השם
"הגאומטרייה של הפחד", ובהם קנת ארמיטאג', לין
צ'דוויק, אדוארדו פאולוצי, רג' בטלר, רוברט אדמס וברנרד
מדוז. הם השתמשו בטכניקות תעשייתיות ובחומרים
דקים ותקיפים כדי ליצור דימויים מטרידים ומשוננים
שתמציתם ייאוש, התרסה וחרדה לצד הפניית עורף
מודעת לצורותיו המוצקות והמעוגלות של מור. ב־1960
הכריז אנתוני קארו, שהיה עוזרו של מור, שהוא ופסלים
צעירים אחרים מתעבים את "רעיון דמות האב" וש"כאשר
חושבים בפיכחון על הנרי מור, התשואות מחרישות את
האוזניים".[10] עם זה, קארו הודה שמור העניק לדור הצעיר
ביטחון עצמי ותרם תרומה חשובה למושג האמנות
הציבורית. בשנות ה־70 חדלו מבקרי האוונגרד, רוזלינד
קראוס וקלמנט גרינברג, מלעסוק במור ותייגו את עבודתו
בתארים "פופוליסטית" ו"שמרנית".[11]

למור לא היו ממשיכים לא מבחינת התוכן ולא מבחינת
הצורה, מפני שככל הנראה "הוא מיצה את שפתו האישית
עד כדי כך, שכל מי שהחל לדבר בה נלכד במלכודת
החיקוי".[12] אמנים צעירים הגדירו אפוא את עצמם בניגוד
אליו. בשנות ה־60 יצר ברוס נאומן שלוש סדרות של
עבודות שעסקו בקונפליקט האדיפלי הזה, ובהן יצירתו
השנונה "כמוסת אחסון יושבת לה"מ" (1966). "משקלו
של מור באמנות הבריטית", אמר אז נאומן, "היה גדול
מאוד שנים רבות, וחשבתי שיבוא יום והפסלים הצעירים
יזדקקו לו. כך עלה במוחי הרעיון של כמוסת אחסון".[13]
ואכן, השפעתו של מור על הפסלים הבריטים המודרנים,
כגון קארו, אניש קאפור, ריצ'רד דיקון וטוני קראג ניכרת
בניסוייהם החדשניים בצורה ובחלל, בשימוש שהם עושים
בחומרים, בדו־שיח שהם מנהלים עם הטבע וביחסי־
הגומלין בינם ובין הקהל.[14]

אף שמור ראה עצמו מונע על־ידי כוח יצירתי שאין לו
הסבר, כתביו והשיחות עמו מגלים הרהורים רגישים
ונוקבים על יצירתו ועל אמנות בכלל. הפסל הטוב לדעתו
הוא זה האוצר בתוכו אנרגיה פנימית: "אם הפסל ניחן
בחיים ובצורה משל עצמו, הוא יחיה ויתרחב, וייראה גדול

מן האבן או העץ שגולף מהם. תמיד צריך להיווצר
הרושם... שהוא צמח אורגנית, נוצר מתוך לחץ שבא
מבפנים".[15] ואכן, רבים מפסליו מייצרים את האנרגיה
הזאת, ומגלים את היושרה הגדולה של אמן זה ואת
דמיונו המופלג.

באוסף מוזיאון ישראל שמורות 79 יצירות מאת הנרי מור
הפסל, הרשם ויוצר ההדפסים. התערוכה והקטלוג
שופכים אור על הנושאים העיקריים שהעסיקו את האמן:
דמויות שוכבות, יושבות ועומדות, ראשים, קבוצות
משפחה וכן אלבומים ורישומים מן המקלט מתקופת
המלחמה. המאמר הפותח מבקש לרדת לחקר
האובייקטים העטופים והקשורים שיצר ולאפשר מושג
המאבק בעיניו. רישומיו, הדפסיו, פסלי־ההכנה ופסלי
הברונזה הגדולים שיצק מור – שואפים כולם לחדור
מבעד לפני השטח של החיים ולתאר את הרגשות
הבסיסיים ביותר של האדם.

---

9   "לפי השקפת עולם שמאלנית, התפוצה הבינלאומית של יצירת מור
הפכה סמל לסוג חדש של קולוניאליזם... הביקורת האמנותית ראתה
בחומרה רבה יותר דווקא את חזרתו של מור על עצמו ולא כל־כך
את ההאשמה הנוגעת להפקת מהדורות רבות מדי ופסלים גדולים
מדי". Cohen, "Who's afraid of Moore?" pp. 265–66.

10   Caro, "Master Sculptor," p. 21

11   שם, עמ' 21–23.

12   Kosinsky, *Sculpting the 20th Century*, p. 266

13   Van Bruggen, *Nauman*, p. 110

14   Kosinsky, *Sculpting the 20th Century*, pp. 28–29

15   James, *Moore on Sculpture*, p. 58

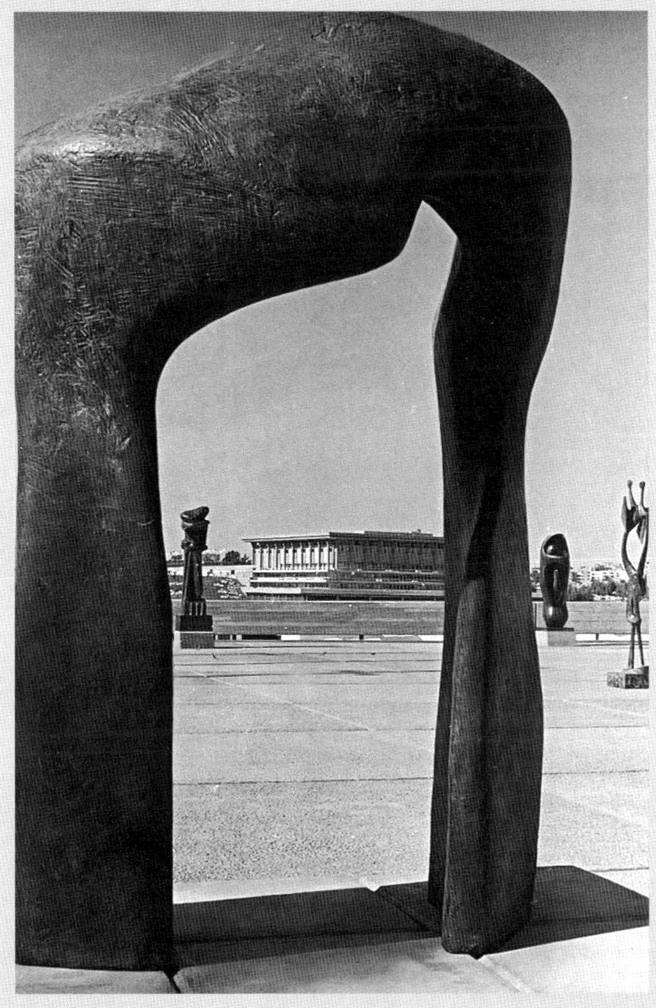

פסליו של מור ברחבה ע"ש אידה קראון בתערוכת מור במוזיאון ישראל
צילום: מוזיאון ישראל, על־ידי יצחק גורן, 1966
Moore sculptures displayed on the Ida Crown Plaza
(framing the Knesset) during his exhibition at the Israel
Museum. Photo: Israel Museum, by Jack I. Goren, 1966

מור בירושלים: בהוקרה לשרלוט ברגמן

ייחודו של אוסף הנרי מור, שהתגבש במוזיאון ישראל במהלך השנים, נובע מן הקשרים הרבים של המוזיאון עם האמן ועם תומכיו ואספניו. עושרו של האוסף נזקף לזכותם של הרבה תורמים נדיבים, והראשונה בהם היא שרלוט ברגמן. עם מותה ביולי 2002, ציוותה גברת ברגמן את האוסף שלה כולו, כ־50 רישומים ופסלים מאת מור – לטובת המוזיאון. ספר זה והתערוכה שהוא מלווה הם מחווה לחברות החמה ששררה בינה לבין מור ונר לזכרה.

קשריו של מור עם מוזיאון ישראל נרקמו בשנים המעצבות של בית־הנכות בצלאל, אשר קדם למוזיאון. כבר ב־1944 הוצגו בו, בשיתוף עם המועצה הבריטית בירושלים, 5 רישומים מאת מור במסגרת התערוכה "רישומים וציורים בצבעי־מים מאת אמנים בריטים מן המאה ה־16 ועד המאה ה־20". תערוכה זו ביטאה את נחישותו של מנהל בצלאל ואוצרו, פרופ' מרדכי נרקיס, לשמר את חיותה של האמנות בארץ־ישראל גם בתקופת מלחמת העולם השנייה, כשהשאלות של יצירות היו חיזיון נדיר. תריסר שנים אחר־כך הקדיש בית־הנכות בצלאל תערוכה שלמה ליצירתו של מור, והציג בה 4 פסלי ברונזה ו־13 תצלומים והעתקים של פסלים ושל רישומים. מארגני התערוכה היו אנשי המועצה הבריטית והקונסול הבריטי הכללי בירושלים, ויליאם וילסון. עם נעילתה, ביקש וילסון מהאמן לשגר לנרקיס עותק חתום של ספר שעסק באמנותו. במכתב נוגע ללב, שהשיב לו נרקיס ממיטת חוליו בפברואר 1957, נכתב שהספר היה לו למרפא: "לו היו בעולם עוד אנשים כמוך, הייתי בוודאי נרפא".

ב־1965 הזמינו טדי קולק, יו"ר מועצת המנהלים של מוזיאון ישראל דאז, וקרל כץ, האוצר הראשי של אגף בצלאל, את מור לחנוכת המוזיאון בירושלים, אך הדבר לא נסתייע. ארבעה חודשים אחר־כך הוקדש ביתן בגן האמנות על־שם בילי רוז להצגתם של יותר מ־40 פסלים ורישומים מאת מור – כולם בהשאלת שרלוט ברגמן, ממייסדות המוזיאון ומעמיתי־הכבוד שלו.

שרלוט ולואיס ברגמן החלו לרכוש את יצירותיו של מור כבר ב־1934, עוד לפני שזכה לתהילה. אף שבני הזוג התגוררו בארצות־הברית מאז פרוץ מלחמת העולם השנייה, הם נהנו מיחסי קרבה אל האמן, ובמסעותיהם התכופים לאירופה ביקרו אצלו באנגליה. היצירות שרכשו על פני יותר מ־35 שנה, נקנו ישירות מן האמן, והן

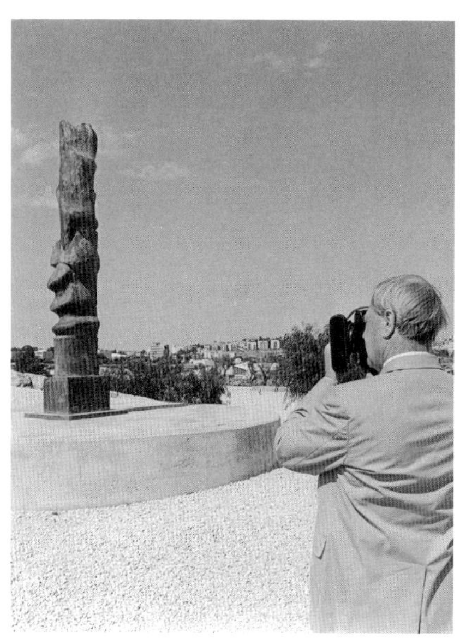

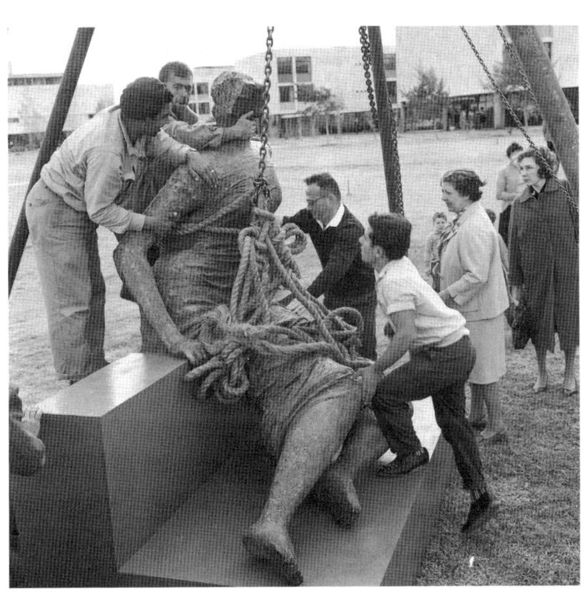

הצבת "אישה עטויה יושבת" בקמפוס אדמונד ספרא, האוניברסיטה העברית
בירושלים, גבעת רם; שרלוט ברגמן מימין (בחליפה לבנה). צילום: ורנר בראון, 1962

Installation of *Draped Seated Woman* at the Hebrew University of
Jerusalem's Edmond J. Safra Campus, Givat Ram. On the right
(in white suit): Charlotte Bergman. Photo: Werner Braun, 1962

מייצגות חתך נאה של יצירתו למן הרישומים ופסלי־
ההכנה ועד לפסלים ממוצעי־הממדים. אוסף הרישומים
שלהם הוא מן האוספים הפרטיים המשובחים.

בחליפת המכתבים ביניהם, אשר התפרסה על פני 40
שנה, הביעה שרלוט ברגמן לא פעם אחת את התלהבותה:
"רוב ה'מורים' שלי שמורים בביתי, והחדר המיוחד
שהקדשתי להם הוא אגדי!" כתבה ב־1964, "אני מקווה
שבקרוב תראה אותו". בתשובה סיפר לה מור על
הפרויקטים שהוא עובד עליהם, על התערוכות ועל חיי
היומיום. ברגמן הרחיבה את ספרייתה בכל הנוגע למור,
אספה קטעי עיתונות עליו ועודדה את מכריה לרכוש
מיצירותיו. ב־1962 היא הכירה בינו ובין דונלד ברואר,
מנהל מרכז האמנות בלה־הוויה שבקליפורניה, ושנה לאחר
מכן הוצגה במקום תערוכה שכללה מאה יצירות מאת
מור.

הפסל הראשון של הנרי מור שתרמה גברת ברגמן
לישראל הוא הפסל גדול־הממדים "אישה עטויה יושבת",
שהוצב בקמפוס האוניברסיטה העברית שבגבעת רם,
ירושלים בנובמבר 1962.[1] בג'רוזלם פוסט נכתב אז ש"את

הפסל תרמה אספנית אוהבת אמנות מארצות־הברית,
החפצה בעילום־שמה, לזכר לואיס ברגמן המנוח, איש
לונדון וניו־יורק, שהיה מסור לאמנות ושם לנגד עיניו את
המטרה להפכה נגישה לדור הצעיר". ואכן, גברת ברגמן
חשבה ש"יש לחשוף את הצעירים לאמנות טובה אפילו
הם אינם נוטים אליה, וכי לצעירים הישראלים יש להראות
את הטוב ביותר".[2] בשנות ה־60 העתיקה שרלוט ברגמן
את מקום מגוריה מניו־יורק לירושלים, ובנתה את ביתה
בשטח מוזיאון ישראל. בבית זה – בין יצירות חשובות
מאת בראק, דופי, רואו, מאיול ופיקאסו, ובחדר השינה
שפסלי־ההכנה של הנרי מור ורישומיו פיארו את כתליו –
בילתה את ימיה, עד הגיעה לשיבה טובה.

חברים ופטרונים אחרים של הנרי מור היו גם הם מתומכיו
החשובים של מוזיאון ישראל. מרכז הנרי מור לפיסול
בגלריה לאמנות של אונטריו, מקום המשכן הציבורי הגדול
ביותר בעולם של עבודות הנרי מור – נוסד רובו ככולו
בסיועם של סם ואילה זקס. אילה זקס היא שהעשירה

<hr>

1   גברת ברגמן סיכמה עם מור שבסיס הבזלת של הפסל יגולף בארץ
לפי הנחיותיו.

2   דברי ברגמן בהודעה לעיתונות שהוציאה האוניברסיטה העברית.

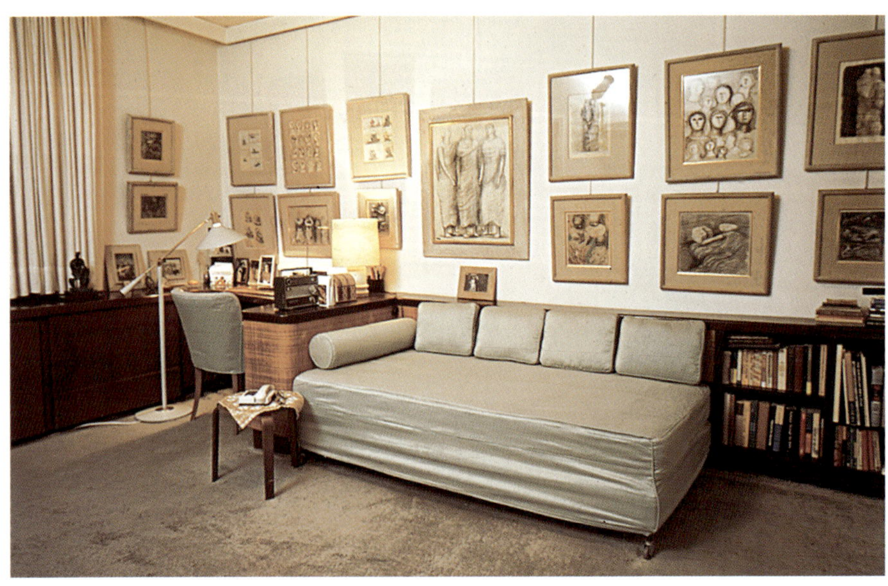

פסלי־הכנה ורישומים של מור מוצגים בחדרה של שרלוט ברגמן בביתה שבמתחם מוזיאון ישראל
צילום: מוזיאון ישראל, על־ידי אבשלום אביטל, 2002

Moore maquettes and drawings displayed in Charlotte Bergman's home on the
grounds of the Israel Museum. Photo: Israel Museum, by Avshalom Avital, 2002

את אוסף המוזיאון בפסל "אישה" (עמ' 50), הנחשב לפסל החשוב ביותר של מור באוסף שלה.

ב־1966 ערך מוזיאון ישראל בשיתוף עם המועצה הבריטית תערוכה ובה 68 יצירות מובחרות מאת מור; כעבור חודשיים הוצגה התערוכה גם במוזיאון תל אביב לאמנות. ד"ר וילם סנדברג, יועץ מוזיאון ישראל דאז, כתב בפתח הקטלוג שליווה את התערוכה את המילים האלה:

הפשטות רבת העוצמה
של צורותיו הנדיבות
הפתוחות והסגורות גם יחד
המתמידות בקשר הדוק עם הטבע
הצורות השכובות כהרים
אברי האנוש המפורדים כשברי סלעים
ההתראות הנשלחות כאצבעות מורמות
הם ביטוי לאנושות
שכמותו רק מועטים בדורנו[3]

מור הגיע לישראל לרגל התערוכה. הוא צילם את פסליו בגן בילי רוז (עמ' 11), וערך סדנה באגף הנוער. באחד התצלומים נראה האמן בפעולה עם קבוצת ילדים

המפסלים בחומר (עמ' 14). לאחר שובו כתב לסנדברג: "אני שמח מאוד שהגעתי – לפני כן לא היה לי מושג איך הדברים נראים – נהניתי מאוד להיות בירושלים במחיצתך... לפני זמן קצר קיבלתי את תצלומי הצבע שצילמתי. הבוהק ואור השמש מדהימים".

מ־1965 עד 1972 היתוספו לגן בילי רוז 3 פסלי ענק חשובים של מור – "מוטיב ניצב מס' 7" (עמ' 63) הושאל תחילה על־ידי גלריה מרלבורו בלונדון ב־1965: 4 שנים אחר־כך הפכה ההשאלה למתנה, הודות למור ולידידים הבריטים של מוזיאון ישראל בהנהגת לורד ארנולד גודמן וגברת דוריס מוריסון. ב־1967 תרמו סלסט וג'ואל סטארלס משיקגו את הפסל השני, "דמות שוכבת: צורה חיצונית" (עמ' 38). הפסל השלישי, "פסל בשלושה חלקים: חוליות" (עמ' 7-46), הגיע לגן באמצעות היועץ השני של המוזיאון, סר פיליפ הנדי. ב־1968 כתב הנדי למור שהשגתם של 3 פסלים מעשה־ידי האמן עומדת בראש תכנית הרכישות שלו. "לדעתי", כתב הנדי, "[המוזיאון] הוא המקום הראוי ביותר בשבילם. הגבעות

---

3 הנרי מור: פסלים ורישומים, קטלוג תערוכה, מוזיאון ישראל, ירושלים, תשכ"ו-תשכ"ז (1966), בלי מספרי עמודים.

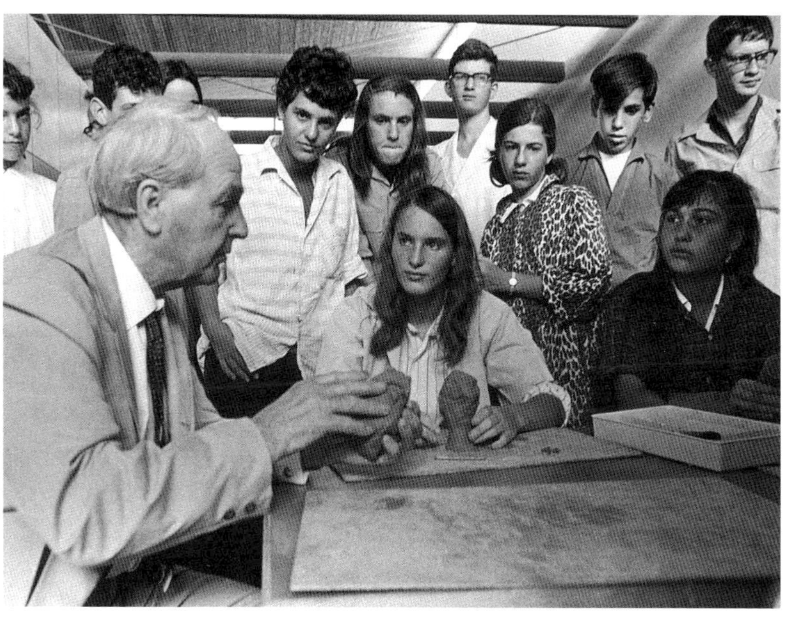

מור מפסל בחומר עם תלמידים באגף הנוער של המוזיאון. צילום: רולף מ' קנלר, 1966
Moore sculpts with students at the Israel Museum's Youth Wing.
Photo: Rolf M. Kneller, 1966

ועצי הזית נפלאים; וכך גם הסלעים והאור". בתגובה הבטיח האמן לעזור ככל שיוכל.[4] ב־1972 תרמו מור והידידים הבריטים של המוזיאון את "חוליות", עבודה מונומנטלית שיצק הרמן נואק מברלין, למוזיאון ישראל.

הצבת "חוליות" בגן הפסלים היתה משימה לא קלה. מור ייעץ להנדי להשתמש בתבניות קלקר של הפסל כדי להחליט היכן יהיה מיקומו הטוב ביותר. בתשובה כתב לו הנדי: "האתר לשלישייה[5] הוא במרכז הגן, ונדמה שכל הגן יתגבש סביבו.... טדי קולק יצא מלשכתו בעירייה כדי להגיע לכאן והתרשם מאוד". אחרי שראה תצלומי הדמיה של הפסל בגן, כתב מור להנדי: "נראה לי שהמיקום שבחרתם מצוין ומושלם מבחינת יחסי הגדלים". ב־1 בדצמבר 1972 היו מור, אשתו אירינה ובתו מרי אמורים להגיע לישראל לטקס הסרת הלוט מעל הפסל, ואולם סערה בים עיכבה את הגעת הפסל לארץ, ומור ומשפחתו ביטלו את בואם. כשלבסוף הגיע הפסל מבית היציקה, חזר כבר הנדי לאוקספורד, וייעצו השלישי של המוזיאון, ג'יימס סוויני, העלה מעט את מיקום הפסל במעלה הגבעה כדי שייראה כנגד השמים.[6]

ב־1973 העניק מור את "תבליט מס' 1" (עמ' 45) למוזיאון ישראל והוכתר בו פטרון.[7] באותה שנה התקבלו שתי תרומות חשובות נוספות של יצירות מאת האמן – דגם־ ההכנה ל"פסל בשלושה חלקים מס' 2: קשת" (עמ' 48) ואלבום גולגולת הפיל (עמ' 79), אשר הוצג בסתיו 1973. תערוכה זו, שהיא הראשונה ב־32 השנים האחרונות המוקדשת להנרי מור, מציגה יחד את כל יצירות מור השמורות במוזיאון: פסלים, פסלי־הכנה, רישומים והדפסים, ומשקפת את מערכת היחסים הנפלאה, בת 60 השנה, ששררה בין מור לאספנים שתמכו בו ולמוזיאון ישראל.

---

4   מור להנדי, 1 ביולי 1968. במהלך ביקור של הנדי אצל מור באותה שנה תרמו האמן ורעייתו למוזיאון את הציור "הקתדרלה השוקעת" מאת סרי ריצ'רדס.

5   הכוונה היא לשלוש היחידות של "חוליות".

6   הנדי וסנדברג הציבו את דגם הפסל במרכז הגן, ואילו סוויני ונואק חשבו שראוי לו שיוצב במקום גבוה יותר, כנגד השמים. נוגוצ'י הציע בשבילו אזור נבדל בגן. מור תמך בהצעה של הנדי אך הציע להציב את הפסל על במה מוגבהת, והתנגד "לאחסן אותו בפינה". סוף דבר, באפריל 1973, הועבר "חוליות" למעלה הגבעה.

7   באוקטובר 1972 ביקשה גולדה מאיר ממור להשתתף בספר "עבודות מקוריות מעשה־ידי האמנים החשובים ביותר בזמננו" לציון 25 שנים להקמת המדינה, אבל כללי קרן הנרי מור החדשה אסרו עליו לחלוק סדרת הדפסים שלמה; ב־1983 קיבל האמן תואר ד"ר כבוד מאוניברסיטת תל־אביב. מור גם תמך באגודת הציירים והפסלים של הקיבוץ הארצי, ונפגש עם אמנים ישראלים שביקרו באנגליה.

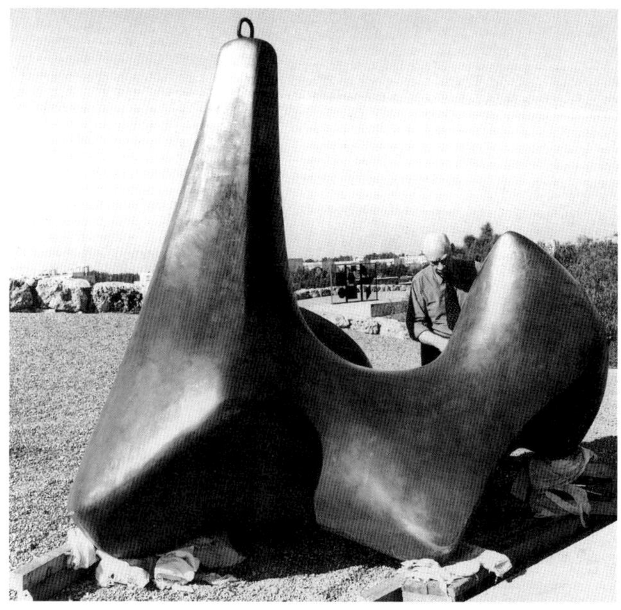

ג'יימס סוויני בודק אחד מחלקי "פסל בשלושה חלקים: חוליות"
צילום: מוזיאון ישראל, על־ידי ניר ברקת, 1972

James Sweeney, advisor to the Israel Museum, examines part of *Three Piece Sculpture: Vertebrae*. Photo: Israel Museum, by Nir Bareket, 1972

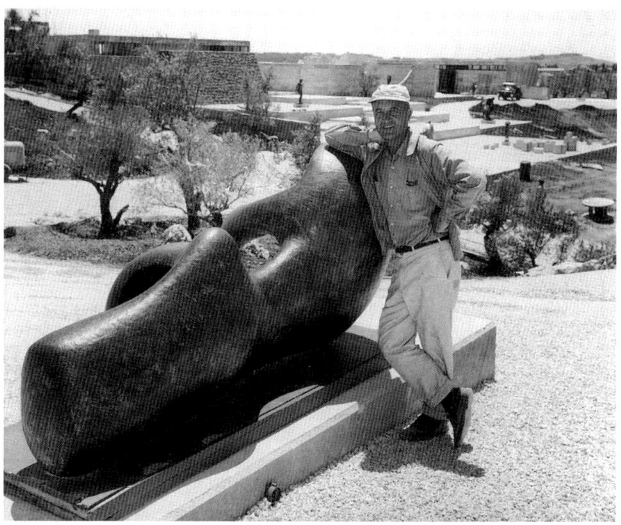

איסאמו נוגוצ'י, מעצב גן האמנות ע"ש בילי רוז, עם "דמות שוכבת: צורה חיצונית"
צילום: רולף מ' קנלר

Isamu Noguchi, designer of the Billy Rose Art Garden, with Moore's *Reclining Figure: External Form*. Photo: Rolf M. Kneller

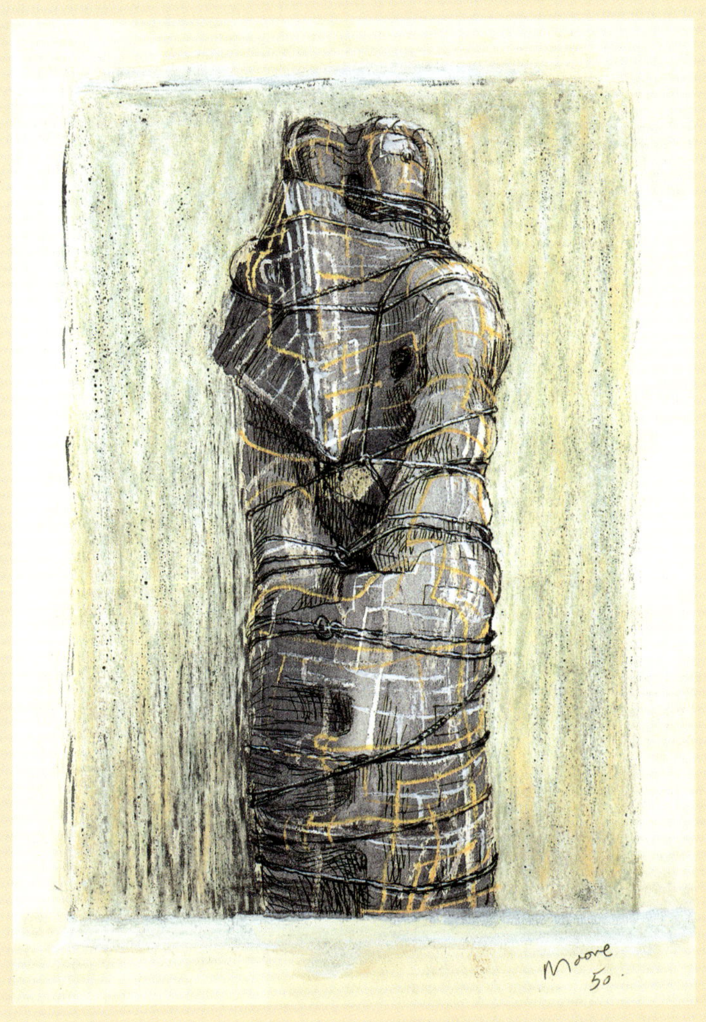

מדונה וילד עטופים: יום, 1950

Wrapped Madonna and Child: Day Time, 1950

פענוח התעלומה של הנרי מור

המסתורין ממלא תפקיד גדול וממריץ בחיינו: אי־הידיעה לצד הרצון לדעת, התהייה והניחוש, השאלה והמחקר. בלי הרף אנו נמשכים אל הלא נודע ומוקסמים ממנו.

הנרי מור, 1974[1]

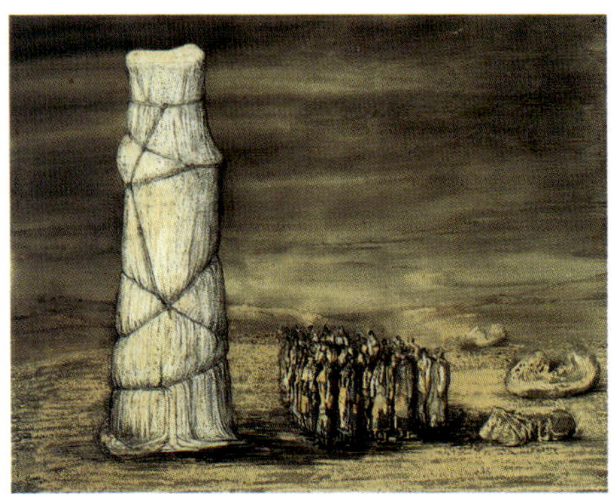

קהל מביט בחפץ קשור, 1942
עיפרון, גיר שעווה שמנוני, פחם, צבעי־מים (מגוון), עט ודיו, 432 x 559 מ"מ
המוזיאון הבריטי, לונדון; מעיזבונו לורד קלארק

Crowd Looking at a Tied-up Object, 1942
Pencil, wax crayon, charcoal, watercolor wash,
pen and ink, 432 x 559 mm
The British Museum, London, from the Estate of Lord Clark
HMF 2064

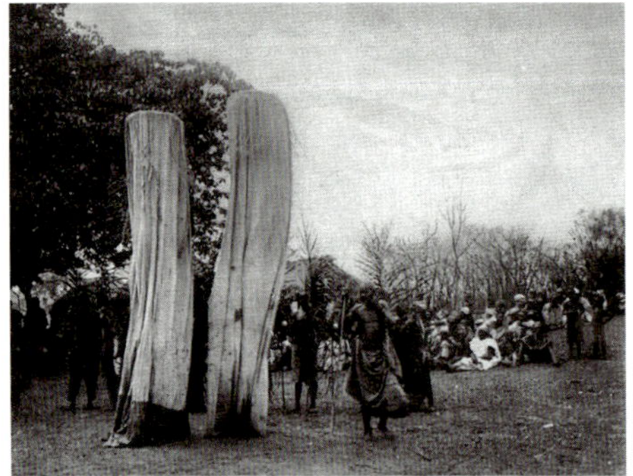

תצלום של בני שבט ניופ (צפון ניגריה) מתוך *Kulturgeschichte*
Afrikas, מאת לאו פרובניוס, ציריך, 1933, לוח 66

Photograph of Nupe tribesmen (northern Nigeria)
From Leo Frobenius, *Kulturgeschichte Afrikas*,
Zurich, 1933, plate 66

בשנת 1942 יצר מור את הרישום המפורסם ביותר שלו "קהל מביט בחפץ קשור".[2] ברישום נראית קבוצת אנשים בתוך מרחב פתוח, דמוי־חלום, הנושאים את עיניהם אל "אובייקט לבן מחופה בד" או "מצועף".[3] השמים כהים, אך שעת היום לא ברורה. על הארץ, סמוך לקבוצה, נראות 3 אבנים המזכירות את הדמויות השוכבות של מור. המראה כולו, ובייחוד החפץ העטוף והקשור המושך את עיני האנשים, חידתי ביותר. אלן וילקינסון העלה את הסברה, שכמקור לדימוי שימש תצלום שבו נראים בני שבט ניופ מצפון ניגריה סביב שתי תלבושות ענק מבדים גולשים, המשמשות בריקודי פולחן הדאקו.[4] אף שספר זה נמצא בספרייתו של מור, נותרת התעלומה בעינה: מה עושים האנשים הללו במרחב השומם, ומהו המושא המרתק את מבטם? כדי לפתור אותה, עלינו לחקור את דימויי האובייקטים העטופים והקשורים של מור.

סביר להניח שהעבודה "קהל מביט בחפץ קשור" עוסקת בחוויותיו של מור כאמן בעת מלחמת העולם השנייה. הנוף הצחיח יוצר רושם של שדה קרב נטוש. ברוח זו טוען רוברט מלוויל, שהרישום "קשור בלי ספק לרצונו [של מור] להמשיך בעבודת הפיסול, אשר נדחקה הצדה כאשר גויס כאמן מלחמה, והוא [הרישום] צופן בחובו הבטחה חידתית."[5] היות שמור לא היה יכול לצקת את פסליו בזמן המלחמה, ברישום שלפנינו הוא עוטף וקושר אחד מהם, כמו שומר על לחות החומר באופן סמלי. הקהל הממתין מסביב, מחכה לראות איזו יצירת־מופת תתגלה עם הסרת הלוט.

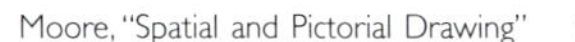

1   Moore, "Spatial and Pictorial Drawing"
2   מור כינה סוג זה בשם "רישום תמונה" וציין: "ברישום תמונה אני מתכוון להצבת הנושא בחלל", שם.
3   הערותיו של מור הרשומות על המתווה ל"קהל מביט בחפץ קשור" (HMF 2045).
4   Wilkinson, *Drawings*, p. 42 גם קנת קלארק רואה בצורה "סוג של פטיש, אובייקט פולחני של קהילה פרימיטיווית..." Clark, *Moore Drawings*, p. 120
5   Melville, *Moore: Sculpture and Drawings*, p. 26 מלוויל ממשיך: העטיפה מסתירה כנראה פסל חדש של הנרי מור אף שהפסל עצמו רק יודע שהוא ניצב ועצום־ממדים. כעת אפשר להשתכנע בקלות שתחת הכסות מסתתרת גרסת אחד "המוטיבים הניצבים" (1955-56), שהגבוה והגדול בכולם נקרא "צלב גלנקילן". שם, עמ' 27.

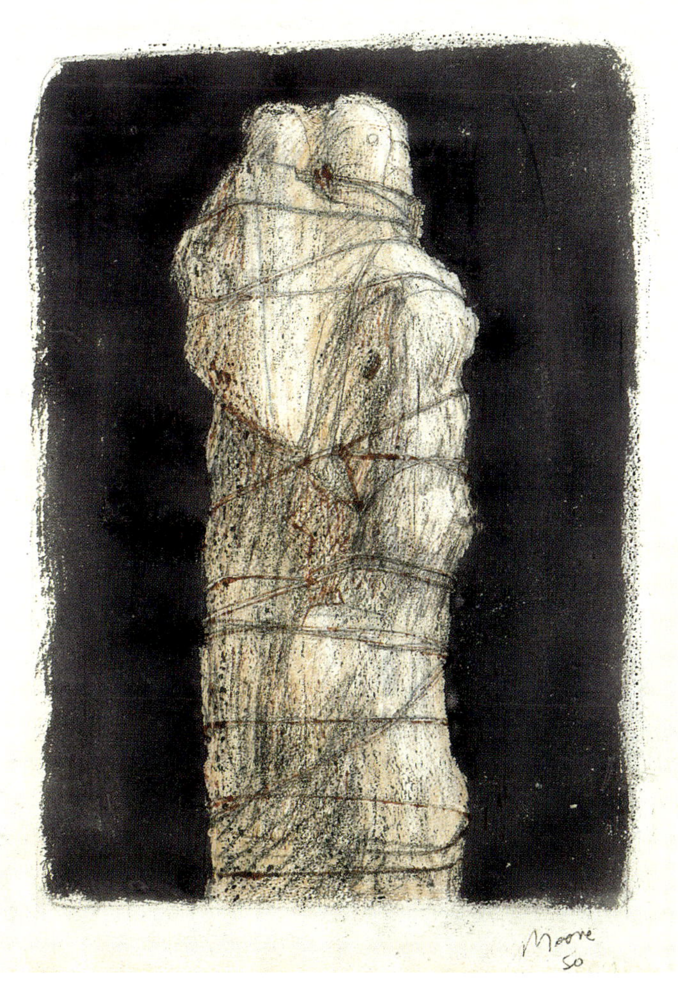

מדונה וילד עטופים: לילה, 1950
Wrapped Madonna and Child: Night Time, 1950

מור עצמו יצר קשר בין האובייקט הקשור ובין לימודיו בכיתת הפיסול בבית־הספר המלכותי לאמנות והנוהג לשמור על החומר במצבו הלח על־ידי כיסויו בבד רטוב וקשירתו בחוט.[6] ב־1938, בעת ביקור בסטודיו החדש של מור בהמסטד ציין מקס ארנסט את "המראה המרשים של העבודות בסטודיו, מחופות באורח מסתורי בסדינים לבנים, שהסיט הפסל מכל עבודה ועבודה וחשף לפי ראות עיניו".[7] סביר להניח, שהמראה הזכיר לו את יצירתו הסוריאליסטית של מאן ריי, "החידה של איזידור דוקאס", המורכבת ממכונת תפירה עטופה בד יוטה וקשורה בחבל. ייתכן מאוד, שגם מור הכיר יצירה זו, המעוררת אף היא מסתורין וציפייה להסרת הלוט.

את "קהל מביט בחפץ קשור" ציטט מור ברישום משנת 1946, "נערה קוראת לאישה וילד". במבט ראשון, וכפי שעולה משם היצירה, לפנינו סצנה ביתית. ואולם, המראה הנשקף מבעד לחלון והמתוחם על־ידי הווילונות אינו אלא "קהל מביט בחפץ קשור". שילוב הטקס החידתי הנערך בחוץ בתפנים שעניינו פעילויות נשים ובמוטיב האם והילד, פירושו אולי, שמושא ההסתכלות העטוף והקשור עוסק אף הוא במוטיב זה: בפנים האם והילד חבוקים, ואילו בחוץ הם נעשים לחפץ עצום־ממדים, נסתר וקשור, המרתק את המבט. כך, מועצם העיסוק של מור באם ובילד ולובש נופך מסתורי.

שני רישומים מרהיבים שהורישה שרלוט ברגמן למוזיאון שופכים אור על "קהל מביט בחפץ קשור", ומסייעים לפענח חלקית את פשר התעלומה. "מדונה וילד עטופים: לילה" (ממול) ו"מדונה וילד עטופים: יום" (עמ' 16), שציורו שניהם ב־1950, 8 שנים אחרי "קהל מביט בחפץ קשור", מתארים אובייקט עטוף וקשור.[8] אף שבשני הרישומים אפשר להבחין במעורפל בצורת אישה ובצורה קטנה יותר של ילד, הרי ששמות הרישומים הללו הם שמבהירים את נושאם. ואף־על־פי־כן, השמות חידתיים לא פחות מן הדימויים. מדוע המדונה והילד עטופים וקשורים, ומדוע בחר מור לתארם כך פעמיים, ביום ובלילה?

על פסלו "מדונה וילד" (נורתהמפטון) מ־1943-44 כתב מור: "סגפנות ואצילות, ומגע של הוד (אולי אף ריחוק

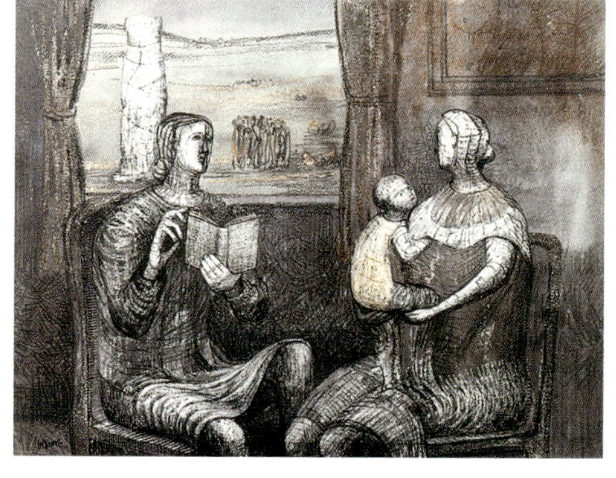

נערה קוראת לאישה וילד, 1946
עיפרון, גיר שעווה שמנוני, גיר שמנוני צבעוני, צבעי־מים (מגוון), עט ודיו,
445 x 610 מ"מ
אוסף ליידי וולסטון, קמברידג'

Girl Reading to a Woman and Child, 1946
Pencil, wax crayon, colored crayon, watercolor wash,
pen and ink, 445 x 610 mm
Lady Walston, Cambridge
HMF 2385

---

6   Wilkinson, *Drawings*, pp. 41–42

7   Penrose, *Scrap Book*, p. 102. סוזן קומפטון מעלה את האפשרות
     שהחפץ העטוף בעבודתו של מור מקורו בהערה של ארנסט
     Compton, *Moore*, p. 254

8   מור יצר עוד רישומים שכותרתם "מדונה וילד עטופים" או "חפץ
     קשור" ב־1950 וב־1951, אשר מזכירים מאוד את אלה שבאוסף
     מוזיאון ישראל (HMF 2712, 2713, 2716, 2717).

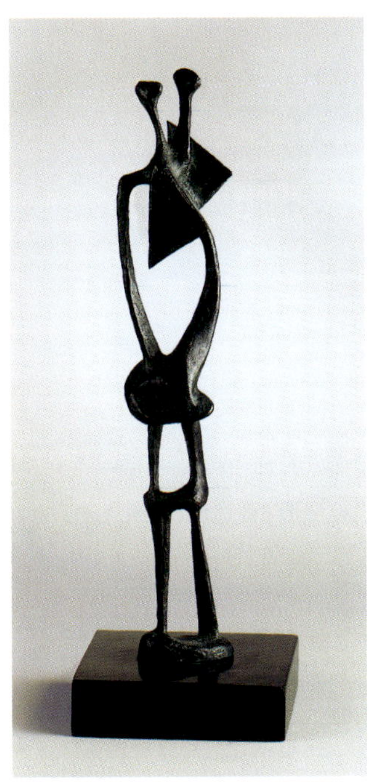

פסל־הכנה לדמות עומדת, 1950
Maquette for Standing Figure, 1950

40

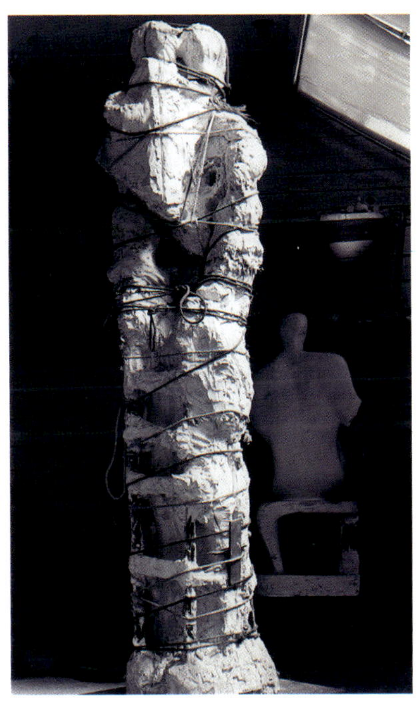

דפוס הגבס לפסל "דמות עומדת"
צילום: הנרי מור, 1950

Studio photograph of tied plaster mold of
Standing Figure. Photo: Henry Moore, 1950

קדוש), שאינם קיימים ברעיון החולין של האם והילד, צריכים ללוות את תיאור המדונה והילד".[9] התכריך הלבן ב"מדונה וילד עטופים" בוודאי מעניק לדימוי את הסגפנות וההוד שמור מדבר עליהם, והקשירה של האם והילד משקפים את התשוקה לאיחוד גופני ורגשי. ברישומים ובפסל כאחד הילד שמור ומוגן בזרועות אמו. רישומי היום והלילה יוצרים חוויה כוללת, על פני יממה שלמה, ונותנים מענה למשאלתו של מור שפסליו ייראו בחוץ, בכל תנאי, ביום ובלילה. כמו ב"קהל מביט בחפץ קשור" גם כאן הנושא ממוקם במרחב. האפלה והאור ממקדים את תשומת־לבנו לדימוי האיקוני, ועם זה יוצרים "נוף" סביב הדמויות הקשורות. שכבות הגיר השמנוני, הדיו, הגואש והמגוון יוצרות את מרקם הרקע, וזה "שובר את רודנותם של פני הנייר השטוחים ומחלץ מהם את המרחב".[10]

ואולם, המקור החזותי של "מדונה וילד עטופים" הוא פסל אחר של מור מ־1950, "דמות עומדת" (פסל־ההכנה למעלה משמאל). במבט ראשון אין דמיון בין היצירות. ה"דמות" הדו־ראשית צנומה וזוויתית, וכמו "צומחת

באנכים תזזיתיים".[11] כדי לצקת אותה בברונזה, יצר מור דפוס גבס וקשר אותו בחבלים. תצלום דפוס זה, שצולם בידי האמן בסטודיו שלו, מגלה דמיון מדויק לדימוי המתואר ב"מדונה וילד עטופים".[12] ברישומים אלה הגבס נהפך למעטפת דמוית־בד, והדמות הדו־ראשית למדונה והילד. הצורה הדומה לשריון שמתחת לראש הילד היא אפוא הכתף המשולשת של "הדמות העומדת", והריק שבמרכז הרישום הוא הד לחלל הפעור בחזהו של הפסל. מקור ההשראה של הרישומים הוא על כן מראה הדפוס הקשור של הפסל – שלב טכני, שהתגלגל והיה לרישומים דרמטיים המטביעים את חותמם על המתבונן.[13]

---

9 James, *Moore on Sculpture*, p. 220
10 מור, צוטט ב־*Auden Poems*
11 Wilkinson, *Moore Collection*, p. 113
12 אני מודה למרטין דייוויס, מנהל המידע בקרן הנרי מור, על עזרתו למחקרי.
13 שתי יצירות אחרות של מור הקשורות זו לזו בקשר דומה הן הפסל "דמות כפולה עומדת" מ־1950 (LH 291) והרישום "שתי דמויות עטופות" מ־1951 (HMF 2717).

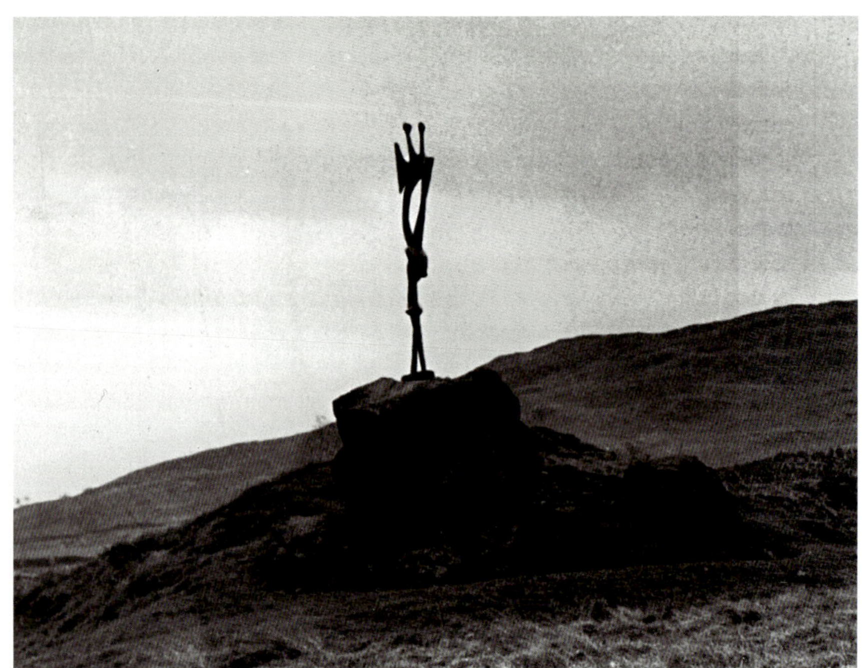

הפסל "דמות עומדת" בגלנקילן
Installation photograph of *Standing Figure* in Glenkiln

בתצלומי הפסל הגדול, שנעשה בעקבות פסל־ההכנה ל"דמות עומדת" והוצב באחוזת גלנקילן, נראית הדמות הדו־ראשית בזווית הרואית ומונומנטלית. ובמילותיו של מור: "נועצת מבטה בחלל... כאילו הראש האחורי עוזר לראש הקדמי להסתכל לאותו כיוון ומכפיל את מבטו". זאת ועוד, "הפסל מוצב על אדמת בור מבודדת בסקוטלנד, ואופיו החשוף של הנוף מבליט את השלדיות, הנוקשות והנזירות שבו". הקשר הפיוטי בין הפסל לטבע גרם למור לכנותו "פסל בנוף – איש עומד".[14] הסביבה השוממת הנראית בתצלום והאווירה הדרמטית העולה ממנו מזכירות את הסביבה והאווירה שב"קהל מביט בחפץ קשור".[15]

ב־1942, אותה שנה שבה צייר את "קהל מביט בחפץ קשור", החל מור לרשום נשים מלפפות צמר. הנושא הזה מוסיף נדבך לפרשנות של הקשירה והחבל ביצירתו. ברישומיו אלה אחת הנשים מגישה קדימה את ידיה הפתוחות, שחוט צמר כרוך סביבן; וחברתה מושכת את החוט ומלפפת ממנו כדור צמר. נושא זה שב ועלה

ביצירתו ב־1948 ("שתי נשים מלפפות צמר", עמ' 22) וגם ב־1949. רישומים אלה הם חלק מקבוצת עבודות שהוקדשה לתיאור נשים גדולות־ממדים קוראות או סורגות בתפנים ביתי. עניינו של מור במלאכות נשים בא לידי ביטוי כבר ב־1927, בדיוקן אמו תופרת. צמר, ליפוף, קשירה וחוטים הם אפוא סמל לפעילות נשית או אימהית ביצירתו. תיאוריו את האם והילד, את המשפחה ואת הדמויות השוכבות אחרי המלחמה "חידשו את האמון בקביעותם וביציבותם של אלה – ואישרו מחדש את הישרדותם של האנושות ושל האיחוד בין הטבע לאדם".[16] רישומים כגון "שתי נשים מלפפות צמר" נועדו לציין את ההמשכיות של המשפחה ושל הקהילה.

---

14   Wilkinson, *Writings and Conversations*, p. 275
15   ב־1966 יצר מור תחריט "קהל מביט בחפץ קשור". החפץ העטוף והקשור בתחריט מזכיר צלב, ואולי יש בו אזכור ל"מוטיב ניצב מס' 1: צלב גלנקילן" מהשנים 1955-56 (LH 377).
16   Feldman Bennet, "Drawings," p. 16

עיסוקו של מור במלאכות נשים הלך והעמיק ברישומים שנושאם שלוש אלות הגורל.[17] לפי המיתולוגיה היוונית, אלות הגורל טוות וגוזרות את חוט (פתיל) החיים של כל אדם. ברישום מ־1950 (עמ' 23) נראות שלוש האלות: מימין, לאקסיס, הקוצבת את משך החיים, אוחזת בפלך ומייצגת את הלידה; משמאל, קלותו הטווה, המסמלת את החיים; ובתווך, אטרופוס ובידה מספריים, המופקדת על גזירת החוט וניתוק פתיל החיים. הרקע הכהה עשוי לרמוז ללילה, אמן של אלות הגורל. אלות הגורל, כך האמינו, פקדו את הילוד בעת לידתו וקבעו את גורלו, המסומל בחוט שטוו. אותו חוט, אולי סמל לחבל הטבור, קושר את האם והילד ב"מדונה וילד עטופים".

דימוייו הקשורים והעטופים של מור משקפים גם את העניין שהיה לו במה שכינה "המאבק הנסתר".[18] אמנות גדולה, לתפיסתו של מור, חייבת להכיל קונפליקט או יסוד מטריד ומסתורי: מאבק מסתורי זה הוא הוא נושא הדימויים העטופים והקשורים. ב־1966, כמעט חצי יובל אחרי שצייר את "קהל מביט בחפץ קשור", קבע מור ש"יש זיקה הדוקה בין הרישום ובין הבנתי את הפואמות של אודן – המסתורין שמתחת לתכריך קרוב במידה זו או אחרת למסתורין שבשירה. זהו אותו יסוד של הלא־נודע המרתק אותי למערות ולפתחים במדרונות הגבעות – אינך יודע מה יש בהם, עד שאתה מתקרב וחוקר אותם. מסתורין זה מצית את הדמיון...".[19] לבעליו הראשונים של הרישום, סר קנת קלארק, אמר מור: "ראיתי אבן קשורה שהובלה במשאית, וחשתי עד כמה מסתורי יכול להיות אובייקט כזה, המגלה את צורתו באמצעות החבלים המתוחים עליו, ובה־בעת מכסה עליה ומעורר את סקרנותנו".[20]

העטיפה והקשירה ביצירתו של מור מרמזים אפוא על כמה משמעויות. מור עודד את מחקר יצירתו, אך דחה אותו כשהציע פרשנות לנפשו. בחששו מן המחובות לאמת או לשלול את הניתוח היונגיאני שכתב אריך נוימן ליצירתו,[21] סירב להמשיך ולקרוא בו מעבר לפרק הראשון. אותה גישה דו־ערכית באה לידי גם בהודאתו: "משחר נעוריי עסקתי בכפייתיות בנושא האם והילד",[22] ובדחייתו המודעת את הניסיון לרדת לפשרה של אותה כפייתיות: "החלטתי שאיני רוצה שיערכו לי פסיכואנליזה, וגם איני רוצה להבין את המקור להתנהגותי".[23] ואף־על־פי־כן, פענוח התעלומה של "קהל מביט בחפץ קשור" חושף חלק נכבד מעולמו הפרטי ביותר של האמן, והבד העוטף מגלה יותר משהוא מכסה. דפוס הגבס הקשור של "דמות עומדת" מתגלגל ונעשה לדימוי סמלי ומסתורי,

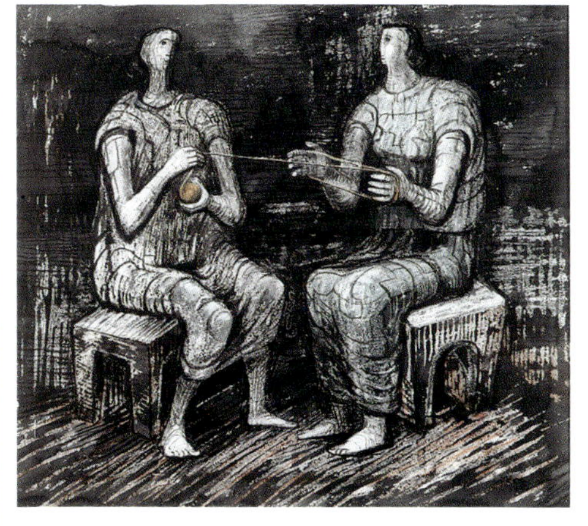

שתי נשים מלפפות צמר, 1948
עיפרון, גיר שעווה שמנוני, גיר שמנוני צבעוני, צבעי־מים (מגוון), עט ודיו,
מכחול ודיו, גואש, 567 x 648 מ"מ
קרן מור דנאוסקי

Two Women Winding Wool, 1948
Pencil, wax crayon, colored crayon, chalk, watercolor
wash, pen and ink, brush and ink, gouache, 567 x 648 mm
The Moore Danowski Trust
HMF 2498

המבטא את הכמיהה להיטמעות. ב"דמות עומדת", שהיא אולי האמן עצמו, משולבים האם והילד, ומערכת היחסים המקודשת שלהם מקילה במעט את קלישותם של החיים.

---

17 "שלוש אלות הגורל" מתוארות ב־1948 (HMF 2163, 2497) שם הן מכונות "נשים מלפפות צמר" וגם במחברת המתווים "פרומתאוס" מ־50־1949 (HMF 2554), שהיא כנראה מתווה לרישום שבאוסף מוזיאון ישראל.
18 James, *Moore on Sculpture*, p. 91
19 Moore, *Introduction to Auden Poems*
20 Clark, *Moore Drawings*, p. 120
21 Neumann, *Archetypal World*
22 Wilkinson, *Writings and Conversations*, p. 213
23 Hedgecoe, *Moore*, p. 151

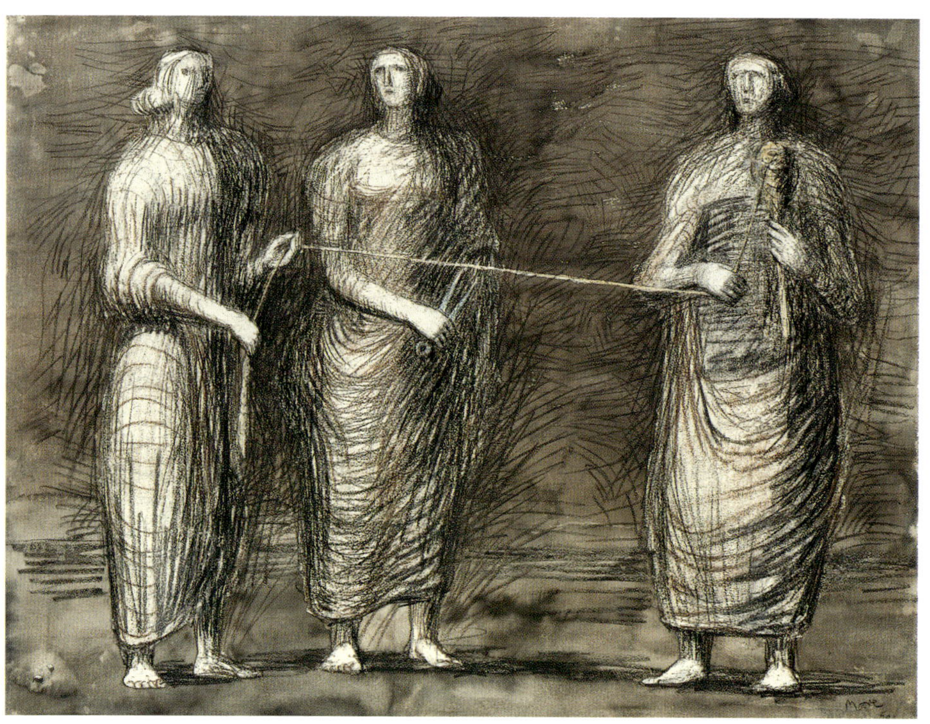

שלוש אלות הגורל, 1950
Three Fates, 1950

39

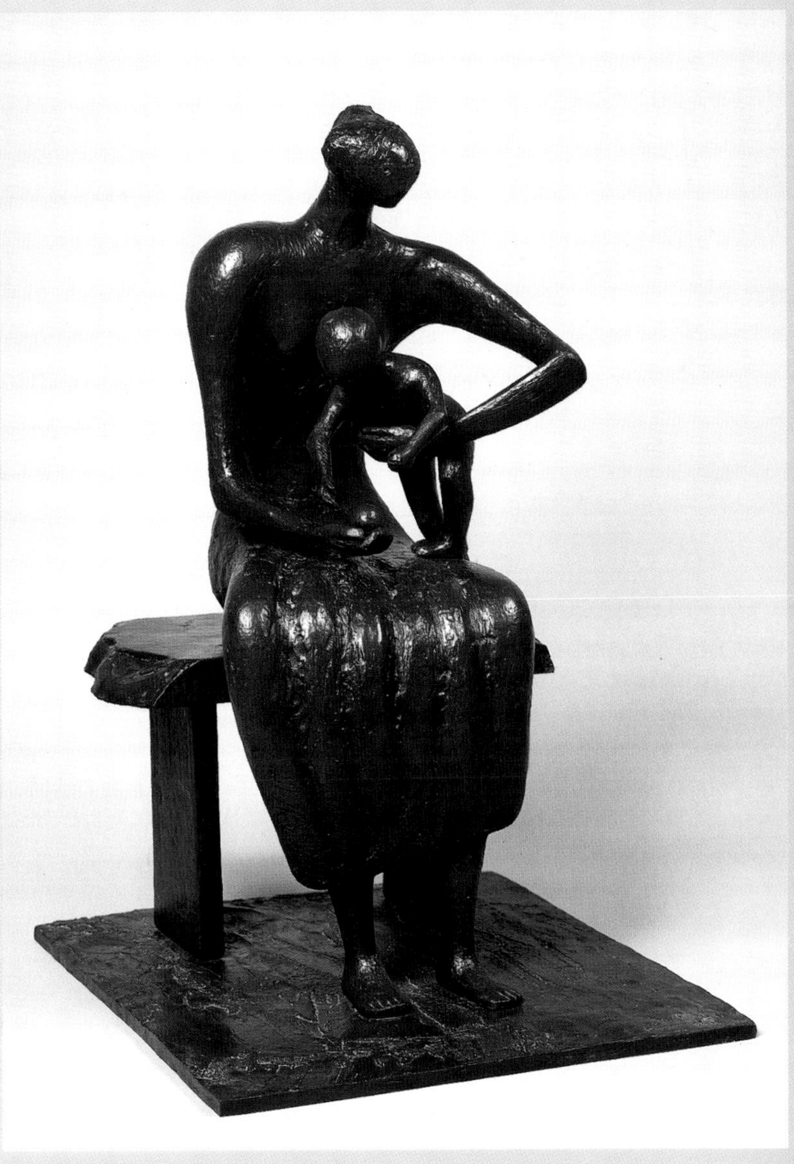

אם וילד מס' 1: מושיט יד לתפוח, 1956
Mother and Child No. 1: Reaching for Apple, 1956

קבוצות משפחה

הנרי מור היה השביעי מבין שמונה ילדים. אמו, מרי, "אישה שהתברכה באישיות מיוחדת, במרץ ובנחישות",[1] מילאה תפקיד מרכזי בחייו של בנה הצעיר. בעיני מור היא היתה

> נשית לחלוטין, התגלמות האישה והתגלמות האם... אני מניח שאני לוקה בתסביך אם... היא היתה בשבילי היציבות המוחלטת, אותו הדבר בחייו של אדם שברור כי הוא שם לשם הגנתו... כך שאין זה מפתיע שסוג הנשים שפיסלתי היו נשים בשלות ולא צעירות.[2]

מרי מור סבלה מדלקת פרקים קשה. מור נזכר: "בחורף, כשהייתי חוזר מבית־הספר היא נהגה לומר לי: 'הנרי, נערי, בוא עסה לי את הגב'. הייתי מעסה אז את גבה במשחה". חוויה זו עיצבה את דמות האישה הבשלה בפסליו. "גיליתי", אמר, "שבבלי דעת אני מעניק לגב הפסל את צורת הגב, שעיסיתי לעתים קרובות כל־כך כילד, ושמזמן שכחתיו".[3] פיטר פולר מקשר את ה"ביטחון והאושר של סביבת הילדות של מור... לחזונו הפיסולי הבוגר".[4] גם עבודות האם והילד של מור חופפות פעמים רבות אירועים מחייו האישיים – לידות אחיינו ואחייניתו, נישואיו לאירינה ובואם לעולם של בתו מרי ונכדו גאס.

מוטיב האם והילד היה לו למור "אובססיה יסודית".[5] בשנות ה־20 הוא יצר לפחות פסל אחד ממין זה מדי שנה. העבודות הפרימיטיוויסטיות הללו, המגולפות ישירות באבן, מתארות אם עצומת־ממדים המערסלת את פעוטה היונק, תינוק הישוב על ראש אמו, או עולל היונק משדיים נטולי גוף – בכולם נשמרו אופיו וצורתו של גוש האבן כדי להביע באמצעותם את הסימביוזה בין האם לילד. מוטיב זה גם משווה נופך "אימהי" לאמן, אשר "מוליד" פסל מתוך האבן.

בין 1932 למלחמת העולם השנייה עברה עבודתו של מור תהליך של הפשטה. האם והילד היו לגוש חומר גדול וצורה קטנה – זיווג אשר סימל את הינקות, הקודמת לרכישת השפה, וסיפק תובנות פסיכולוגיות לקשר שבין האם לילד. כמה מהעבודות הללו מעידות על העניין שגילה מור בסוראליזם ובקונסטרוקטיוויזם. ב־1938, לאחר שראה במוזיאון המדע של לונדון מודלים מתמטיים ובהם

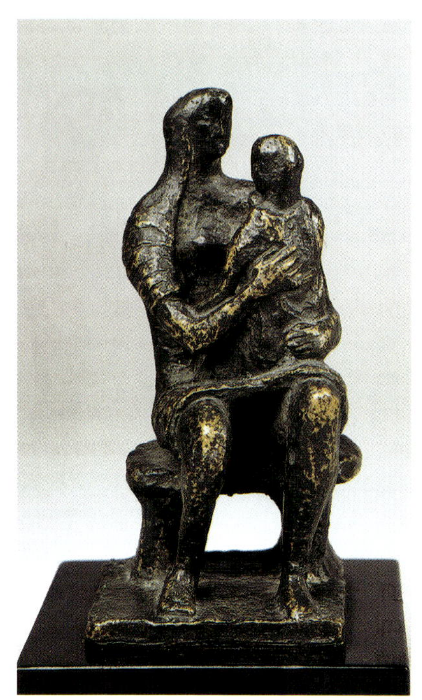

מדונה וילד, 1943
ברונזה, ג 14.6 ס"מ
אוסף פרטי
Madonna and Child, 1943
Bronze, h. 14.6 cm
Private collection
LH 216

Berthoud, *Life of Moore,* p. 21   1
Moore, *Observer,* p. 30   2
Roditi, *Dialogues,* pp. 191–92   3
Fuller, "Mother-spaces," p. 13   4
James, *Moore on Sculpture,* p. 220   5

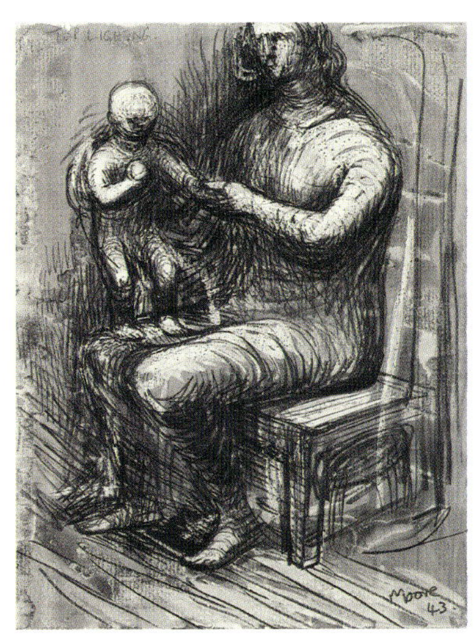

מתווים למדונה וילד, 1943
Madonna and Child Studies, 1943 | 17

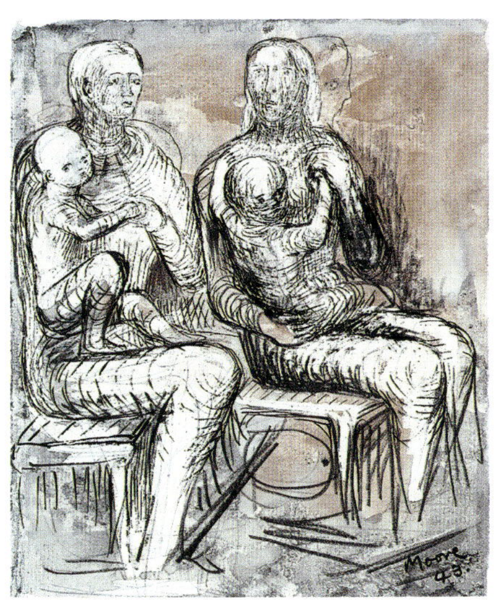

מדונה וילד, 1943
Madonna and Child, 1943 | 16

חוטים, מתח האמן מיתרים בין האם לילד, ובכך הדגיש את הקשר הדיאדי ביניהם.

ב־1943 הוזמן מור לגלף פסל של המדונה והילד לכנסיית סנט מתיו בנורתהמפטון. מור, שנרתע מהתמודדות עם המסורת העשירה של האמנות הדתית, היסס להיענות להזמנה ונעתר לספק רק רישומים ודגמים קטנים מחומר. פסל מברונזה שנוצק מאחד הדגמים הללו (עמ' 25) מראה מדונה כבדת־גוף, ארצית מאוד, משחקת בחיבה עם ילדה. שמלתה מכסה רק מחצית מירכיה, ועל משקלה מלמדים קימורי השרפרף שתחתיה.[6]

ברישומי המדונה וילד שלו מור מתחבט בשאלת הצגת הקשר בין האם לילד. ב"מתווים למדונה וילד" מ־1943 (מס' 17), אמנם הילד מייצג את ישו, אך הוא מנסה תוך כדי משחק להתייצב על ברכי אמו ואוחז תפוח בידו; הפן האנושי הזה מאפיין גם את פסל הברונזה מ־1956, "אם וילד מס' 1: מושיט יד לתפוח" (עמ' 24), שבו חצאית האם דומה לגזע עץ, ומרמזת לאימא אדמה.[7] ב"מדונה וילד" מ־1943 (מס' 16) אם נשגבת אוחזת ברוך ביד ילדה ומגעה משדר קשר חם. על אף הכותרת "שתי נשים וילדים" מהשנים 1943-44 (עמ' 28), הרישום מתאר ככל

הנראה את המדונה והילד לצד הקדושה אנה ויוחנן המטביל בינקותו. מתווה העיפרון המצויר בראש הדף מזכיר רישומי רנסנס של עליית הבתולה השמימה. העמידה החזיתית של הילד בחיק המדונה והמושב דמוי הכס המלכותי (ברישומים שבעמ' 27), והגומחה (ברישום שבעמ' 30, מס' 20) יוצרים דימוי בעל נופך דתי-פולחני. הניסויים של מור בסגנונות מנוגדים (מס' 19) מעידים על הקושי שלו לבטא רוחניות.[8] פסל האבן הסופי של המדונה והילד ניחן, לדברי האמן, ב"סגפנות ובאצילות, ובנגיעה של הוד... ברוך ובגאווה שקטה". והוא מוסיף: "ניסיתי לתת תחושה של נינוחות ורוגע מוחלטים, כאילו המדונה יכולה להישאר כך, במצב זה, לנצח".[9] תיאורים אלה של המדונה והילד הם היסוד לפסלי המשפחה של מור.

ב־1943-44 פנה אל מור המחנך הנרי מוריס, שביקש להציב פסל בשטחי מכללה כפרית המתוכננת לקום

---

6 אני מודה לסם סילווסטר על דבריו מאירי העיניים בנוגע לטיבה הארצי של המדונה הזאת.

7 התפוח שהילד מחזיק או מושיט אליו יד חייב להינגס ולא להימצץ, ובזה יש אולי רמז לסדיזם אוראלי ינקותי. ראה Schneider, "Mother and Child," 263, n. 8

8 Garrould, *Moore: Complete Drawings*, vol. 3, p. 192

9 James, *Moore on Sculpture*, p. 223

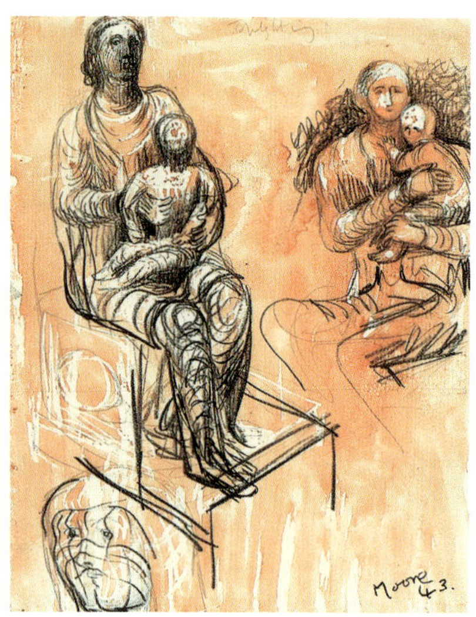

מתווים למדונה וילד, 1943
Madonna and Child Studies, 1943

18

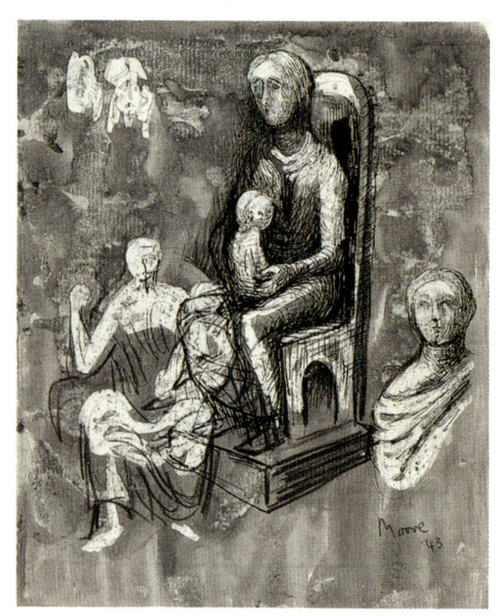

מתווים למדונה וילד, 1943
Madonna and Child Studies, 1943

19

באימפינגטון שבמחוז קמברידג'שיר; מור מילא מחברת ברישומי קבוצות משפחה. כעבור זמן כתב, "קבוצת המשפחה, על כל צורותיה, נולדה מתוך ההטמעה שלי את רעיון המכללה הכפרית [של מוריס] – מוסד שאמור לספק את צורכי המשפחה בכל שלבי החיים".[10] בעקבות הרישומים הכין מור כ־14 דגמי טרקוטה, אשר נוצקו מאוחר יותר בברונזה. ההזמנה הזאת אמנם בוטלה בהעדר מימון, ואולם אחד הדגמים הוגדל ונוצק בברונזה ("קבוצת משפחה", 1948-49) והוא הוצב ב־1950 במכללת ברקלי, סטיוונג'. במתווה מפורט לעבודה (עמ' 29), הזרועות השלובות והברכיים הצמודות מעוררים תחושה של אחדות משפחתית. מור השתמש כאן בשיטה שהוא פיתח – קווי נפח המשווים לרישום תלת־ממדיות מעניקים לו איכות של פסל.

כמו סדרת העבודות שעניינן המדונה והילד, גם רישומי המשפחות של מור התגבשו בד בבד עם שינוי מבנה המשפחה בימי מלחמת העולם השנייה. במשפחות רבות, הגיוס לצבא והפציעות בקרב הרחיקו את הגברים מהבית. בתום המלחמה, השיבה למסורתיות, שיפור הביטחון והעלייה ברמת החיים הביאו לגידול ניכר בשיעור הנישואין

והלידות. עבודותיו של מור שימשו מודל למשפחה למופת.[11]

מור העיד כי ברישומים מ־1942, שבהם תיאר כורי פחם, גילה "את הגוף הגברי ואת איכויותיו בתנועה".[12] דמויות הכורים התגלגלו כעבור זמן לאבות בתיאורי המשפחות של מור, אם כי הרקע הנוקשה והזכרי של הכורים עומד בניגוד חד לשלווה העולה מהעבודות המאוחרות להם. במקור אחר לעבודות הללו אפשר להבחין ברישום (עמ' 30, מס' 23), שבפינתו הימנית־עליונה נראים מדונה וילד נושאים ארשת מלכותית במיוחד ומתחתם, הורים הסוגרים על ילדיהם במחוות הגנה. האם מלכותית בצבעי אדום וכחול, הטיפוסיים בדרך־כלל למדונה. לעתים אימהותיו הנאצלות של מור עומדות זקופות, כמו בקומפוזיציה המעניינת מ־1949 בקירוב של תשע קבוצות משפחה (עמ' 31, מס' 33), המגדירה מערכות יחסים באמצעות מיקום ותנוחות – אך האם והפעוט לעולם אינם נפרדים זה מזה.

Moore: War and Utility, p. 21   10
Stallabrass, "Mother and Child," pp. 15, 17   11
James, Moore on Sculpture, p. 216   12

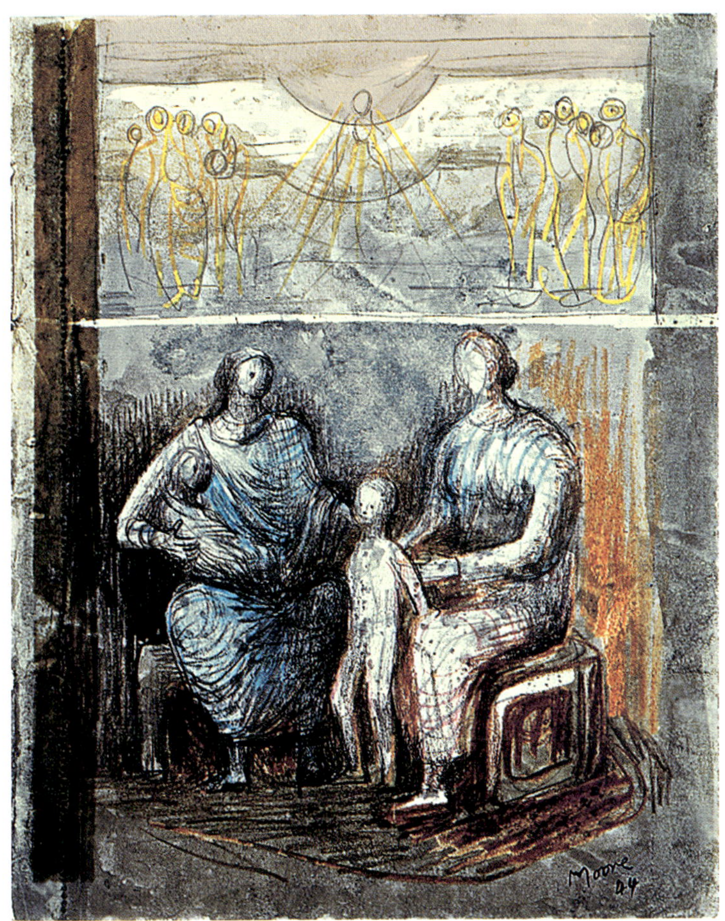

שתי נשים וילדים, 1943–44
Two Women and Children, 1943–44

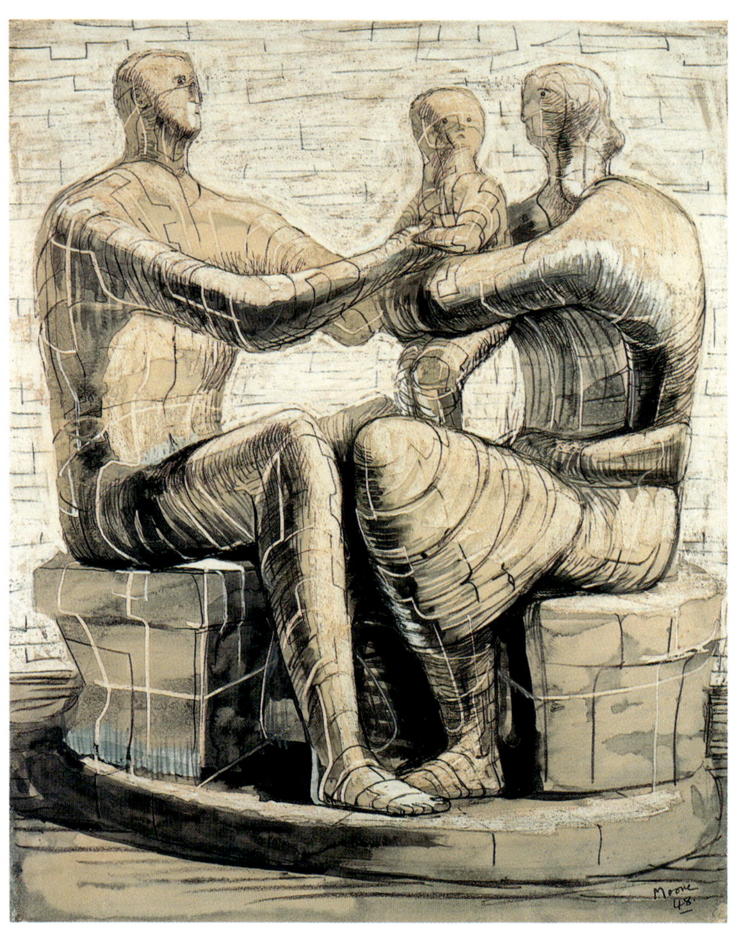

קבוצת משפחה, 1948
עיפרון, גיר שעווה שמנוני, גיר שמנוני צבעוני, צבעי־מים (מגוון), עט ודיו, מכחול ודיו,
635 x 521 מ"מ
אוסף אילה זקס-אברמוב, בית אילה, תל־אביב

Family Group, 1948
Pencil, wax crayon, colored crayon, watercolor wash, pen and
ink, brush and ink, 635 x 521 mm
Ayala Zacks-Abramov Collection, Beit Ayala, Tel Aviv
HMF 2506

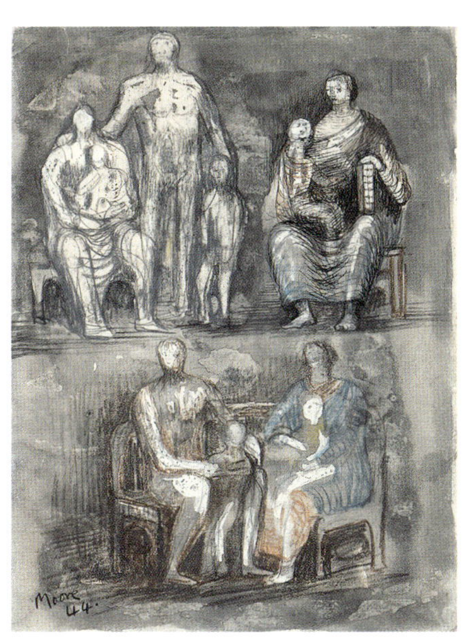

קבוצות משפחה ומדונה וילד, 1943–44, בקירוב
Family Groups and Madonna and Child, ca. 1943–44 | 23

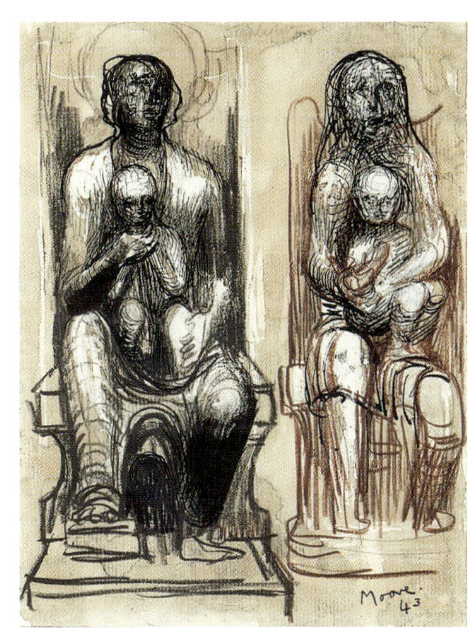

מתווים למדונה וילד, 1943
Madonna and Child Studies, 1943 | 20

ב"קבוצת משפחה" מהשנים 1943-44 (עמ' 31, מס' 24),
גבר נוגע ברכות באשתו ובילדם הבוגר, שעומד בין רגלי
אביו ואוחז ספר בידיו. אף כי מור צייר נשים קוראות,
אימהות הקוראות לילדיהן, ואימהות וילדים המאזינים
לקורא אחר, הרי שברוב עבודותיו מסמנת הקריאה דווקא
את הקשר שבין האב לילד הבוגר. אביו של האמן, ריימונד
ספנסר מור, כורה שהתקדם לדרגת סגן־מנהל מכרה,
היה אדם אינטליגנטי ומשכיל; הוא היה נחוש בדעתו
לחסוך מבניו את ה"עבודה בבור המכרה" והתעקש
להעניק לכל ילדיו חינוך נאות.

ברישום רגיש במיוחד מ־1947 בקירוב (עמ' 32), מתאר
מור את בתו היחידה, מרי, מחזיקה ספר. עבודה זו היא
חלק מסדרת רישומים־מן־החיים המתארת את מרי: אחרי
הרחצה, ישנה, משחקת או יונקת משדי אמה. העבודה
"מתווים לבת האמן" קרובה יותר למושא ההתבוננות,
היא מפורטת מאוד ומשקפת את האינטימיות בין האמן
לבתו. מור הכיר בכך שלידתה "עוררה מחדש בפיסול
שלי את מוטיב האם והילד" וכי רישומיו "מנסים לרדת
לעומק הקשר בין האם לילד". שלושת המתווים של מרי,
שופעי חיוניות וצבעוניות עשירה, מדגימים את תפיסתו
ולפיה "רישומים הנעשים מתוך אהבה שונים בעיניי

מרישומי התבוננות גרידא, שכן האמן מעורב רגשית
במושא ההתבוננות".[13]

בתם הקטנה של בני הזוג מור סיפקה השראה גם
לכיסאות *נדנדה*, סדרה של רישומים ופסלי ברונזה קטנים
המרחיבים את העיסוק במוטיב האם והילד. אוסף המוזיאון
כולל 3 עבודות שובבות מתוך סדרה זו. ב"חמישה מתווים
לכיסאות נדנדה" מ־1949 בקירוב (עמ' 37) מור עורך
ניסויים בתנוחות, בשיווי משקל ובקימורי הכיסא בעוד
האם מניפה את ילדה אל־על בעת משחק. חמשת
הרישומים ה'נקראים' ברצף מזכירים צילום תנועה,
ומבטאים חיות ודינמיות. שתי העבודות "מתווים לפסל"
(עמ' 34 ו־35) הן רישומים־בתוך־רישומים, תחומים
במסגרות. כל חלק מתאר את אחד הנושאים המרכזיים
בעבודתו של מור: כיסאות נדנדה, קבוצות משפחה,
ודמויות שוכבות או עומדות. על רקע דחוס, מצויר בגירי
שעווה ובגירים צבעוניים, יוצר מור לא רק רעיונות
לפסלים, כי אם תמונה מאורגנת היטב.

Wilkinson, *Writings and Conversations*, pp. 66, 307 | 13

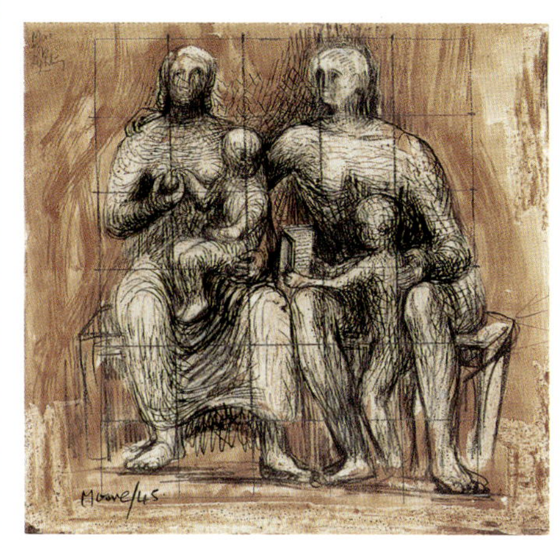

קבוצת משפחה, 1943–44 בקירוב
Family Group, ca. 1943–44 | 24

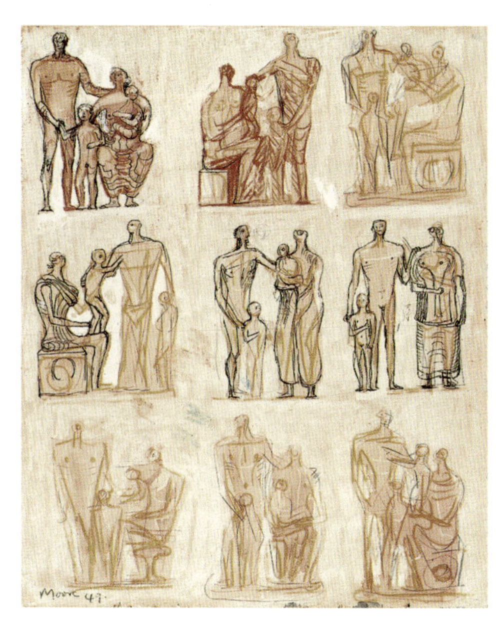

קבוצות משפחה, 1949 בקירוב
Family Groups, ca. 1949 | 33

פיתוח נוסף של מוטיב האם והילד מופיע בסדרתו של
מור *צורה פנימית/חיצונית* משנות ה־50 וה־60 (פסל מן
הסדרה בעמ' 36). הסדרה שואבת השראה מתגליפי
המלנגאן (פסלי עץ שנועדו לטקסי קבורה וגם בהם יש
משחק בין פנים לחוץ) המיוצרים בניו־אירלנד, והעבודות
בה הן מהבודדות מהתקופה שלאחר המלחמה, המבוססות
על אמנות לא־מערבית. מור ראה בה "עובר המוגן על־ידי
צורה חיצונית, רעיון של אם וילד, או האבקן בפרח, כלומר,
דבר־מה צעיר ומתפתח, מוגן בתוך קליפה חיצונית". מוטיב
זה מרחיב את זה שבסדרה *ראש קסדה* (רישומים מן
הסדרה בעמ' 68), שעסקה אף היא בצורה גדולה המגוננת
על צורה קטנה ושברירית או מכילה אותה בתוכה. מור
ראה ביחס שבין הצורות ובתלות של הקטנה בגדולה ביטוי
של "שתי חוויות אנושיות בסיסיות: היות ילד והיות
הורה".[14] תחושת ההיטמעות, העולה בעוצמה מעבודה זו,
קשורה לתקופה הסימביוטית המוקדמת בחיי הילד, שבה
הוא חווה את עצמו כחלק בלתי נפרד מהאם.

תיאורי האם והילד, המדונה והילד וקבוצות המשפחה של
מור משרים תחושת שלווה ביתית, יוצרים אינטימיות
וחמימות פיזית ורגשית ומאירים את קשר ההורות באור
אידאלי.[15] עבודותיו הנטורליסטיות והמופשטות כאחד,

משדרות רגש וקרבה באמצעות מחוות הגוף, ולאו דווקא
על־ידי הבעות הפנים. בבחירת החומרים והיחסים בין
הצורות מבקש האמן להעביר לצופה את תחושת הקשר
בין התינוק לאם כפי שהוא נחווה מבפנים. רישומיו ופסליו
חורגים מהחוויה הפרטית ובוחנים שאלות ראשוניות,
אוניוורסליות, על החיים, הגדילה, היצירתיות והאהבה.
בתוך יחידה משפחתית אוהבת מתאר מור "אושר
המושתת על חיבה אנושית".[16]

---

14 James, *Moore on Sculpture*, p. 247

15 עבודתו היחידה של מור המבטאת עוינות בין האם לילד היא "אם
וילד" משנת 1952 (LH 315). כאן נראה כי הפעוט היונק עומד
לטרוף את שד אמו, תיאור המזכיר את התיאוריה הפסיכואנליטית של
מלאני קליין בנוגע לסדיזם אוראלי בקרב תינוקות. ראה *Read, Moore:*
Life and Work, p. 176

16 Clark, *Moore Drawings*, p. 255

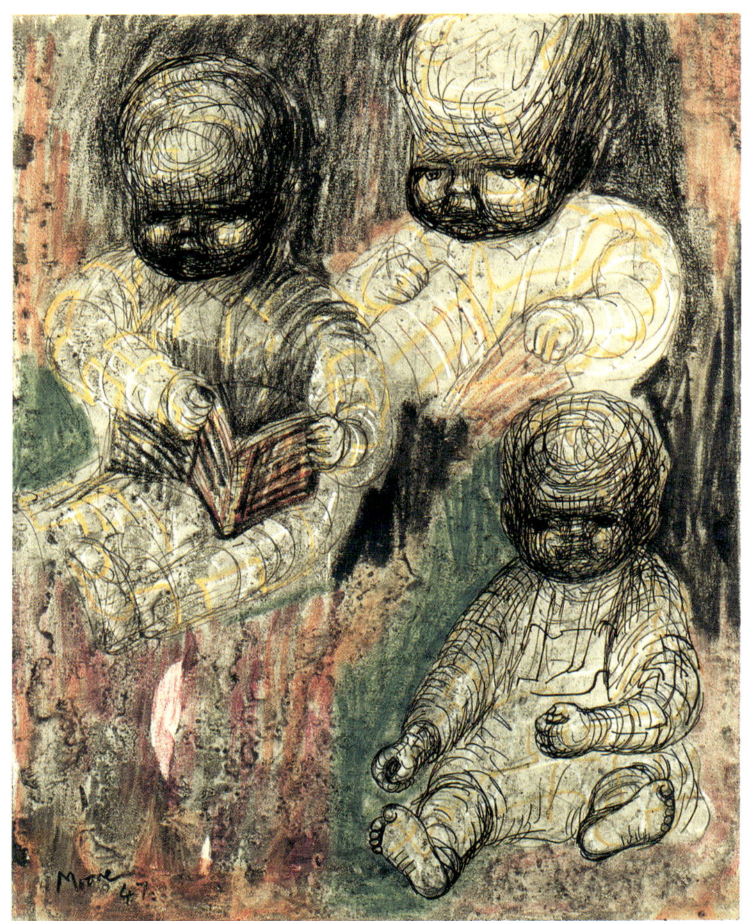

מתווים לבת האמן, 1947 בקירוב
Studies of the Artist's Child, ca. 1947 | 30

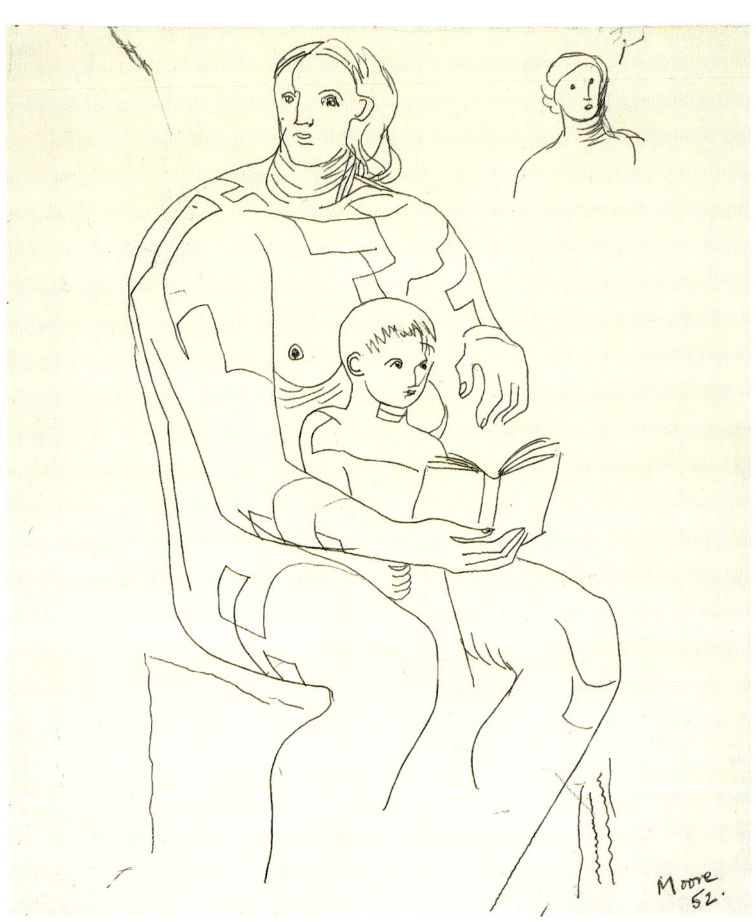

אם וילד, 1952
Mother and Child, 1952 50

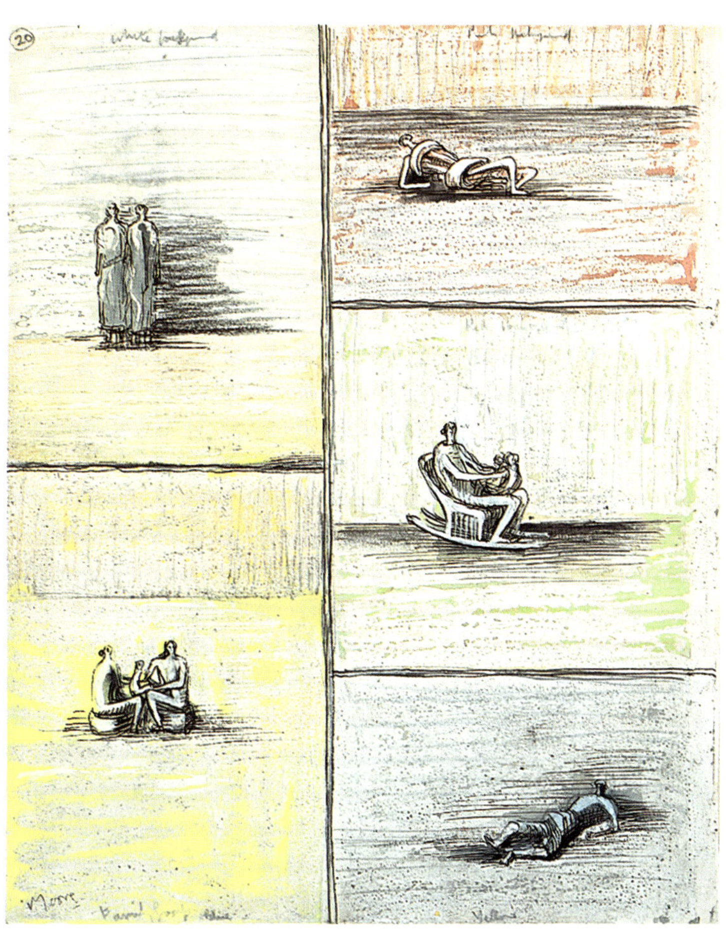

מתווים לפסל, 1950–51
Studies for Sculpture, 1950–51
א44a

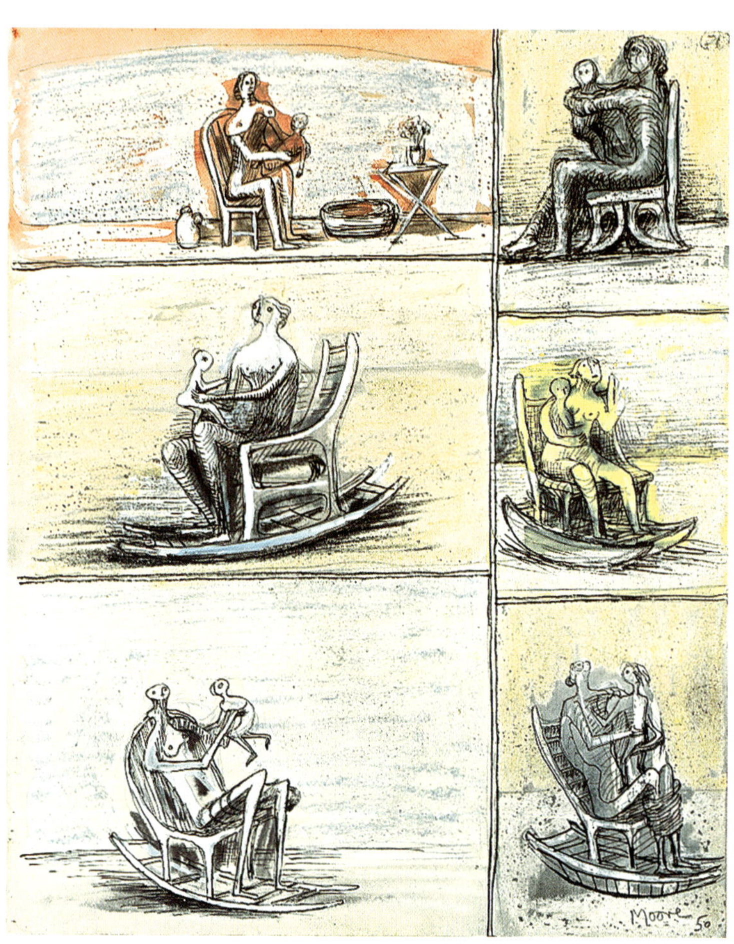

מתווים לפסל, 1950–51
Studies for Sculpture, 1950–51　45אַ

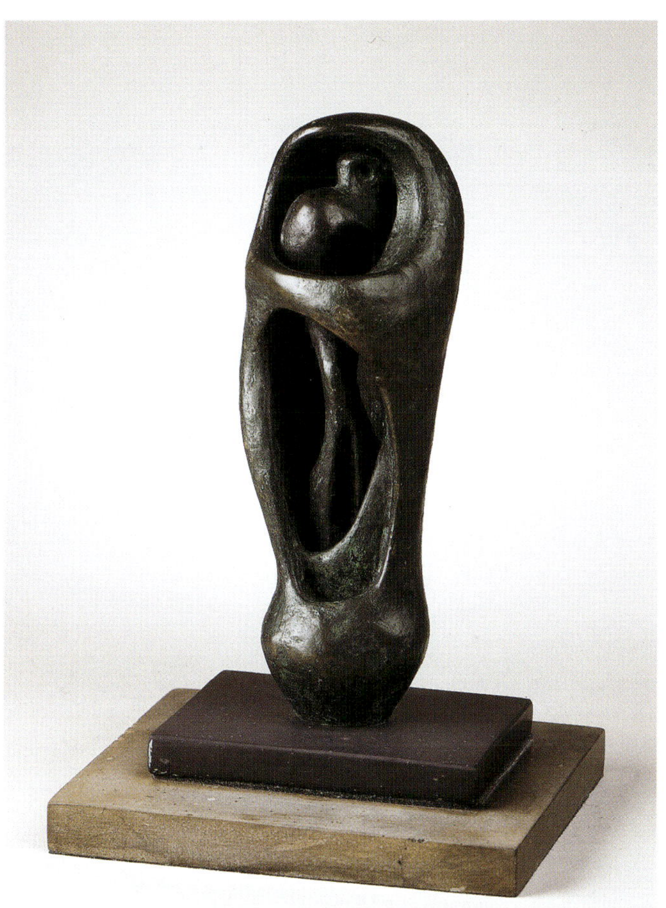

פסל־הכנה לצורה פנימית/**חיצונית זקופה**, 1951
Maquette for Upright Internal/External Form, 1951

46

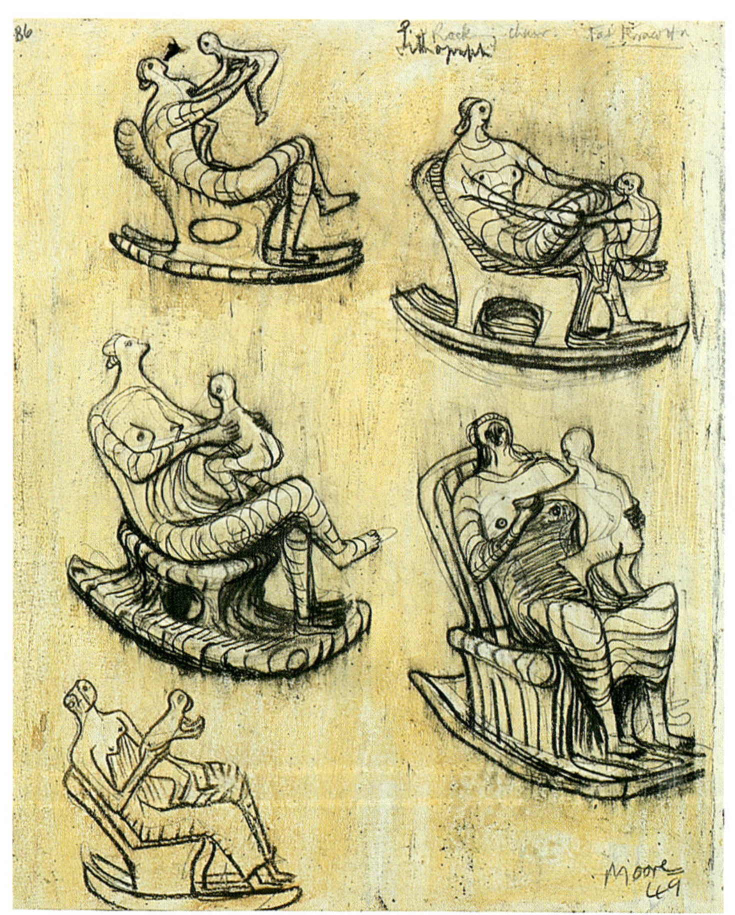

חמישה מתווים לכיסאות נדנדה, 1949 בקירוב
Five Studies for Rocking Chairs, ca. 1949

32aא

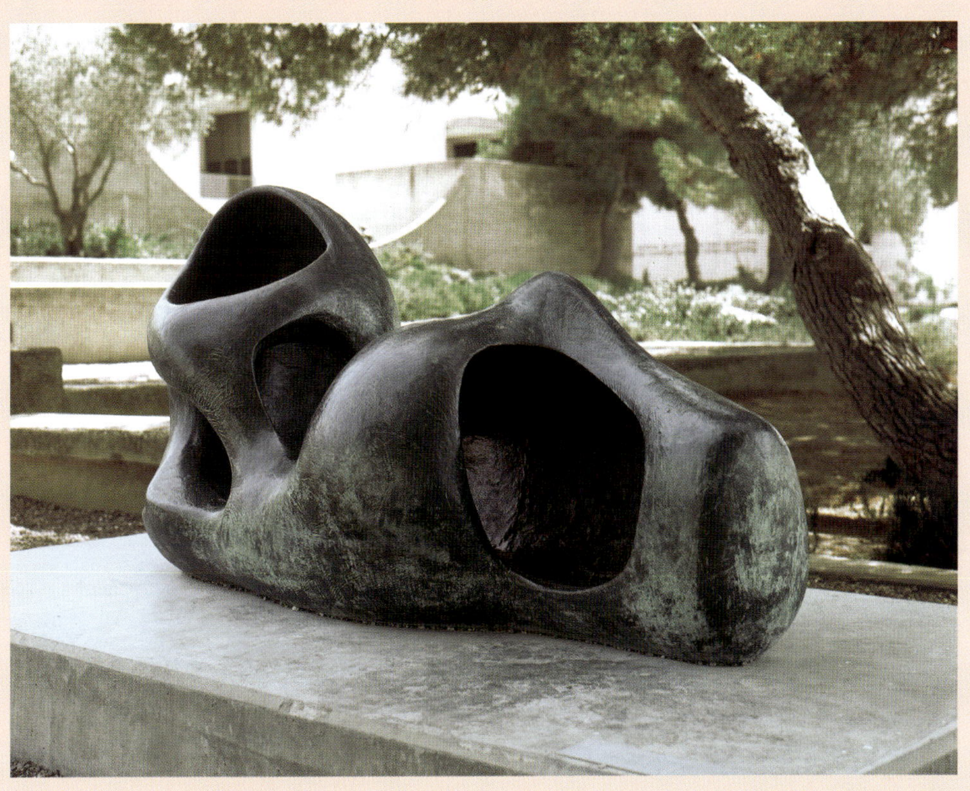

דמות שוכבת: צורה חיצונית, 1953–54
Reclining Figure: External Form, 1953–54

54

הדמויות השוכבות

הנרי מור נמשך לפיסול הדמות השוכבת "משיכה כפייתית ממש". אף שפיסל את דמות האדם בעמידה ובישיבה, בדמות השוכבת מצא "חופש מרבי, מבחינת הקומפוזיציה ועיצוב החלל".[1] תנוחתה האופקית של הדמות יוצרת בסיס איתן המבטל את הצורך בכן הצבה, ומאפשר לאמן לערוך ניסויים בקומפוזיציה. יציבותה של התנוחה גם מביעה קביעות ומנוחה – יסודות חיוניים בעבודתו של מור.

בייחוד בדמויות השוכבות שלו שאף מור לבטא חמימות, חיות, ותחושה של צורה אורגנית. בכלל, הטבע היה לו מקור השראה מרכזי – הפתחים דמויי-המחילות מזכירים סלעים ששחקום הרוח והמים,[2] התנוחה האופקית מקבילה למפגש השמים והארץ, והדמות הנשית העירומה מרמזת לאימא אדמה כמקור החיים. נשותיו השוכבות של מור, כבדות-גוף ומחוברות לקרקע, הן דמויות אידאליות, נעדרות מאפיינים אישיים. תנוחתן מזכירה את פסלי צ'אקמואל ממקסיקו (900-1050 לספירה, מהתרבות הטולטקית-מאית) – פסלים ששימשו מזבח בדמות לוחם טולטקי שוכב וקערה למנחות על בטנו. מור התפעל מהדמויות הגדולות והנשגבות הללו, אשר הזכירו לו הרים, סלעים וחלוקי אבן שנשחקו במי ים.

טיבן האורגני של הדמויות השוכבות של מור קשור גם למגמה הפונקציונליסטית באדריכלות בשנות ה-30. בשעה שהאדריכלות השילה מעליה אלמנטים קישוטיים נטולי ערך פונקציונלי, יצר מור פסלים שעמדו בזכות עצמם, ועם זה קיימו דיאלוג פורה עם בניינים וסביבותיהם. כזה הוא פסלו של מור "דמות בהסבה" מ-1938 (פסל-ההכנה בעמ' 40), שיועד למרפסת ביתו של האדריכל סרג' צ'רמאייף בסאסקס, אשר יצר זיקה בין המבנה האופקי בעל הסגנון המודרני, לבין הנוף הנפרס לפניו: "הדמות שלי השקיפה לעבר המרחב המשתרע של גבעות הדאונז, ומבטה אסף אליו את קו הרקיע".[3]

אוסף המוזיאון מדגים היטב את התמורות שחלו בפיסול הדמויות השוכבות של מור; בהדרגה הן נפתחות – בקבוצת עבודות אחת, תנוחותיהן מכתיבות את מיקום החללים בצורה; בעבודות אחרות, לא נטורליסטיות, נקיקים רבי-הבעה מחברים את שני צדי הפסל, ובכך

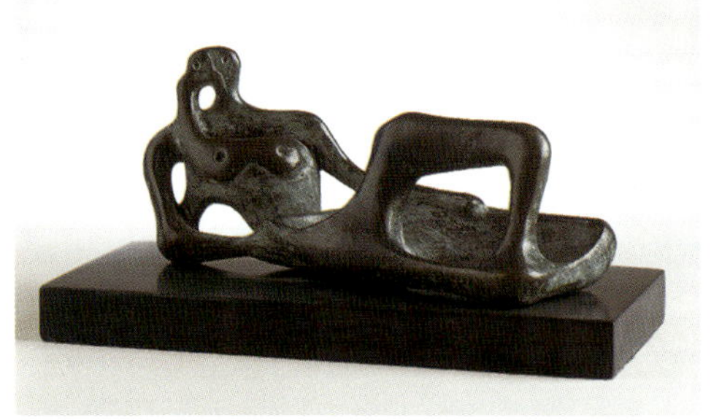

דמות שוכבת, 1945
Reclining Figure, 1945

26

James, *Moore on Sculpture*, pp. 264–65   1
Sylvester, *Moore*, p. 5   2
James, *Moore on Sculpture*, p. 99   3

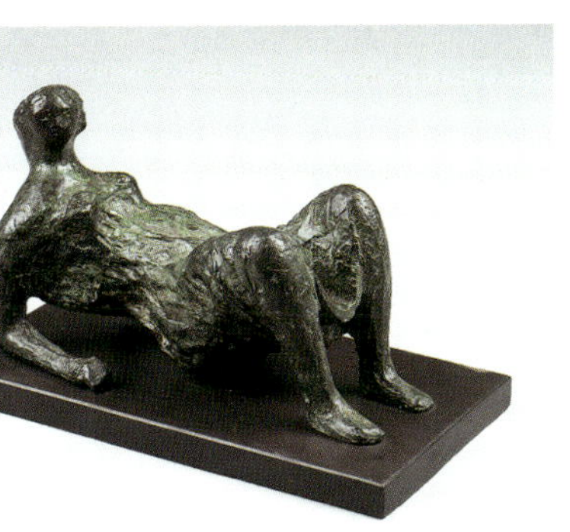

פסל־הכנה ל**דמות עטויה שוכבת (אישה שוכבת)**, 1952
Maquette for Draped Reclining Figure, 1952 | 51

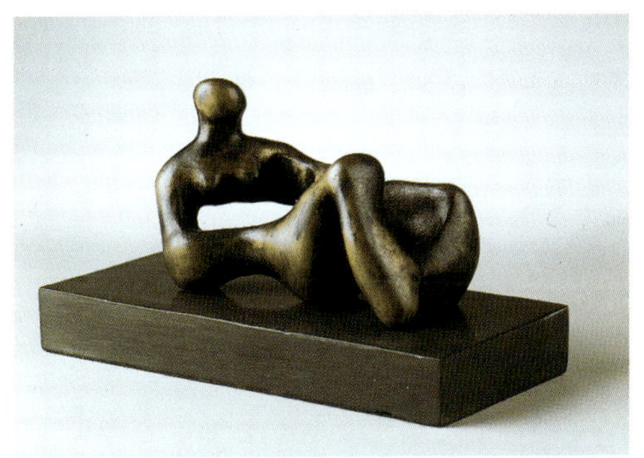

דמות בהסבה, 1938
Recumbent Figure, 1938 | 8

מדגישים את נפחיותו. בשנות ה־60 פנה מור להפשטה חלקית ולקיטוע הצורה האנושית וגייס לשם כך את החלל כמשתתף פעיל ביצירת העבודה; החלל השלילי היה לחלל "חיובי", הרה־משמעות.

בפסל־הכנה ל"דמות עטויה שוכבת" (1952), אפשר לראות צעד ראשון של מור לקראת יצירת חללים בפסליו. זוהי דמות נשית, נטורליסטית יחסית, שנפח גופה נשמר כמעט בשלמותו. פסל הברונזה מזכיר פיסול יווני קלסי, והוא הראשון בכמה עבודות חשובות משנות ה־50, שמתוארות בהן דמויות עטויות בדים.[4] הלבשת דמויותיו המפוסלות של מור צומחת מתוך השימוש בבדים ברישומיו מן המקלט מהשנים 1940-41. בפסל זה, הקפלים והקמטוטים הרבים של הבד מדגישים את מוקדי המתח בצורה. החומר מהודק על כתפי האישה, אך רופף יותר בין ירכיה. אף שהדמות רוגעת ונטורליסטית, תנוחתה הערנית מזכירה את פסלי צ'אקמואל השעון שזרועותיו תומכות, כמו כאן, בפלג גופו העליון. פסלים ורישומים אחרים משנות ה־30 המאוחרות ועד שנות ה־50 מסוגננים יותר. גופיהם המפותלים, פשוקי הברכיים הנתמכים על מרפקים, של פסלים כגון "דמות שוכבת מס' 2" מ־1953 (עמ' 41) משקפים את תפיסתו של מור שלפיה "לעולם אין בחי סימטרייה טהורה".[5] בעבודות האסימטריות הללו נקודות המבט רבות מספור.

בקבוצה אחת של דמויות שוכבות (עמ' 42) הפתחים היחידים הם החללים הטבעיים הנפערים בין ירכיה הפשוקות של הדמות, או בין הזרועות לחזה. בפסלים אחרים, הגוף הנשי הופך לרשת דמיונית של נקבים ונקרות. גריעות החומר הללו מעידות על העניין של מור במערות ובגוף הנשי – יסודות שעוררו בו תחושה של מסתורין.[6] פתח מפתיע בבית החזה של כמה דמויות שוכבות (למשל למעלה מימין) מדגיש את השדיים המחודדים. כמה דמויות (כגון זו שבעמ' 43, מס' 29) מרימות יד כדי לתמוך בראשן, ובכך פוערות חלל נוסף. ב"דמות שוכבת" מ־1945 (עמ' 39), איברי האישה נחים בתוך גופה דמוי־הסירה, וחלל משונה נוצר סמוך לראשה. שסע בראשה של "דמות שוכבת" מ־1938 (עמ' 43, מס' 9) יוצר דימוי כפול־ראש, של ילד השוכב לצד אמו, או אולי שתי דמויות מתנות אהבים. מור מעניק לנשותיו השוכבות תווי פנים מינימליים בלבד; לעתים רק נקבים זעירים משמשים עיניים, כשם שהפטמות מנוקבות (למשל עמ' 43, מס' 29).

כפי שצוין לעיל, בדמויות השוכבות המאוחרות יותר של מור מידת ההפשטה הולכת וגדלה. דמויות אלה, במילותיו של האמן, "נשלטות פחות על־ידי שיקולים של ייצוג",

---

4   עבודות אלו נעשו בעקבות הביקור הראשון של מור ביוון, ב־1951.
     ראה Wilkinson, *Moore Collection,* p. 120
5   Wilkinson, *Writings and Conversations,* p. 198
6   ראה את הציטוט הפותח במאמר "פענוח התעלומה של הנרי מור",
     עמ' 17 בקטלוג זה.

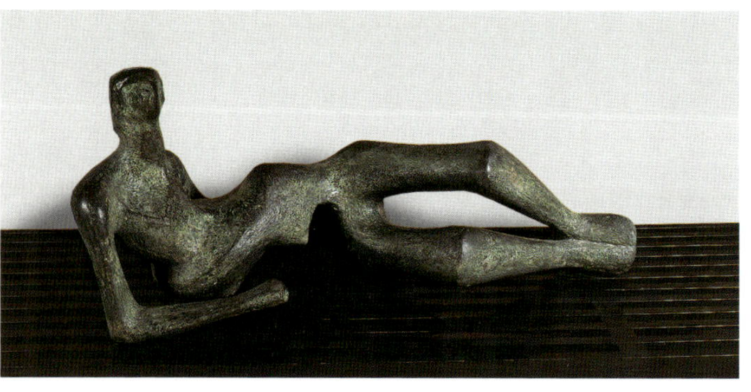

דמות שוכבת מס' 2, 1953
Reclining Figure No. 2, 1953
52

ומפעילות "צורות ואת היחסים ביניהן בחופשיות רבה".[7]
טיפוסית למגמה זו היא "דמות שוכבת: צורה חיצונית"
מהשנים 54-1953 (עמ' 38). בפסל זה, הדמות, שהיתה
במקור נתונה בתוך צורה דמוית־מערה, איננה, ובמקומה
נותר חלל ריק. ביצירות אחרות ביתר האמן את הצורה
הנשית לשניים או לשלושה חלקים, ויצר דמויות
המורכבות מנפחי גוף נפרדים.[8] בכך יצר אפשרות
ל"וריאציות תלת־ממדיות רבות מאלה המוצעות בעבודה
העשויה מקשה אחת".[9] החלל הנפער בין החלקים חיוני
ומאיר עיניים. בעבודות "מתווים לפסל: דמויות שוכבות
בשניים ובשלושה חלקים" (עמ' 44 למעלה), "תבליט מס'
1" (עמ' 45), "דמות שוכבת בשלושה חלקים" ו"פסל
בשלושה חלקים: חוליות", משחק מור בהצבת הדמות
וחלקיה בדרכים שונות.

בפסל־ההכנה הקטן "דמות שוכבת בשלושה חלקים"
מ־1961 (עמ' 44 למטה), הדמות העירומה מבותרת
לחלקים נפרדים: הראש ופלג הגוף העליון, הבטן,
והרגליים. מור יוצר מחלקי הגוף צוקים ותצורות סלעים,
והמתכת המחורצת מוסיפה לאופיו הבראשיתי של הפסל.
לעומתו, "חוליות" מהשנים 1968-69 (עמ' 46-7)
המונומנטלי מורכב מצורות חלקות ולטושות, המעניקות
לברונזה בוהק מישושי. 3 היחידות המרכיבות את העבודה,
הניצבת על גבעה בגן האמנות במוזיאון ישראל, מתאחדות
לישות אחת רק במבטו של הצופה. הדמות השוכבת כבר
אינה נראית בבירור, ועל יסודות הצורה הנשית מאפילות
3 החוליות הסמוכות, אשר לכאורה שלובות זו בזו. העניין

של מור בעצמות, המתגלה גם בדגם־הכנה ל"פסל
בשלושה חלקים מס' 2: קָשָׁת" מ־1964 (עמ' 48), מקורו
בשאיפה להפיח בעבודותיו תחושה של חיות פנימית.
בעיניו, העצם היא מקור התנועה והאנרגיה, "המבנה
הפנימי של הצורה החיה".[10] "חוליות", המשתנה עם שינוי
זווית הראייה, אוצר בתוכו אנרגיה אדירה. צורתו בוקעת
את קליפתה, ופורצת השמימה בעוצמה.

---

7   James, *Moore on Sculpture*, p. 258
8   אמנם כבר ב־1934 יצר מור דמויות רבות־חלקים, אך אלה היו
    ניסיונות בוסר, ובסוף שנות ה־50 חזר אליהם ופיתח עוד את המוטיב.
9   Hedgecoe, *Moore*, p. 338
10   Wilkinson, *Writings and Conversations*, p. 198

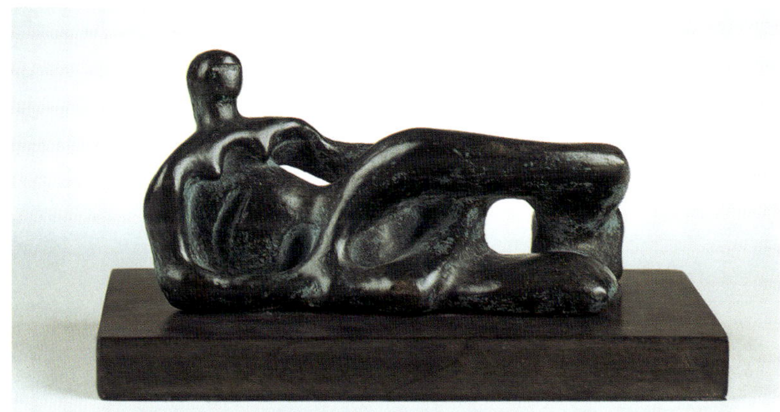

דמות שוכבת (פסל־הכנה לדמות עץ בוקיצה), 1945
Reclining Figure (Maquette for Elmwood Figure), 1945 | 27

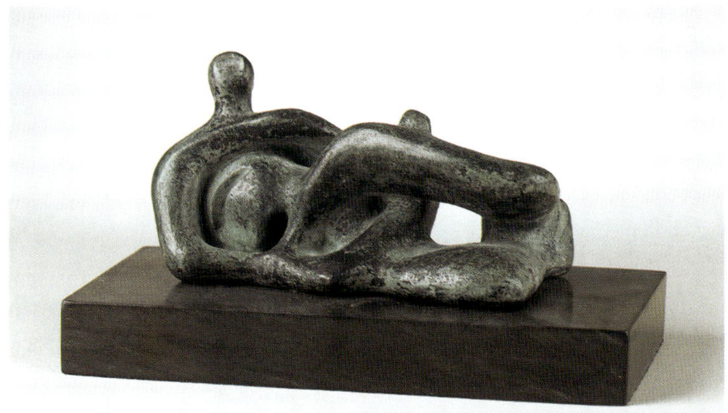

דמות שוכבת, 1945
Reclining Figure, 1945 | 28

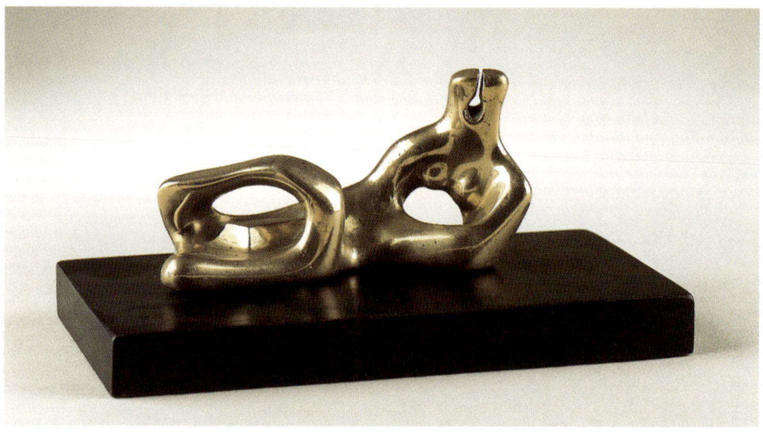

דמות שוכבת, 1938 | 9
Reclining Figure, 1938

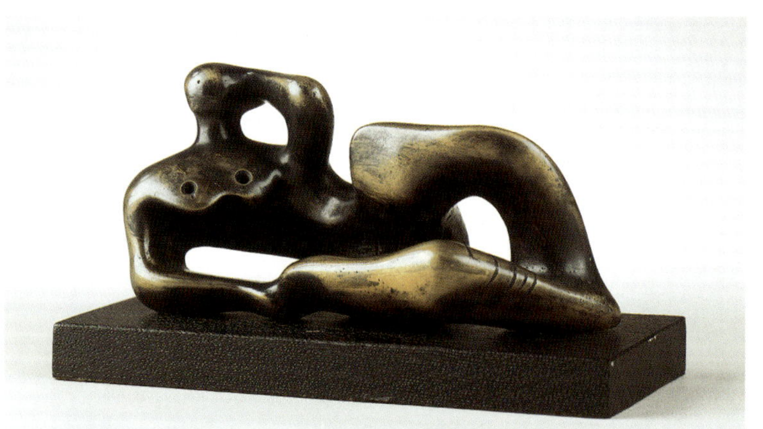

דמות שוכבת, 1946–47 | 29
Reclining Figure, 1946–47

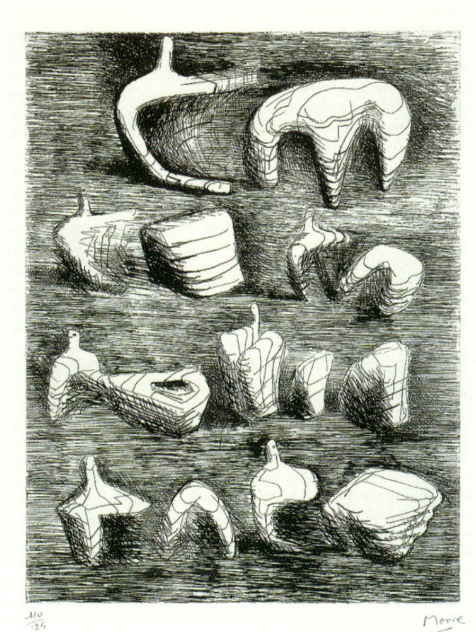

מתווים לפסל: דמויות שוכבות בשניים ובשלושה חלקים, 1967
Studies for Sculpture: Two and Three Pieces
Reclining Figures, 1967

71

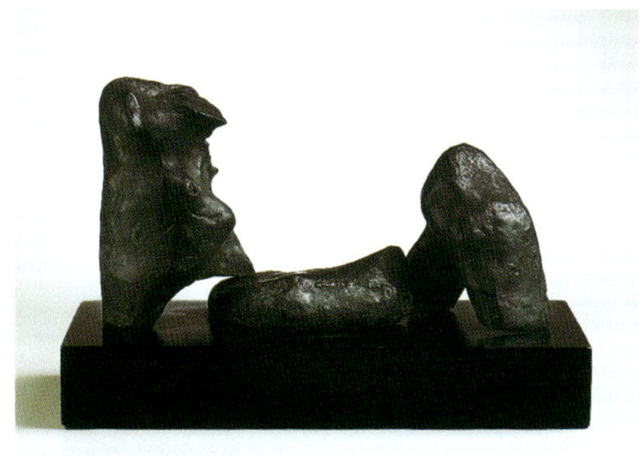

דמות שוכבת בשלושה חלקים: פסל־הכנה מס' 1, 1961
Three Piece Reclining Figure: Maquette No. 1, 1961

65

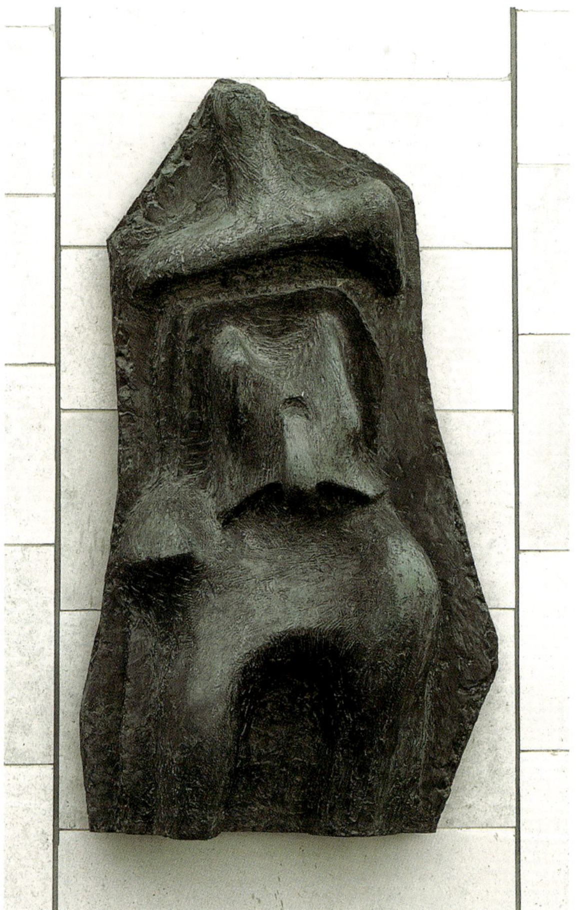

◄

פסל בשלושה חלקים: חוליות, 1968–69
Three Piece Sculpture: Vertebrae, 1968–69 | 73

תבליט מס' 1, 1959
Relief No. 1, 1959 | 63

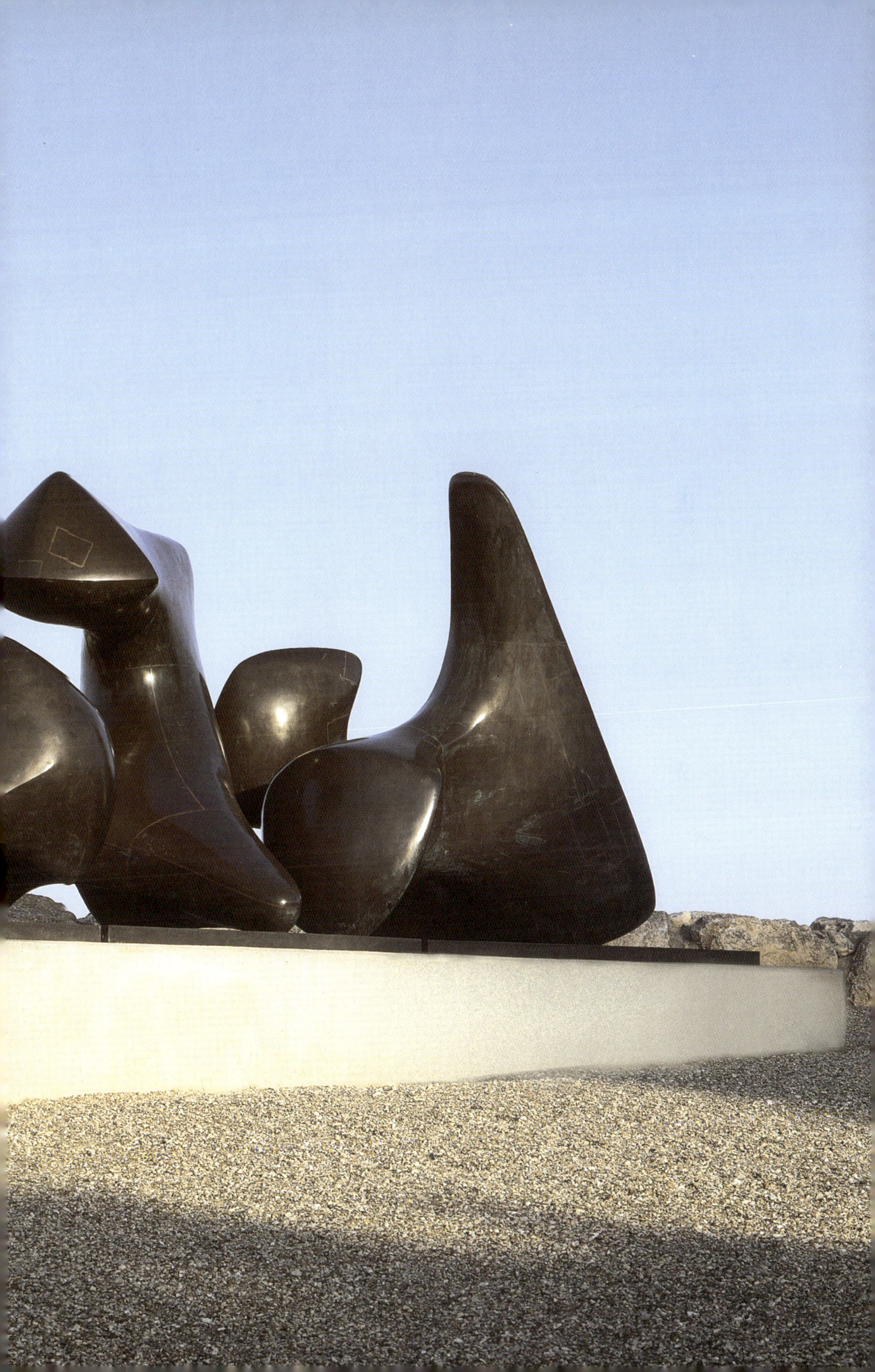

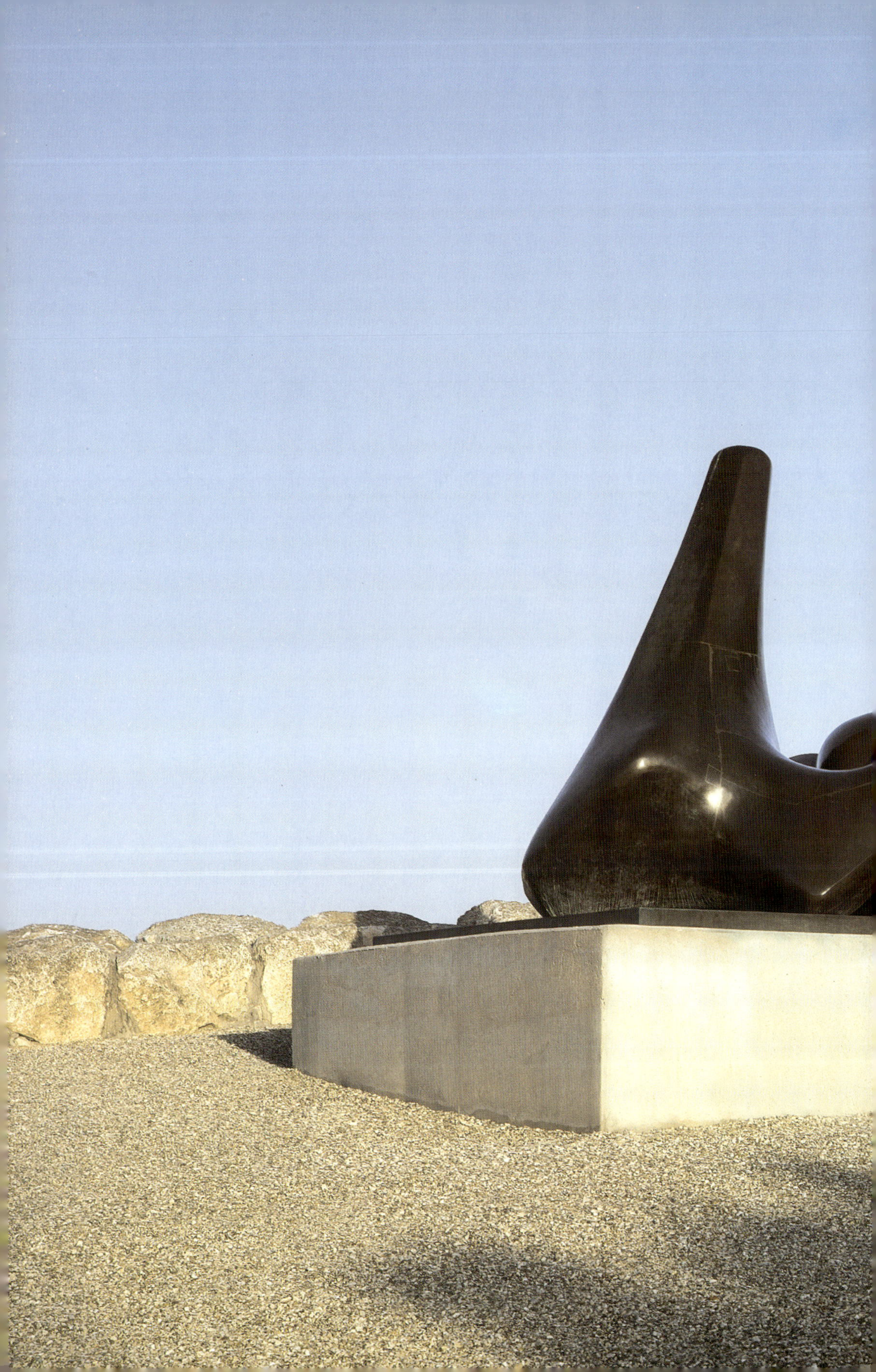

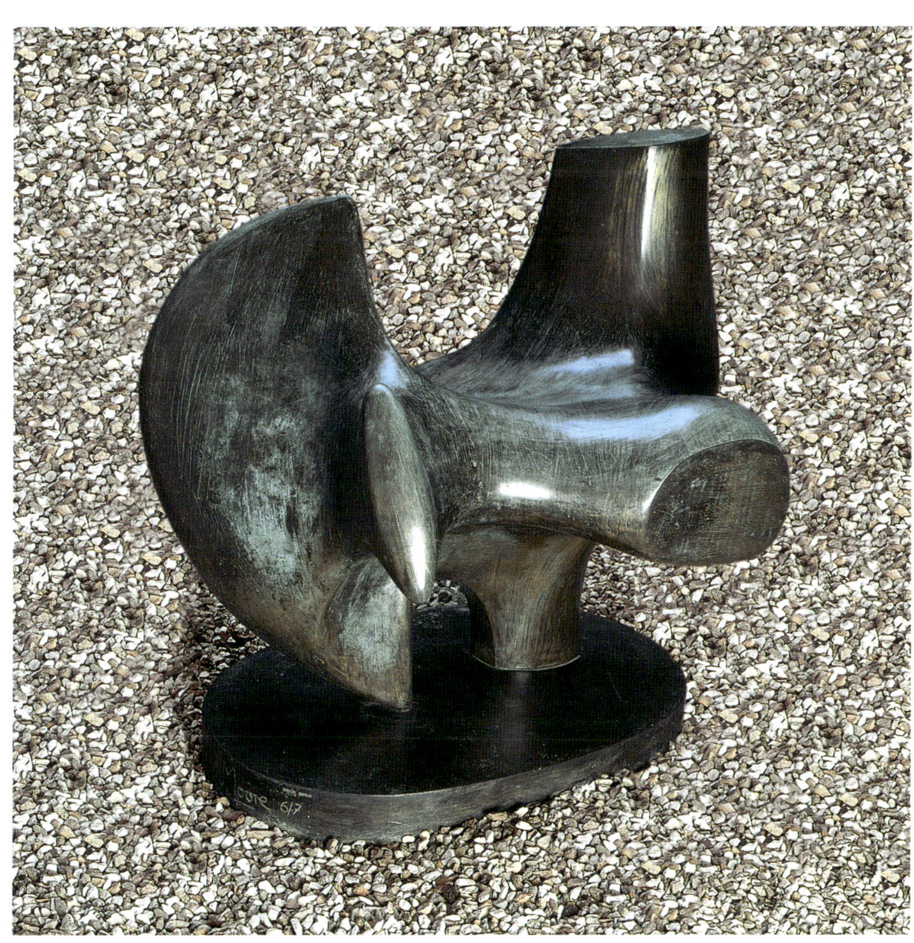

דגם־הכנה לפסל בשלושה חלקים מס' 2: קשֶת, 1964
Working Model for Three Way Piece No. 2: Archer, 1964

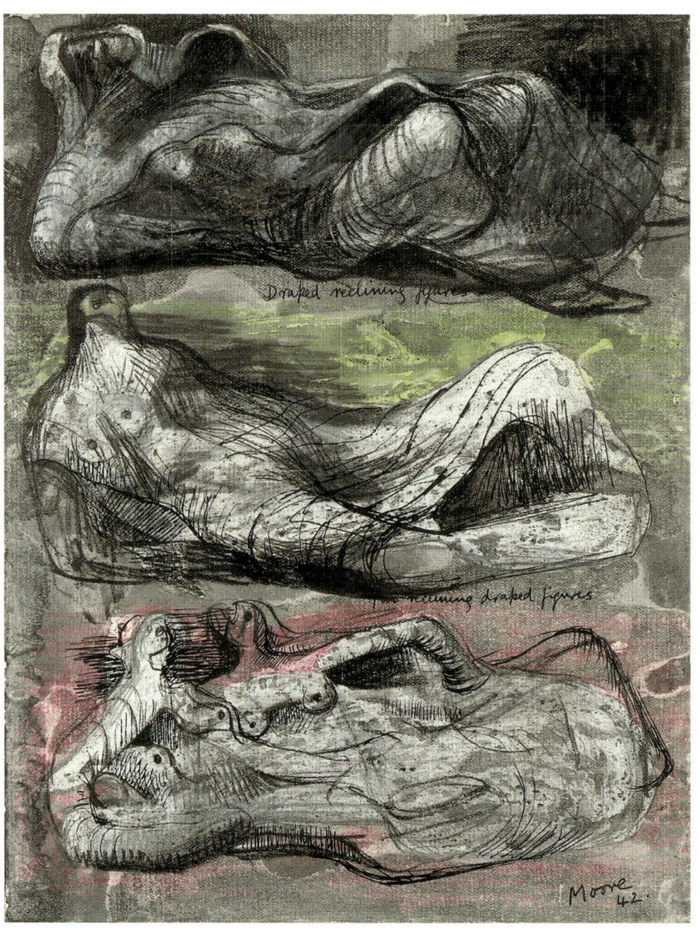

דמויות עטויות שוכבות, 1942
Draped Reclining Figures, 1942
15

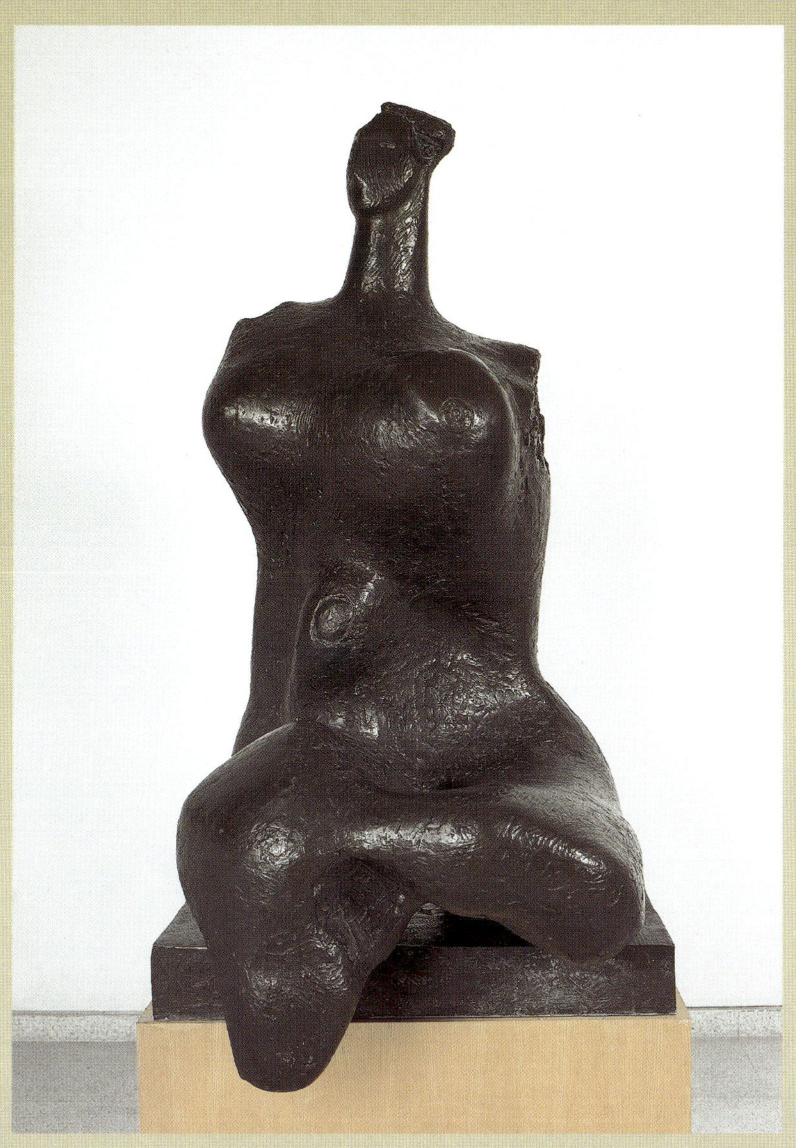

אישה, 1957–58
Woman, 1957–58

60

הדמויות היושבות

נכתב בשיתוף עם יעל אשל

הנשים היושבות בפסלים וברישומים של הנרי מור משדרות עוצמה וביטחון. אלה נשים עצמאיות, לא קשורות עוד לתיאורי האם והילד או המדונה והילד. הן מושפעות מאמנות פרהיסטורית, מאמנות המזרח הקדום ומאמנות אגאית; הן על־זמניות ועכשוויות בעת ובעונה אחת; אין אלה אלות או דמויות מיתולוגיות, אלא "ישויות עליונות, מודרניות, הניצבות למשמר על אוניברסיטה, מוזיאון או כיכר עירונית."[1]

מור העריך מאוד את האמנות המסופוטמית, ובייחוד את הפיסול השומרי, על "שפעת אהבת החיים [שבו], האהבה למופלא ולטמיר שבחיים, האחוזה לבלי הפרד באמירה ישירה בחומר, שמקורה בדחף יצירתי אמיתי. [פיסול זה] ניתן בגודל ובפשטות, בלי כל תוספות עיטוריות."[2] באמנות המסופוטמית היתה תנוחת הישיבה שמורה לאלים ולמלכים, ואילו הדמויות העומדות רק סגדו להם,[3] ואף שאצלם לא יוחדה הדמות היושבת למין אחד, מור השתמש בתנוחה זו כמעט אך ורק לפיסול נשים.

הרקע של הדמות היושבת תורם רבות להתרשמות מעבודותיו של מור. אחדות נתונות במושבים דמויי כס־מלכות – כך למשל "חמש דמויות יושבות" מ־1934 – היוצרים מסגרת סביב הדמות ומדגישים את כובד משקלה המונומנטלי. אחרות יושבות בזקיפות־קומה מלכותית, גם בלי משענת לגבן – "אישה" מהשנים 1957-58 (מימין); פסל־הכנה ל"אישה יושבת: צוואר דק" מ־1960 (עמ' 52) – ויש המוצבות על מבנים דמויי־ספסל, חסרי צורה ממשית, המעניקים תמיכה מינימלית ("דמות יושבת", 1949, עמ' 52; "ילדה יושבת", 1956, עמ' 53). בפסל "אישה עטויה יושבת" מהשנים 1957-58 (עמ' 55), הדמות נשענת בהסבה חלקית על סלעי בזלת כהים בקמפוס האוניברסיטה העברית בירושלים בגבעת רם. הפטינה הירוקה של הברונזה בולטת על רקע האבן השחורה, ועם זה מערה את הפסל בסביבתו הטבעית. יד האישה מונחת על סלע, וידה האחרת תומכת בגופה העצום; אך לא פחות משהן מספקות תמיכה פיזית, ידיים משמשות את

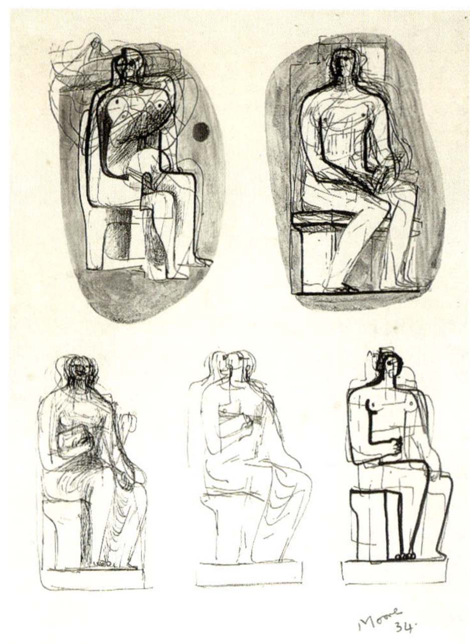

חמש דמויות יושבות, 1934
Five Seated Figures, 1934

6

Grohmann, *Art of Moore*, p. 229 1
Wilkinson, *Writings and Conversations*, p. 101 2
Winter, "Iconography," p. 255; Winter, "Royal Images," pp. 12–42 3
אנו מודות לד"ר טלי אורן, אוצרת לעתיקות מערב אסיה ע"ש רודניי א' סוהר במוזיאון ישראל, על עזרתה.

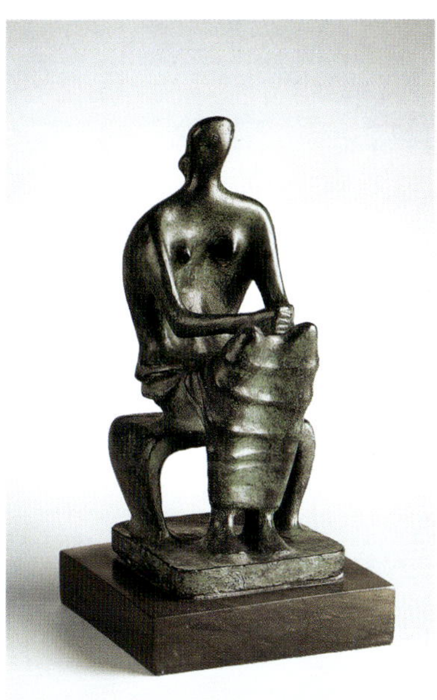

דמות יושבת, 1949
Seated Figure, 1949 | 34

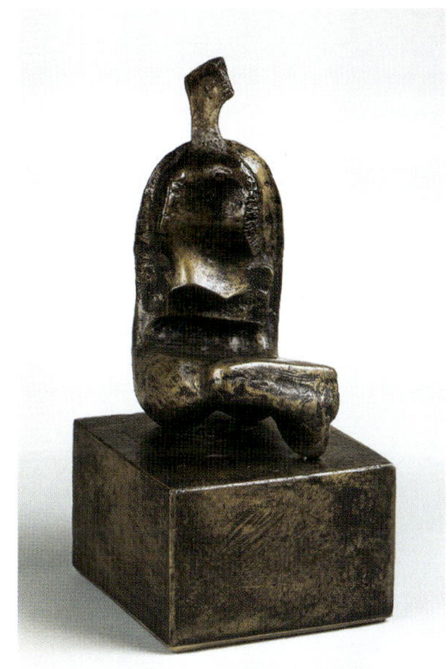

פסל־הכנה לאישה יושבת: צוואר דק, 1960
Maquette for Seated Woman: Thin Neck, 1960 | 64

מור להבעת רגש[4] – כך למשל אצבעות ידיה של "דמות
יושבת" (מס' 34) שלובות זו בזו וידיה מונחות על ברכיה
כבמחוות תפילה.

הקשר בין הדמות לתימוכה הוא יסוד מרכזי בדמויות
היושבות של מור. התלות ההדדית ביניהם היא תמציתו
של הפסלון "אשדודה", צלמית פלשתית מתקופת הברזל
(המאה ה־12 לפני הספירה) הכלולה באוסף המוזיאון.
בתצלום בעמ' 9 נראה מור מחזיק בידיו העתק של
הצלמית, שקיבל לאחר ביקורו במוזיאון ישראל ב־1966.
הוא התרשם מה'הנרי מוריות' של הפסלון. האישה
והכיסא מתמזגים בו לישות אחת, כמו ב"דמות אישה"
שלו מ־1928 (עמ' 53), שבו אגן הדמות הופך מושב של
כיסא ורגליה הפשוקות מדומות לרגלי הכיסא. מקורם של
פסלים מסוג זה ככל הנראה בצלמיות האגאיות של נשים
יושבות מסוף התקופה המיקנית השלישית. מוטיב האם־
האלה[5] של הצלמיות הללו השפיע עמוקות על עבודתו
של מור.

לטרנספורמציות שהכניס מור בגוף האישה אין כל זכר
ברישום נטורליסטי, כגון "עירומה יושבת" מ־1929 (עמ'
54) – אחד מרבים שיצר אחרי שהשלים ב־1924 את
לימודיו בבית־הספר המלכותי לאמנות בלונדון. מבט הדמות
הכבירה מוטה הצדה, ואילו גופה פונה לחזית. מתארים
נוספים סביב צדודית הפנים מרמזים על נקודות מבט
מרובות, ומזכירים, כמו גם גודל הדמות, את ציורי הנשים
העירומות של פיקאסו משנות ה־20 – נשים כבדות־איברים
ועצומות בממדיהן – ורק השרשרת העדינה העונדה לצוואר
הדמות העירומה ממתנת את הרושם הכבד הזה. ב"אישה
עטויה יושבת" (עמ' 55) האמן מגדיל עוד את קנה־המידה,
מתמקד פחות בתווי הפנים ויותר בבד;[6] הקפלים הזעירים
המרובים מזכירים את הפיסול היווני הקלסי ושונים
בתכלית מרצועות הבד האופקיות, הסכמטיות, הכרוכות
על "דמות יושבת" (מס' 34) חשופת החזה.

Wilkinson, *Writings and Conversations*, p. 220   4
Meshorer, *Archaeology*, p. 60   5
בין רגלי הפסל הותקן מרזב כדי למנוע הצטברות אבק וגשם בקפליו.   6
Wilkinson, *Moore Remembered*, p. 179

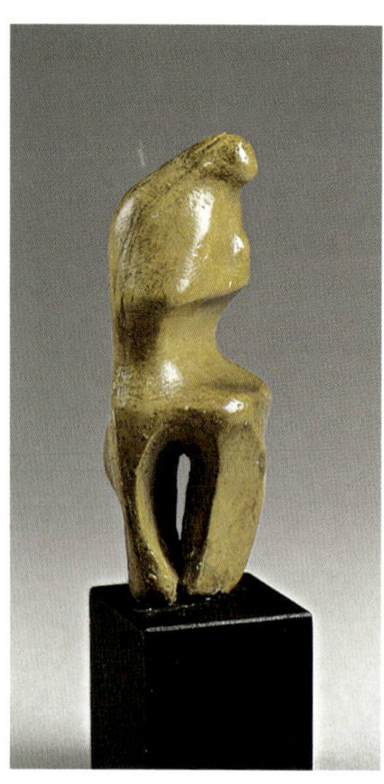

דמות אישה, 1928
Female Figure, 1928 | **1**

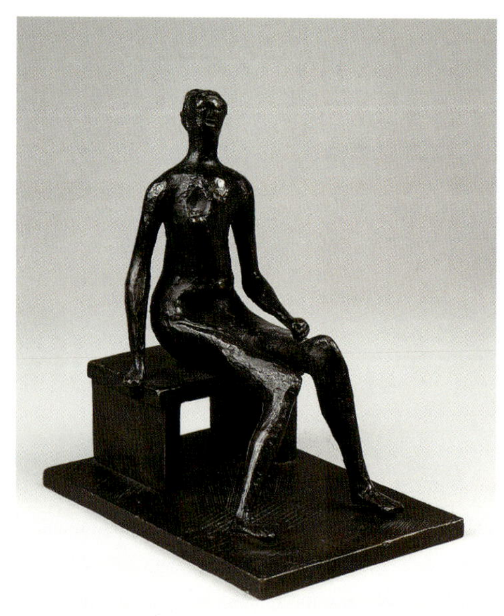

ילדה יושבת, 1956
Seated Girl, 1956 | **58**

סימן ההיכר של נשותיו היושבות של מור הוא ראש קטן במעלה גוף גדול וחושני, אך מידותיו הקטנות אינן מלמדות על ערכו: "בשבילי", הסביר האמן, "הראש הוא החלק החשוב ביותר בפסל. הראש נותן את קנה־המידה לשאר העבודה... יציבה אנושית מסוימת ומשמעות".[7] הראש הקטן ממקד את עיני הצופים בגוף הפסל. ב"אישה" (עמ' 50) וב"אישה יושבת: צוואר דק" מעצים מור את אפקט ההתמקדות בגוף על־ידי קטיעת הידיים והרגליים: ב"צוואר דק", כתפי האישה מעוגלות ורגליה מסתיימות בגדם מרובע; ואילו כתפיה המחוספסות, החדות בקצוות, של "אישה", יוצרות ניגוד לגדמי רגליה המעוגלים והחלקים. ב"אישה" מודגשים מאפיינים נשיים, כמו בתיאורים של אלות פריון פרהיסטוריות. הצורות הגדולות והמעוגלות של הגוף חוזרות כהד בסימונים העגולים על השדיים והבטן. הטבור המחורץ מייצג, אולי, חיים המתפתחים בתוך הרחם, והשדיים נראים גדושים בחלב. פסל זה מזכיר את הרישומים שבהם תיאר מור את הפסל הפלאוליתי "ונוס מגרימלדי". פוריותה של ונוס הודגשה אף היא על־ידי קיטום הזרועות והרגליים.[8]

החיבה של מור לפשטותה הראשונית של פסלי אלילים ציקלדיים, שמְתאריהם חדים, והעניין שגילה בעצם ובאבן צור, הובילו ליצירת סדרת הפסלים *חוד הסכין* בשנות ה־60. ב"צוואר דק", פסל מתוך הסדרה, "הצוואר והראש הדקים, לעומת הרוחב והנפחיות של הגוף, מעניקים לעבודה מראה מונומנטלי".[9] הדמות היושבת משלבת משטחים מעוגלים ומושחזים, ואוצרת בתוכה איכויות של פסל שנחצב באבן. מזיגה זו של עדינות ועוצמה, עצמאות ופגיעות, שלמות ופירוק, מטביעה בחותמה את נשותיו היושבות של מור ומציעה, באמצעותן, חקירה מורכבת ומקיפה על אודות הנשיות.

Wilkinson, *Writings and Conversations*, p. 219 | 7
Wilkinson, *Moore Remembered*, p. 183 | 8
Wilkinson, *Writings and Conversations*, p. 290 | 9

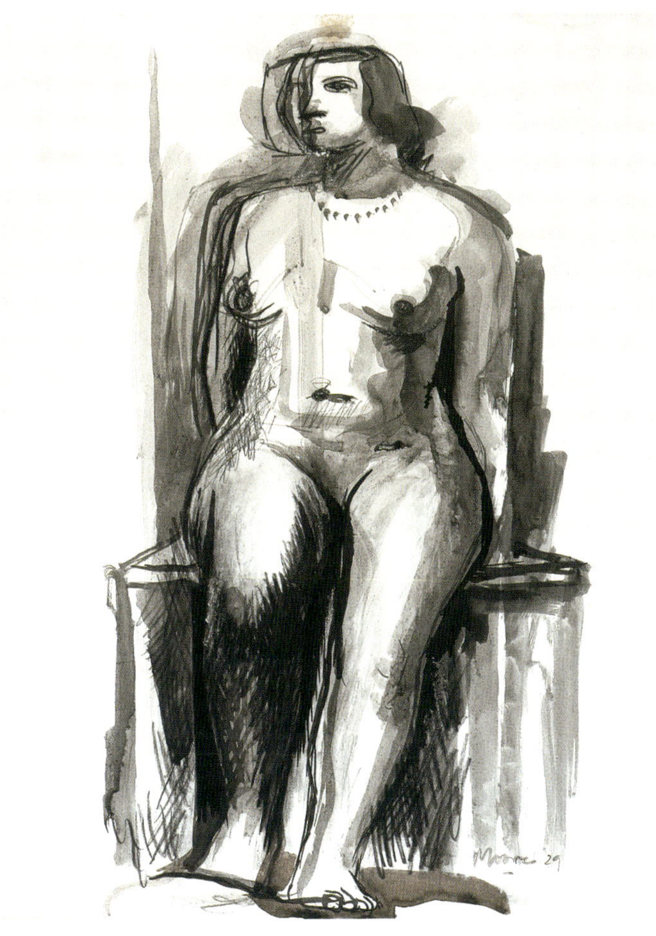

עירומה יושבת, 1929
Seated Nude, 1929 | 2

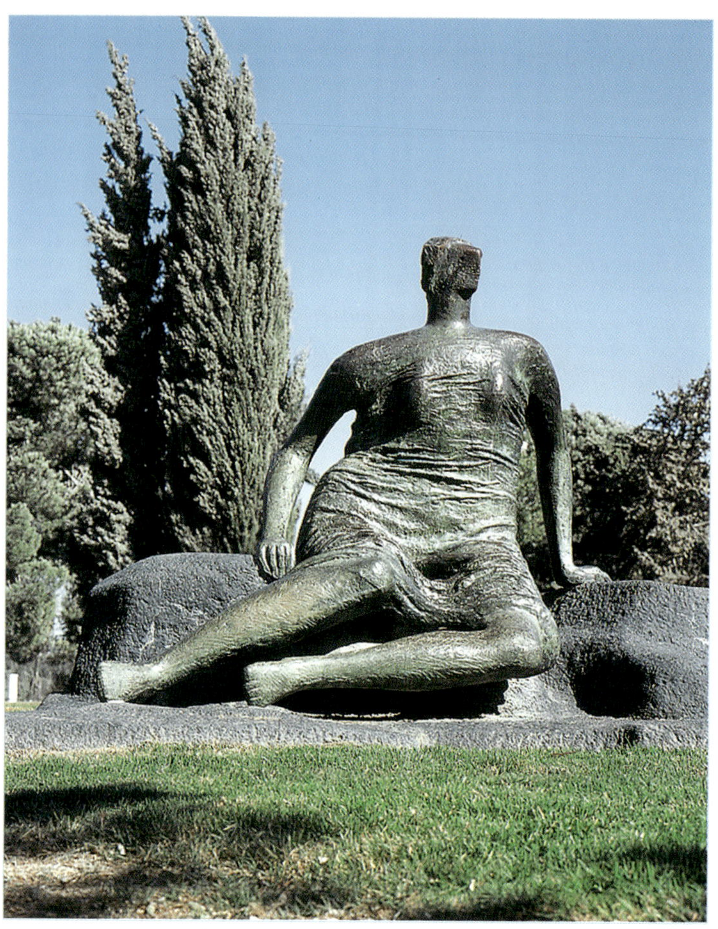

אישה עטויה יושבת, 58–1957

ברונזה, ג 185.4 ס"מ

האוניברסיטה העברית בירושלים

מתנת שרלוט ברגמן, לזכר לואיס ברגמן

Draped Seated Woman, 1957–58

Bronze, h. 185.4 cm

The Hebrew University of Jerusalem

Gift of Charlotte Bergman, in memory of Louis Bergman

LH 428

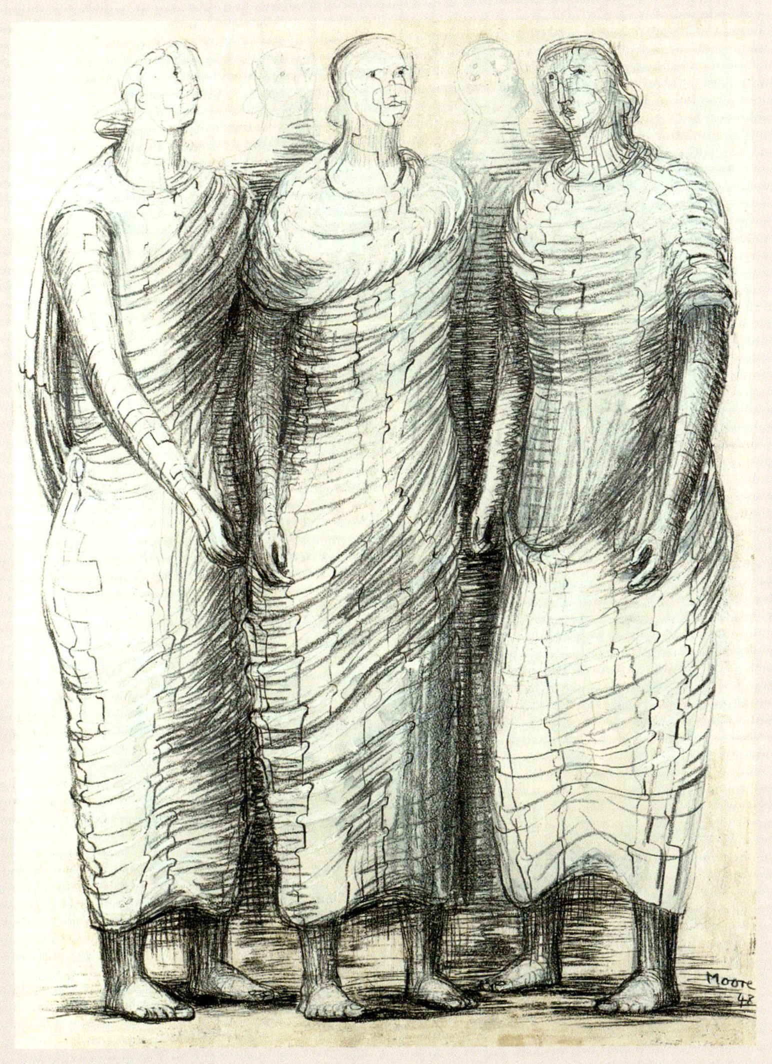

נשים עומדות, 1948
Standing Women, 1948

הדמויות הניצבות

לדמות הניצבת, המתוארת באורך מלא, בשלושה רבעים או בחצי גוף, מקום מרכזי בעבודתו של הנרי מור, והיא משתנה לבלי הכר לאורך שנות יצירתו. דמויותיו הניצבות לובשות ופושטות צורות ומצבים: יש בהן הדורות וחגיגיות, אחרות היתוליות, נסוכות רוח שטות. אוסף מוזיאון ישראל חושף מעברים וניגודים בפסליו אלה – מזוויתיות מודגשת ועד עגלגלות; מקשיות ועד רכות; משלדיות עד כובד גוף.

"דמות שלובת אצבעות" מ־1929, מאוסף מוזיאון תל אביב לאמנות, היא מהתגליפים המעולים של מור משנות ה־20. צורתה הריבועית של הדמות, המתוארת בחצי גוף, משקפת את השפעתן של האמנות הטולטקית והאצטקית וכן את רצון הפּסל לשמור על צורתו של גוש השיש הטרוורטיני. בהטיה הצדה של הפנים דמויי־המסכה נשברת הסימטרייה, והדיוקן החזיתי והצדודית משתלבים יחד, בדרך קוביסטית. בליטת אבן מאחור מייצגת סכמטית את שערה האסוף של האישה. כבתגליפים מוקדמים אחרים, מור כמעט שאינו מפסל צוואר, אולי מחשש להחליש את האבן. מרווחי האוויר היחידים בעבודה מונוליתית זו נפתחים בין הגוף לזרועות. הידיים, אצבעותיהן שלובות תחת השדיים, מזכירות פסלים כגון גודיאה השומרי, ובה בעת מדגישות את נשיותה של הדמות.

"דמות בחצי גוף" מ־1932 בקירוב (עמ' 59) מעידה על המעבר הרדיקלי של מור לשפת פיסול עם זיקה לצורות הביומורפיות של הסוראליסטים. מור השתתף אמנם בתערוכת הסוראליזם הבינלאומית בגלריות ברלינגטון בלונדון ב־1936, אך מעולם לא ראה עצמו שייך לתנועה זו. עם זה, לעבודתם של ארפ, פיקאסו, מירו וטאנגי נודעה עליו השפעה משחררת, ובעקבותיהם נבט ביצירתו רעיון גלגול־הצורה. ב"דמות בחצי גוף" מתוארת למעשה דמות נשית בשלושה רבעים, מהראש ועד אמצע הירך.[1] האמן משתעשע במשחקי אנטומיה: הראש כמעט שאינו מובחן מן הצוואר, שד אחד נמוך מרעהו, והישבן מסובב לפנים. החריתות העדינות בברונזה תורמות לרוח המחויכת הנסוכה על הדמות. עיגולים שבלוניים במקום עיניים מספיקים לסימון כל תווי הפנים, וחריץ צר במורד הכתף הוא רמז היתולי לשער האישה הגולש. אצבעות חרוטות

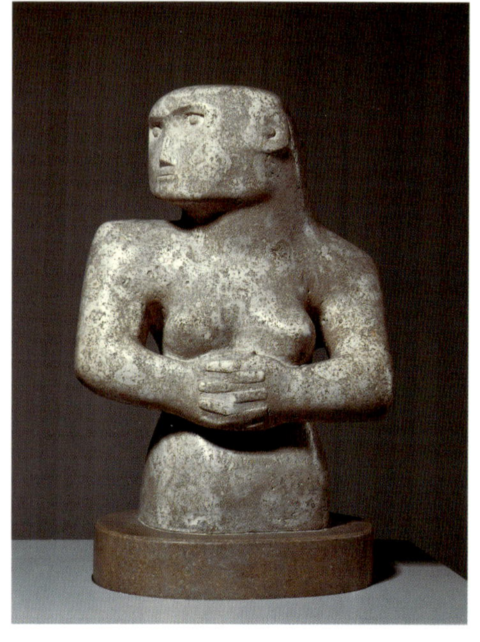

דמות שלובת אצבעות, 1929
שיש טרוורטין, ג' 45.72 ס"מ
מוזיאון תל אביב לאמנות. מתנת סר א' ויקס
באמצעות הידידים הבריטים של המוזיאונים לאמנות בישראל

Figure with Clasped Hands, 1929
Travertine marble, h. 45.7 cm
Tel Aviv Museum of Art. Gift of Sir A. Wix, through the
British Friends of the Art Museums of Israel
LH 60

---

1 פסל זה דומה מאוד לדמות בחצי גוף של מור מ־1931 (LH 98), הגלופה מבהט.

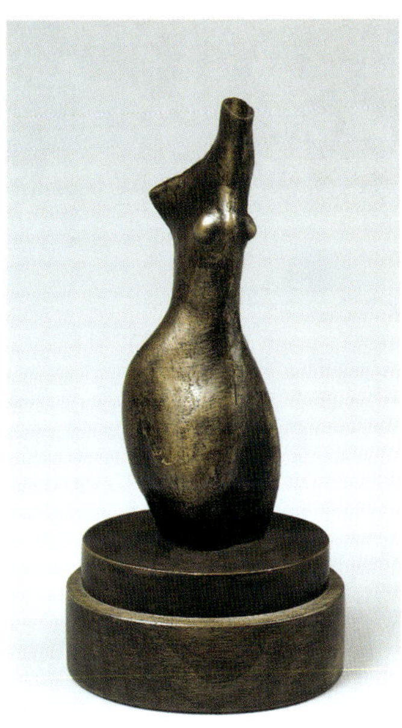

טורסו אישה, 1984
Female Torso, 1984 | 78

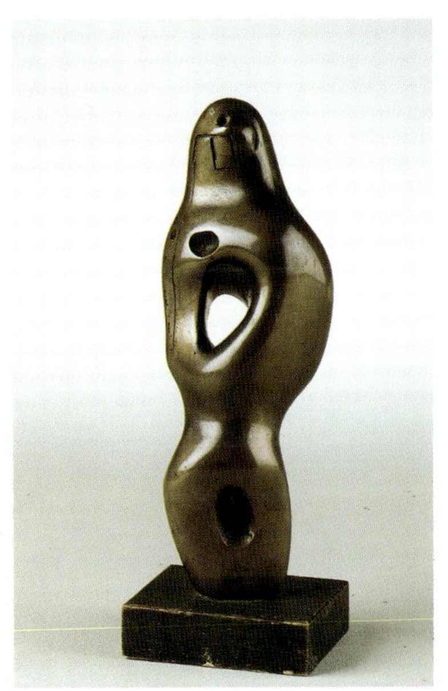

דמות, 1935 בקירוב
Figure, ca. 1935 | 7

בקלישות נוגעות בשדה ובירכה, ונקבובי פטמות וטבור מנקדים את פני השטח.

ב"דמות", מ־1935 בקירוב, נוסק הביומורפיזם של מור לגבהים חדשים: צורות מעוגלות הזורמות בחופשיות ונקבים מייצגים בהפשטה את נושא היצירה. הצפייה בפסל משני עברי החלל המרכזי מגלה הבדלים ניכרים הן במתאר הכללי הן בחריתות המעצבות, המשמשות גם כיסוד עיטורי. כאן מור חופר מחילה בגוף האישה, וברישומו מ־1941, "ארבע דמויות" (עמ' 60), ההצללה האפלה והמסתורית היא המרמזת על עומקי הנשיות החבויים, דמויי־המערה.

בשנות ה־50 הפליג מור בחדשנות יצירתית, עם סדרה של דמויות אנכיות גרומות. ב"דמות עומדת מס' 1" וב"דמות עומדת מס' 3" (שתיהן בעמ' 62), גישת פיסול קווית ומרוקנת מנפחיות מפיקה "עצמות מופחות חיים"[2] ונטולות בשר. בניגוד חד לנשים הקלסיות, מלאות הגוף,

המתוארות בעבודות כגון "נשים עומדות" מ־1948 (עמ' 56), הדמויות הללו, עם קווי גופן המשתרגים, משקפות את העניין של מור בעבודתם של ברנקוזי וג'אקומטי, וכן את הטמעתו את החירות הצורנית ואת העיוות, האופייניים לדימויי הגוף של פיקאסו בתקופה זו.[3]

בפסל־הכנה ל"דמות עומדת" (עמ' 20) הגוף האנושי נבקע ומתרוקן.[4] בליטות באזורי המפרקים מחברות יחד את רצועות המתכת השלדיות המייצגות את הזרועות והרגליים. צורות משולשות מושטחות בגובה הכתף מרמזות על שכמות או מגנים קטנים, ומתוכם עולים שני צוארים וראשים דמויי־אנטנה. גרסת הברונזה המוגדלת של הפסל הוצגה לראשונה בפארק בטרסי שבלונדון, סמוך לאגם, שם בלטה הדמות הכחושה והאנכית על

<hr>

Russell, *Moore*, p. 143   2
Wilkinson, *Moore Collection*, p. 113   3
פירושים נוספים לעבודה זו ואחרות הקשורות אליה ראה במאמר   4
"פענוח התעלומה של הנרי מור" (עמ' 17-23).

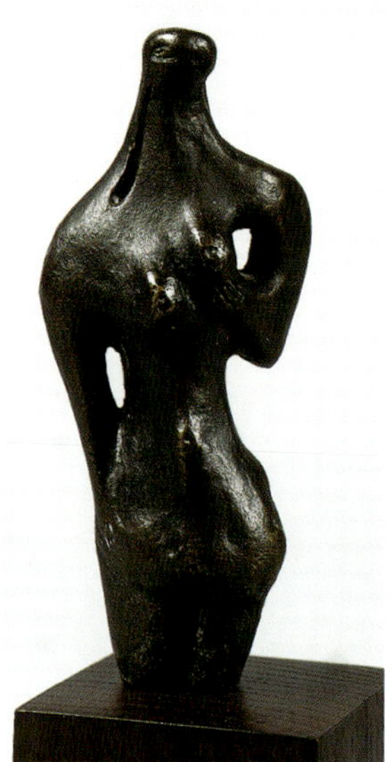

דמות בחצי גוף, 1932 בקירוב
ברונזה, ג 12.7 ס"מ
אוסף פרטי

Half-Figure, ca. 1932
Bronze, h. 12.7 cm
Private collection
LH 116

רקע משטח המים האופקי והשלו. את שורשי העבודה
הזאת נעץ מור בתצלום של בני שבט אפריקני, שבו נראים
הגברים עומדים בלא ניע על גדת הנהר, רגע לפני הטלת
הצלצל אל הדג.[5] בתחילה ראה הפֶּסל בחזונו 4 דמויות
עומדות בשורה, ניצבות על בסיס משותף, אך בסופו של
דבר בחר בשתי יציקות של דמות אחת בלבד.

"דמות עומדת מס' 1" (עמ' 62) היא עבודה נטורליסטית
יותר, אם כי גופה צנום וברכיה ומותניה גרמיים. אמנם
המותן הדקה והחזה הבולט עשויים להתפרש כסממנים
נשיים, אך מינה של הדמות אינו ברור. זרועותיה המורמות
יוצרות תחושת דריכות ומתח. "דמות עומדת מס' 3" (עמ'
62), לבושה חלקית ושקועת-חזה, משדרת בדידות
והשתוקקות.

פיתוח מוטיב הדמות האנכית בעבודתו של מור הגיע
לשיאו בסדרה *מוטיב ניצב* מהשנים 1955-56 (עבודה
מהסדרה בעמ' 63). ראשיתה של הסדרה ביצירה

שהוזמנה לחצר הבניין החדש של חברת אוליווטי במילנו.
בתהליך העבודה יצק מור 13 פסלי-הכנה אנכיים –
מוטיבים ניצבים – שתוכננו כ'תשובה' חזותית לבניין
האופקי. הם כבר אינם מרמזים לגוף; המוטיבים דמויי-
הטוטם כוללים בתוכם מגוון מרתק של צורות אורגניות
המונחות זו על זו באיזון. כאשר ביקש האמן להגדיל כמה
מפסלי-ההכנה, "שלושה מהם התקבצו יחדיו ולבשו בעיניי
מראה של תמונת צליבה".[6] יחד עם "מוטיב ניצב מס' 2"
ו"מוטיב ניצב מס' 7", "מוטיב ניצב מס' 1 – צלב גלנקילן"[7]
מייצג את ישו הצלוב בין שני הליסטים. כשהן נצפות
בנפרד, בלי הנופך הסמלי, משדרות העבודות הפאליות
הללו תחושה של צמיחה אורגנית הנתונה בהתפתחות
תמידית.

Wilkinson, *Moore Collection*, p. 113   5
Wilkinson, *Writings and Conversations*, p. 285   6
LH 377   7

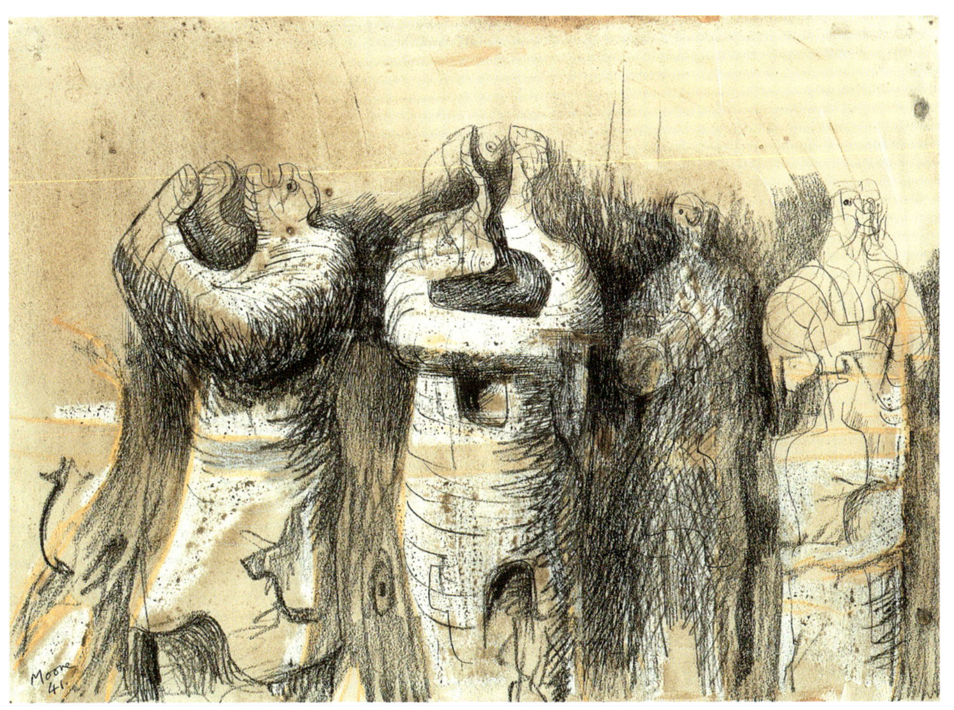

ארבע דמויות, 1941
Four Figures, 1941

11

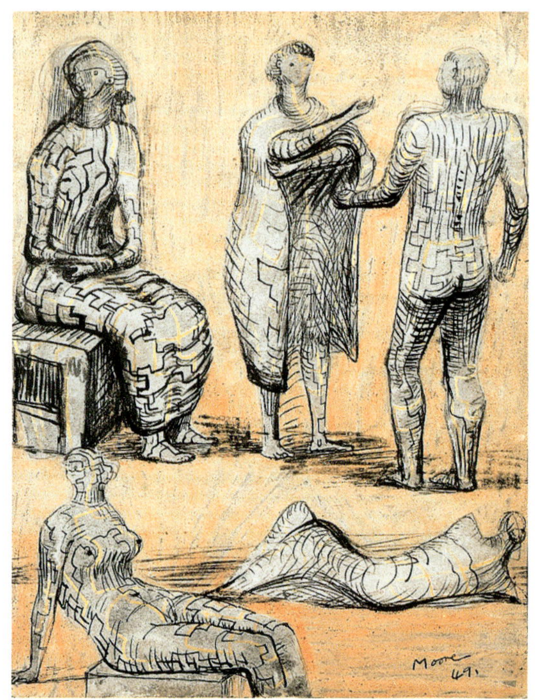

דמויות עומדות, יושבות ושוכבות, 1949 בקירוב
Standing, Seated and Reclining Figures, ca. 1949

35

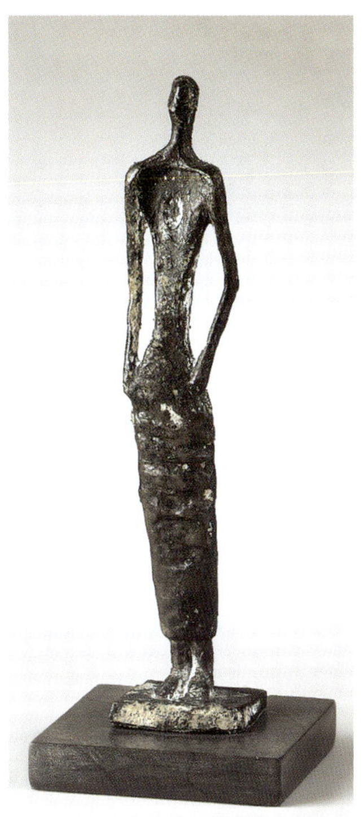

דמות עומדת מס' 3, 1952
Standing Figure No. 3, 1952 | 49

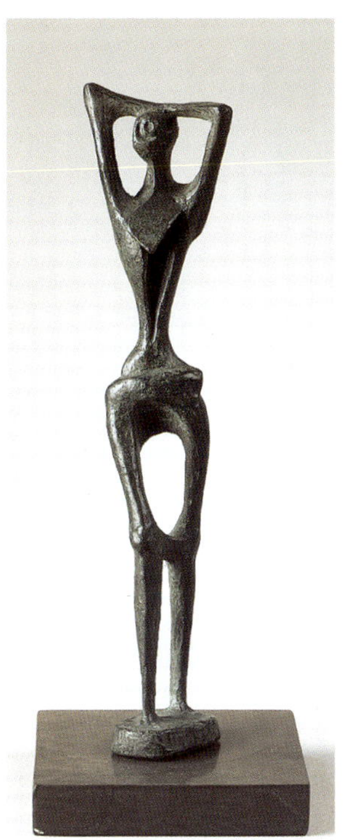

דמות עומדת מס' 1, 1952
Standing Figure No. 1, 1952 | 48

◀ מוטיב ניצב מס' 7, 1955–56
Upright Motive No. 7, 1955–56 | 56

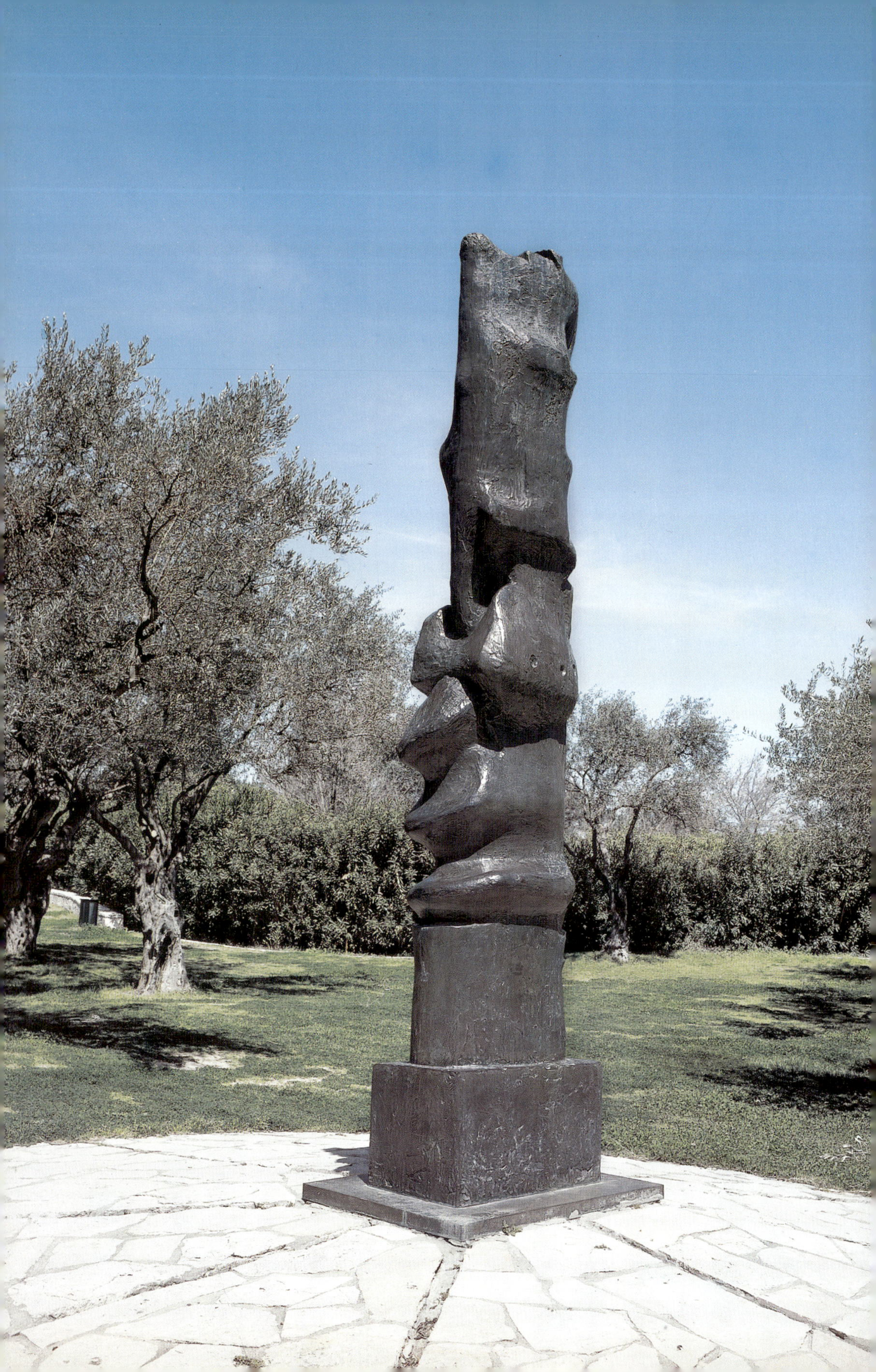

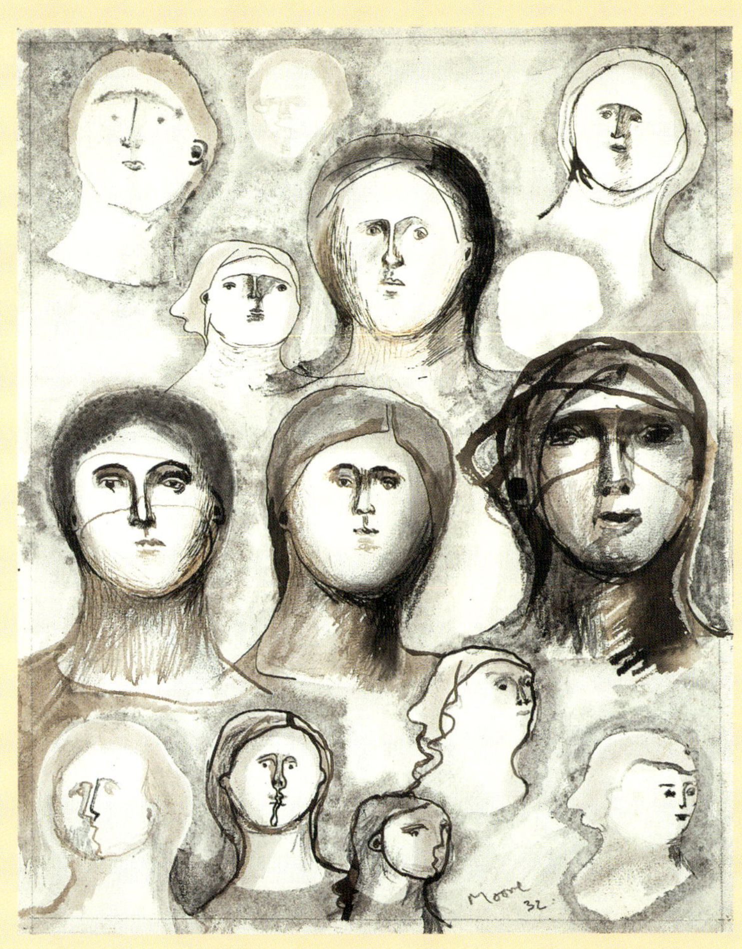

מתווי ראשים, 1932
Studies of Heads, 1932

4

ראשים משתנים

נכתב בשיתוף עם ג'וליאנה אוקס

הראשים המפוסלים של הנרי מור קטנים וכמעט נטולי פרטים; לעתים קרובות הם מתגמדים על־ידי גוף גדול־ממדים ועלולים להיראות חסרי חשיבות, או איבר שהאמן לא העניק לו די תשומת־לב. "אך אין הדבר כך", טוען סר קנת קלארק, "האמת היא, שהוא התעניין בהם יתר על המידה".[1] מור חקר ובדק ראשים של בני־אדם ושל בעלי־חיים למעלה מ־5 עשורים. הרישומים והפסלים מקטגוריה זו שבאוסף המוזיאון נותנים תחושה של עוצמה רבה ושל שלמות.

מור מבודד את ראש האדם ובוחן אותו בשני רישומים משנת 1932. הרישום דמוי־הסריג "שישה־עשר ראשים" (עמ' 66) בוחן את הראש מזוויות שונות. בעוד הפנים דומים וייתכן אף שזהו דיוקנה של אותה אישה, הקווים הזורמים מושכים לכיוון פרשנות דינמית של המודל. ב"מתווי ראשים" (מימין) הארגון חופשי יותר והטיפול בכל אחד מהראשים שונה בגודל, ברמת הפירוט ובהיקף השימוש בחומרי הציור. הראשים במרכז התמונה כובשים את תשומת־לב הצופה בשל גודלם וההצללה הדרמטית שלהם, והראשים שסביבם קטנים ובהירים ויוצרים להם מעין הד. כל אחת מהעבודות היא סקיצה חופשית ובד בבד גם רישום מאורגן היטב.

בין השנים 1937 ו־1940 ערך מור ניסויים עתירי דמיון ומעוף בפיסול משולב במיתרים. הוא שאב את ההשראה לסדרת עבודות זו מתגליפי מלנגאן מניו־אירלנד שהוצגו במוזיאון הבריטי ונראו למור כציפורים בכלוב וכן מהמודלים המתמטיים שהוצגו במוזיאון המדע בלונדון, ובהם נעשה שימוש בחוטים מתוחים.[2] ראשי המיתרים של מור מעוצבים כקערה, צווארם עבה ועיניהם חורים קדוחים. הפסל "ראש מיתר" מ־1958 (עמ' 67, מימין) העשוי טרקוטה מעניק תחושה ארצית, וכשהוא יצוק בברונזה (1986, שם, משמאל) עם פטינה מוזהבת, הראש נראה מודרני ומשקף את התעניינותו המוקדמת של מור במכונה. בשתי הגרסאות בולט ההבדל בין קלות המשקל של המיתר לבין דחיסות הפסל. 8 חוטים חוצים אופקית את הראש הקעור, ובכך מגבירים את המודעות לגבולות החלל של הפסל ועם זה שומרים על פתיחותו.

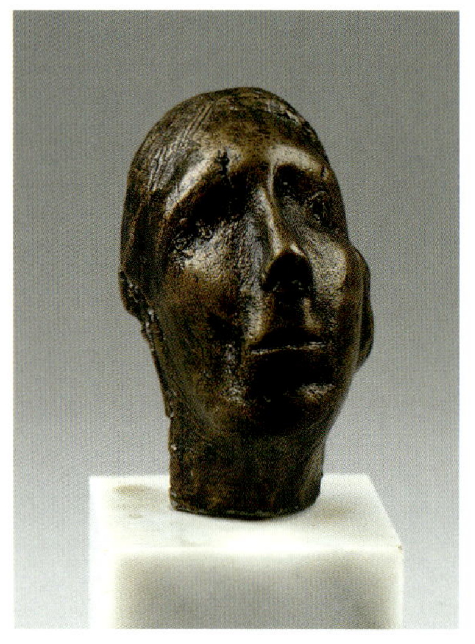

ראש קטן, 1953
Small Head, 1953

53

Clark, *Moore Drawings,* p. 221 1

Grohmann, *Art of Moore,* p. 103 2

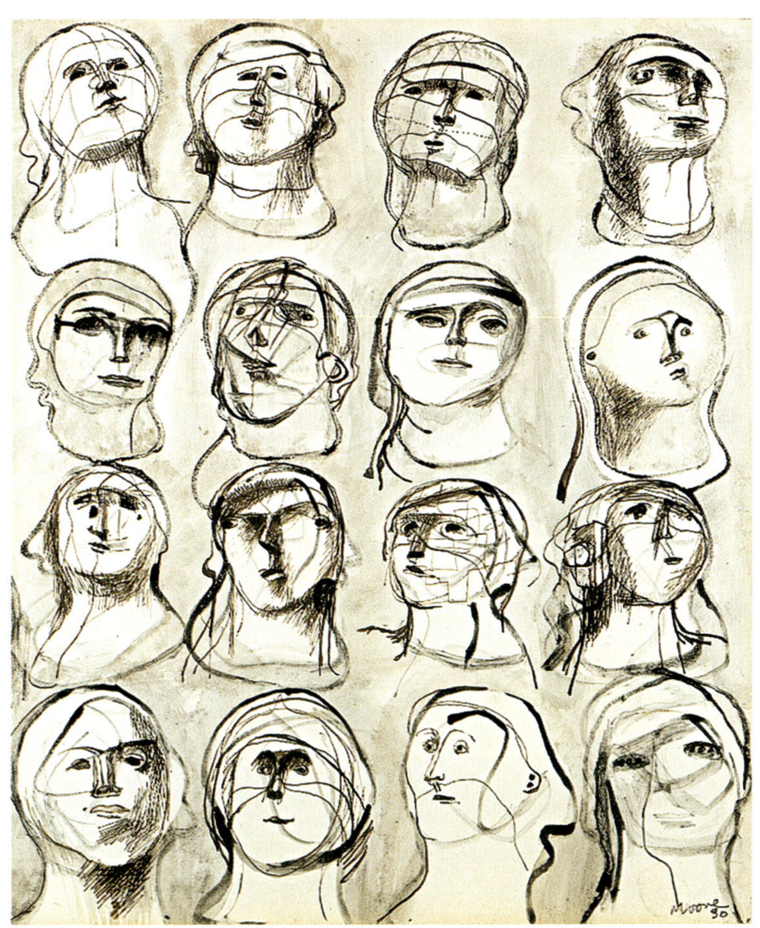

שישה־עשר ראשים, 1932 בקירוב
Sixteen Heads, ca. 1932

3

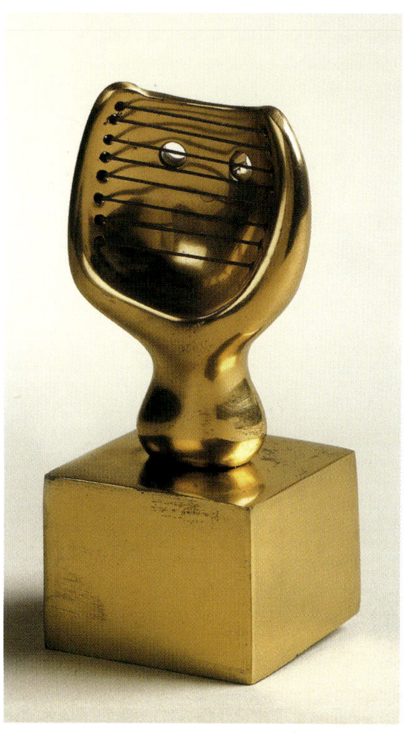

ראש מיתר, 1986
Stringed Head, 1986 | 79

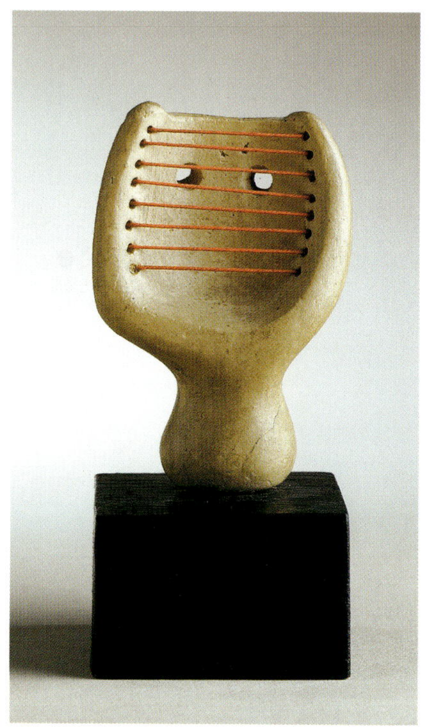

ראש מיתר, 1958
Stringed Head, 1958 | 62

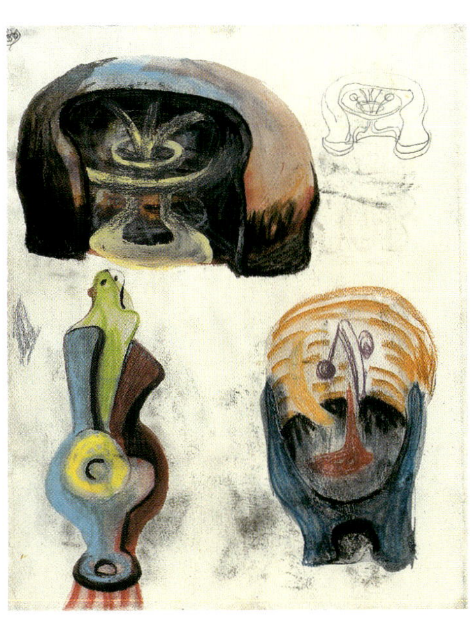

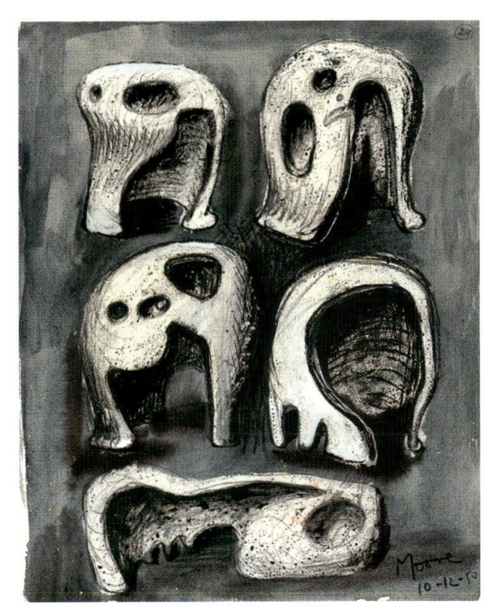

צד ב של **ראשי קסדה**
Verso of *Helmet Heads* | **41b**

ראשי קסדה, 1950
Helmet Heads, 1950 | **41a**

אינטראקציה זו בין החלל הפנימי והחיצוני בולטת
ברישומים ובפסלים של האמן מן הסדרה *ראשי קסדה*,
שבה החל בשנת 1939.[3] ראשי קסדה אלה עשויים
מעטפת חיצונית ובתוכה צורה פנימית ומגלמים
את "המסתורין שבלא לדעת לגמרי מה טיבה של הצורה
הפנימית... כמו שריון מגן – המעטפת החיצונית מגנה
על הפנים הרך".[4] בשנת 1950 פיסל מור כמה ראשי
קסדה ורשם מתווים בנושא. ברישום למעלה מימין,
לדוגמה, הוא רשם 5 מעטפות קסדה כאלה, והדגיש את
חלליהן הכהים המזכירים מערות פעורות־פה. בצדו האחר
(משמאל), הצבוע בצבעים עליזים ומלאי חיים, הצורות
הפנימיות המפותלות, המוגנות, או שמא כלואות, על־ידי
הקסדה – נראות רק בחלקן. ברישום שבעמ' 69 האמן
מדגיש את אנושיותה של הקסדה על־ידי הוספת אוזניים
וזוג חורים המייצגים את העיניים.

הצורות הפנימיות הסבוכות מייצגות את רקמת המוח
הרכה, או את המחשבות והרגשים. "מיד בתום מלחמת
העולם השנייה" ראשי קסדה אלה "עוררו בצופה רושם
מפחיד ומאיים, שכן הם שיקפו את התחושה הקשה

והבלתי־נעימה של אותן שנים".[5] ראשי הקסדה הולידו
כעבור 10 שנים את הסדרה *צורה פנימית/חיצונית* ואולי
הם אף מהווים את מקבילתה הזכרית. בשתי הסדרות
אפשר להצביע על קשר לתאוריות של הפסיכואנליטיקן
ויניקוט על יצירתיות כתהליך פנימי־חיצוני שבו סף־המודע
מתווך בין המאגר הלא־מודע של זיכרונות, פנטזיות ואנרגיה
לבין הפיכתם המודעת של מרכיבים אלה לאמנות.[6]

בד בבד עם יצירת ראשי הקסדה, יצר מור ב־1953 גם
את "ראש קטן" (עמ' 65) – מיניאטורה המתוארת בפירוט
רב מזה שבדמויות הגדולות שפיסל. את "ראש קטן"
מאפיין פתוס, והוא נעשה אולי בהשראת המתווים למלכה
כהכנה ל"מלך ומלכה" מהשנים 1952-53.[7] המבע הכאוב

3   מעניין לציין שב־1932, שנה לפני ביקורו של מור אצל ז'אק ליפשיץ
    בפריז, יצר ליפשיץ כמה עבודות שכותרתן "מתווה לראש", המזכירות
    את המעטפת של *ראשי קסדה*. תודה לסוזן לנדאו, אוצרת ראשית
    לאמנות ע"ש יולה וז'אק ליפשיץ, על ההשוואה הזאת.
4   Gilmour, *Graphics*, p. 43
5   Compton, *Moore*, p. 227. ויל גרומן טוען שציוד מלחמה כגון קסדות
    פלדה ומסכות גז השפיעו על מור. Grohmann, *Art of Moore*, p. 106
6   Deri, "Vicissitudes," in Schneider, "Mother and Child," 263, n.
7   LH 350

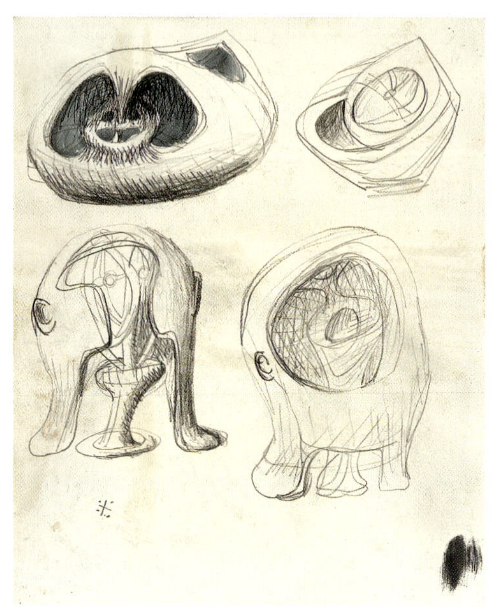

צד ב של **מתווים לפסל**, 51–1950 (עמ' 35)
Verso of *Studies for Sculpture*, 1950–51 (p. 35)

45b

והתיאור המדוקדק והמפורט של העיניים, האף, הפה
והסנטר משקפים את הערצת האמן לדיוק הפסיכולוגי
המובע בפסליו של רודן. מור העניק לפסל ברונזה זה
מרקם מעניין באמצעות חריתה ושפשוף של עיני האישה
השקועות והעצובות והדגיש את העצמות הבולטות מעל
לחייה השקועות.

צורות דמויות ראשים מופיעות גם ב״תבליט קיר: שלוש
צורות״ מ־1955 (עמ' 70), חלק מסדרת תבליטי קיר
שהתפתחו מיצירתו האחרת של מור ״מסך זמן/חיים״
מ־53-1952.[8] האמן עיצב תחילה בגבס רך ואז גילף שלוש
צורות, מנצל את מה שכינה ״ההבלטה והנסיגה של
הצורה״.[9] צורות כדוריות ושקעים עמוקים דמויי־עיניים
מאפיינים את הראשים בתבליט, והעורקים המשתרגים
המעטרים אותם מזכירים את סדרת פסלי הברונזה
דמויות עלה שפיסל מור בשנת 1952.

״צורת חיה״ מ־1959 (עמ' 71) נגזרה מהיצירה ״שלושה
מוטיבים ליד קיר מס׳ 1״ מ־1958; היא קשורה ל״ראש
עז״ מ־1952 וייתכן שאת ההשראה ליצירתה שאב האמן

מעצמות בעלי־חיים שנחשפו בגינת ביתו. בניגוד למנוחה
הרוגעת האופיינית לרוב יצירותיו, כאן ההצגה המעוותת
והאקספרסיוניסטית של גוף בעל־החיים שופעת תנועה
ואנרגיה.[10]

הראש שבה את דמיונו של מור ואפשר לו לבטא פתוס,
לבחון את הצורה הסבוכה של חללים פתוחים וסגורים
ולהביע את המסתורין הגלום בצורות פנימיות וחיצוניות.
הראש העניק לאמן צורה תחומה המכונסת בגבולות,
שמורכבותה מקיפה את מכלול הגוף והנפש האנושיים.
הראשים של מור – מעוטרים או נטורליסטיים, שקועים
בשרעפים או שובביים – הם כלי שבאמצעותו הביע האמן
את מחשבותיו על אודות הצורה האנושית והחלל
המפוסל.

8   LH 344

9   James, *Moore on Sculpture*, p. 275

10   במשך 6 שנים בחרה האגודה הזואולוגית של לונדון להעניק פרסים
בצורת החיות הללו, עד שעלותם נעשתה גבוהה מדי. *Berthoud, Life*
of Moore, pp. 309–10

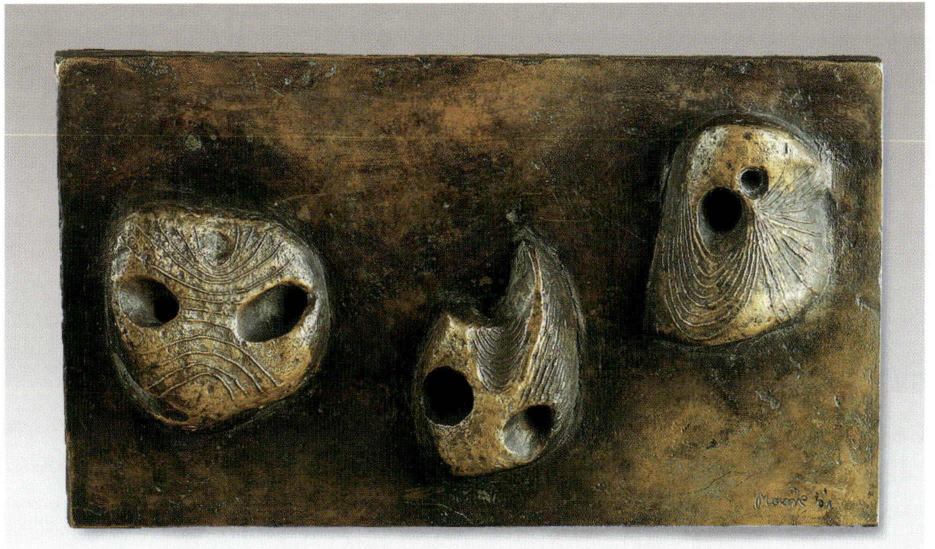

תבליט קיר: שלוש צורות, 1955
Wall Relief: Three Forms, 1955

55

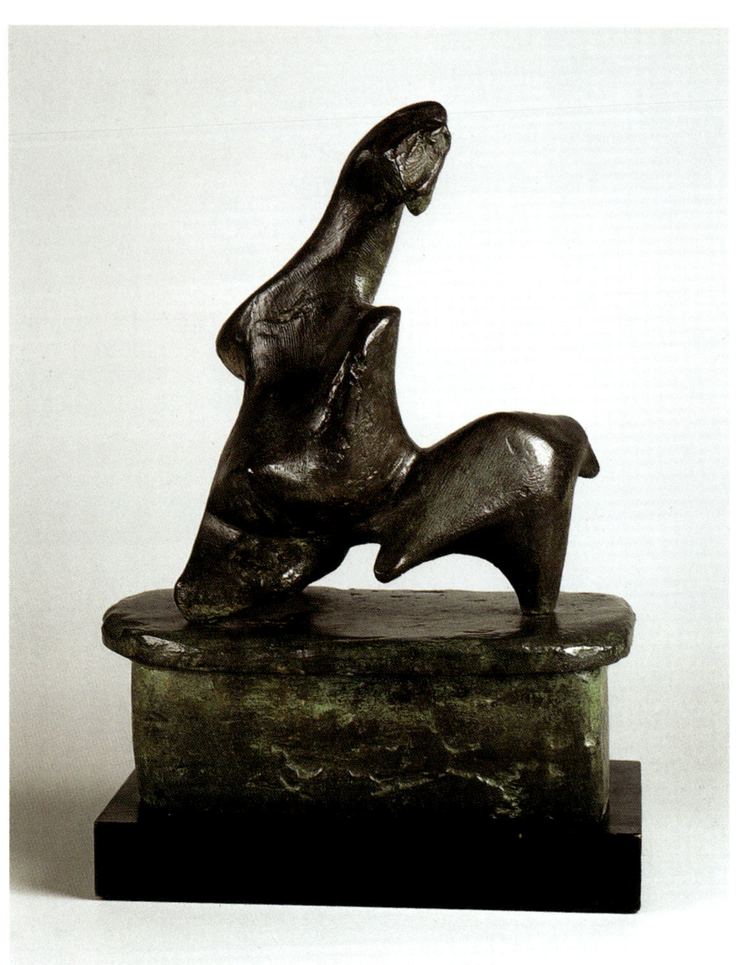

צורת חיה, 1959
ברונזה, ג 34.29 ס"מ
אוסף פרטי

Animal Form, 1959
Bronze, h. 34.3 cm
Private collection
LH 443

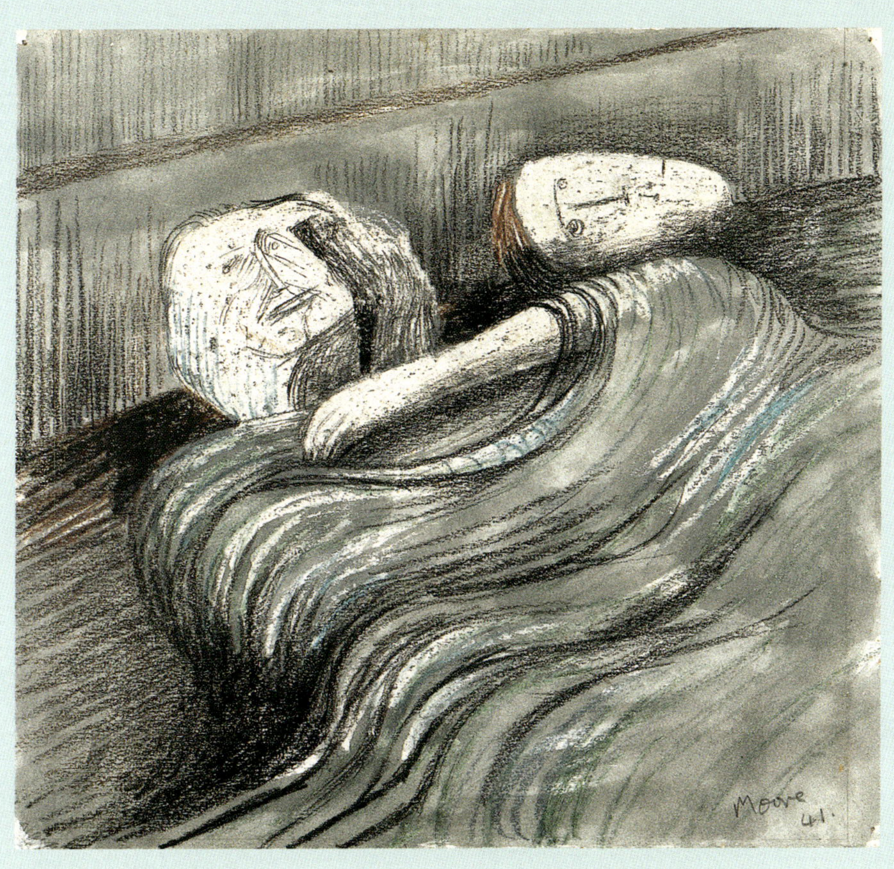

תמונה מן המקלט: שתי דמויות שוכבות, 1941
Shelter Scene: Two Reclining Figures, 1941

14

רישומים מן המקלט

נכתב בשיתוף עם ג'וליאנה אוקס

בעיצומם של מוראות מלחמת העולם השנייה תיאר הנרי מור דווקא דמויות עדינות ושבריריות, לעתים משפחות שלמות, המבקשות נחמה והגנה. "אלמלא המלחמה, המנתבת את דרכו של האדם לחיים עצמם, נראה לי שהייתי אדם הרבה פחות רגיש ואחראי. המלחמה העלתה ועודדה את הפן ההומניסטי ביצירה".[1]

מור חי ופעל בקינגסטון שליד דובר כשהוכרזה המלחמה ב־3 בספטמבר 1939. מחשש פן יפלשו הגרמנים לבריטניה, הוחלט להפוך את הכפר לאזור מלחמה מוגבל, ומור ורעייתו שבו ללונדון. ב־7 בספטמבר 1940 החלו ההפצצות מן האוויר – ה"בליץ" – ביום ובלילה, ואלפים מתושבי לונדון השתמשו במנהרות הרכבת התחתית למקלט מאולתר. כשם שהבריחה אל המנהרות היתה ספונטנית ואינסטינקטיווית, כך גם העניין שעוררה התופעה במור. באחד הערבים הראשונים של ההפצצות הוא הבחין בשורות־שורות של אנשים מסתופפים יחד תחת שמיכות על הרצפה הקרה של תחנת הרכבת התחתית – מראות שהזכירו לו את תיאורי הדמויות השוכבות ביצירתו:

מעולם לא ראיתי שורות כה רבות של דמויות שוכבות. אפילו הפתחים שמהן הגיחו הרכבות נדמו לי כמו החללים שבפסליי. עם זה, היו גם רגעים של אינטימיות. ילדים נמו את שנתם העמוקה ומטרים ספורים מהם חלפו רכבות סואנות בשאון מחריש אוזניים. אנשים שלא היה ביניהם כל קשר, זרים מוחלטים זה לזה, יצרו קבוצות אינטימיות קטנות ומדוקות. הם היו מנותקים לחלוטין מהההתרחשויות שמעליהם, אך עם זה מודעים להן. מתח שרר באוויר. הם הזכירו לי במעט את המקהלה בדרמות היווניות העתיקות, שתפקידה לדווח לנו על אלימות שאיננו עדים לה.[2]

בחודשיים הבאים שב מור ופקד תחנות רכבת תחתית ברחבי לונדון כמעט מדי ערב, וחזה במו עיניו כיצד חיי הפרט הפכו באופן סוראליסטי לנחלת הכלל. תצפיותיו מילאו כמה וכמה מחברות רישומים. סר קנת קלארק, שהיה אז יושב־ראש הוועדה המייעצת של ציירי המלחמה, התרשם מעבודותיו של מור – אף שהיו רק ביטוי ספונטני בינו לבין עצמו של מה שראה – והמלצתו הובילה למינויו של מור לצייר מלחמה רשמי.

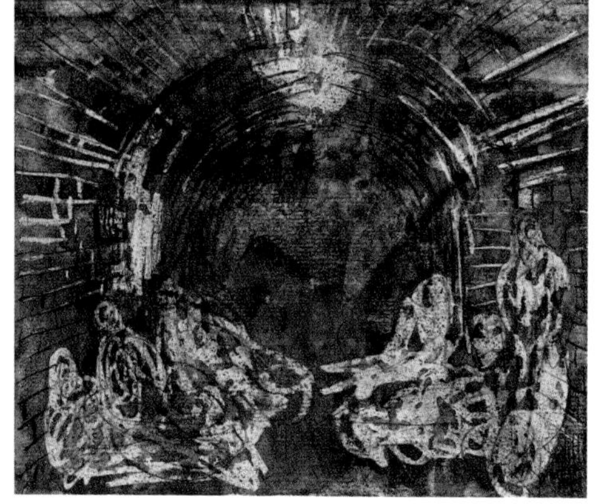

תמונה מן המקלט, 1941
Shelter Scene, 1941

12

Compton, Moore, p. 32   1
Moore: Shelter Sketchbook, p. 9   2

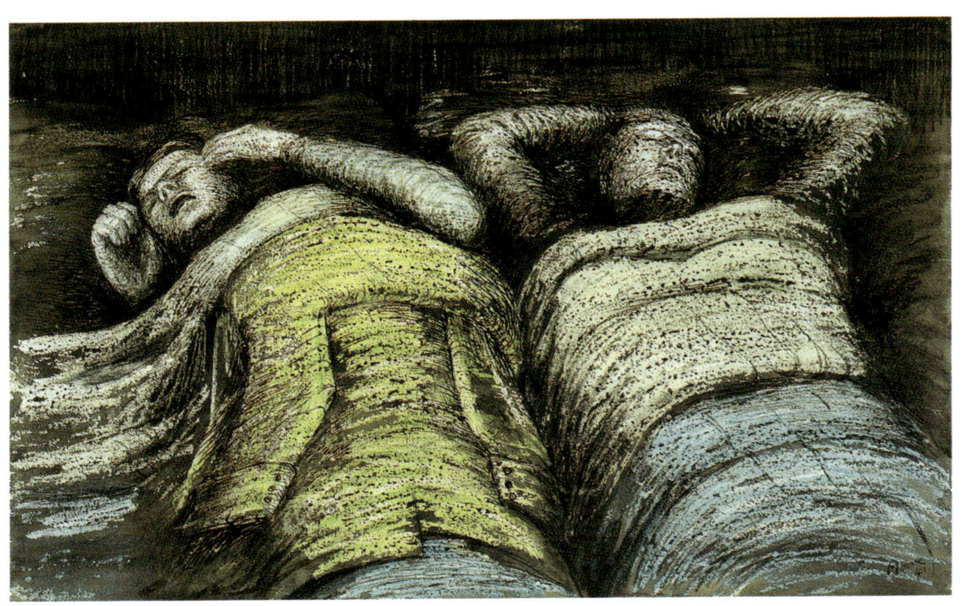

רישום מן המקלט, 1941
Shelter Drawing, 1941

13

משהושלמה המחברת הראשונה של הרישומים מן המקלט, הפצירה הוועדה במור להמשיך ולתעד את רשמיו והזמינה אצלו רישומים גדולים – רובם הוצגו בגלריה הלאומית בלונדון בזמן המלחמה. האוסף שבמוזיאון ישראל כולל 4 מרישומי המקלט, והם מייצגים את מגוון הסגנונות שבאמצעותם ביטא האמן את החוויה האנושית במלחמת העולם השנייה.

ב"תמונה מן המקלט" מ־1941 (עמ' 73), קירות התחנה המעוגלים יוצרים מעין מערה המובילה אל מנהרה חשוכה ומתעקלת. מור מסרטט את הַמְתאַרים ואת הלבנים הכבדות בפירוט מדוקדק, אך את הדמויות האנושיות העומדות, יושבות או שוכבות הוא מתאר כמסה של צלליות מטושטשות ועלומות־שם. וכך מוצג המקלט בו־זמנית כמקום רווי מתח, תוסס ונרגש, אך גם כמקום מפלט שקט ופסיווי. את המנהרה הקודרת דמוית־הרחם צבע מור בגוונים מונוכרומטיים של אפור וכחול־אפרפר. כברישומים רבים מן המקלט, גם כאן שילב 5 אמצעים – עיפרון, גיר, גיר שמנוני, עט ודיו ומגוון – ויצר בהם עושר נפלא ועומק דק ומרומז אף שהקומפוזיציות מונוכרומטיות.

בתארו את קירות המנהרה ואת הדמויות השתמש מור בגיר שמנוני לבן אשר דחה את שכבת המגוון הכהה שנמשחה מעליו. הלובן הבוקע מן הרקע השחור מדגיש את החושך ואת הקדרות.

ב"רישום מן המקלט" וב"תמונה מן המקלט: שתי דמויות שוכבות" (עמ' 72), שניהם מ־1941, התמקד מור בסבילות השקטה של האנשים שנרדמו בתחנת הרכבת התחתית. הדמויות מתוארות באקצרה, כך שלצופה נדמה כאילו הוא מביט בהן מלמעלה למטה, ונוצרת אשליית עומק. האמן חושף רק את זרועותיהם ואת פרצופיהם המטושטשים, אך בניגוד לדמויות השוכבות בנינוחות, התנוחה כאן רחוקה מלהיות שלווה ורוגעת והמתח מוחשי ביותר. ב"רישום מן המקלט"[3] הנטורליסטי מציב האמן זו מול זו נשים דומות, אולם אחת מהן שקטה ונינוחה בעוד חזות רעותה (משמאל) מיוסרת. היא מקרבת אגרופים קפוצים אל עיניה כאילו מנסה להרחיק סיוט. ב"שתי דמויות שוכבות" מביע מור את סערת הרגשות

---

3   "רישום מן המקלט" מבוסס על "מתווה לרישום מן המקלט" (HMF 1667) מתוך מחברת המקלט השנייה.

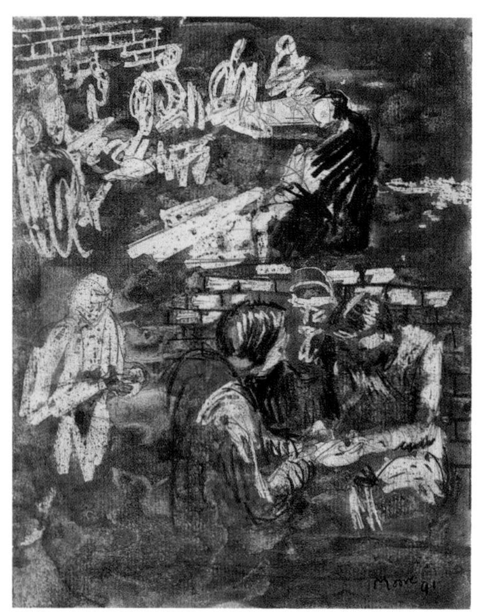

נשים וילדים בבניין שהופצץ, 1940–41 | 10
Women and Children in Bombed-out Building, 1940–41

והמהומה העוברת על נושא הציור באמצעות עיוות הפנים ותנוחת האיברים. הרישום גדוש עמימות. על אף שכותרתו מבהירה שברישום מתוארות שתי דמויות, שרידים קלושים מרמזים על כך שדמות נוספת מופיעה בין השתיים. או שמא מבוקע ראשה של הדמות משמאל בצורה משונה? גם המגדר של אותה דמות איננו ברור. מור מתאר בעיקר נשים, ואילו כאן יש רמיזה לדמות גברית בלסת המרובעת והשלדית ובמצח הגבוה. גולגולת הדמות האדמונית דמוית־הביצה נראית מנותקת מגופה ותווי פניה השדופים נראים בלתי אנושיים. גם הקונפיגורציה של הגופים האנושיים מעוותת, וקשה לקבוע למי שייכת הזרוע המושטת לרוחב השמיכה.

הפרצופים חסרי השקט ב"רישום מן המקלט" וב"שתי דמויות שוכבות" מהווים ניגוד לניחוחת ולסבילות של הגוף הישֵן. בשתי העבודות מגונן מור על האנשים בכך שהוא עוטף אותם בשמיכות ובמעילים, ויוצר בעבורם מעין מקלט בתוך מקלט. ב"שתי דמויות שוכבות", שמיכה הצבועה במגוון אפור ובעפרונות שעווה בצבעי כחול וירוק מתרוממת מעל הדמויות כנחשול ים והקווים הדקים בעט ובדיו מדגישים את החיבור בין הדמויות. ב"רישום מן המקלט", השמיכה והמעילים, שאינם אלא מחסה ארעי, צבועים בעפרונות שומניים בגוונים של זהב וכחול. קיפולי האריג ושכבותיו המעוצבים בקפידה הפכו לימים לרכיב חשוב בפסליו של מור, הבולט למשל ב"אישה עטויה יושבת" (עמ' 55).

הדמויות הכרוכות זו בזו עוברות תהליך הפוך לזה שברישומי ה"טרנספורמציה" של מור משנות ה־30: שם מאניש האמן עצמים טבעיים כגון חלוקי נחל וצדפים, ואילו הדמויות הנמות מהמקלט, ה"קבורות" תחת שמיכות כבדות, הופכות למעין גלמים חסרי תנועה.

אף שמור התמקד במקלטים התת־קרקעיים, הוא תיאר גם בניינים בלונדון המופצצת. "נשים וילדים שהופצץ" מהשנים 1940-41 הוא דוגמה לרישומים כאלה ממחברתו השלישית.[4] התיעוד החפוז הבולט ברישום זה מצביע על הסגנון הדוקומנטרי של צייר המלחמה. כמו במתווים לפסליו המוקדמים, אף כאן מתגודדים 4 אשכולות של דמויות כמו בהֶדבֵק (קולאז') על רקע מבנה לבנים הרוס ויוצרים קהילה זעירה.

לאחר כמה חודשי הפצצות בלתי פוסקות, ציידה הממשלה את המקלטים במיטות שדה ובמזנוני אוכל, וכך תפסה ההתארגנות הממוסדת את מקום

הספונטניות.[5] בהיעדר "הדרמה והמוזרות" הכאוטיים ששררו קודם ברציפים הצפופים, איבד מור עניין בנושא, והוא חדל מלרשום סצנות מן המקלט. יש משום אירוניה בעובדה שמור, אף שרותק למהומה שבמנהרות, הדגיש דווקא את חוסר התנועה שבשינה והסב את תשומת־הלב לדו־קיום של נוחות וזוועה, חיים ומוות בעתות מלחמה.

---

4   מחברת פרומה מן השנים 1940-41 כונתה "מחברת המקלט השלישית". ראה Garroud, *Moore: Complete Drawings*, vol. 3, p 70
5   *Moore: Shelter Sketchbook*, p. 12

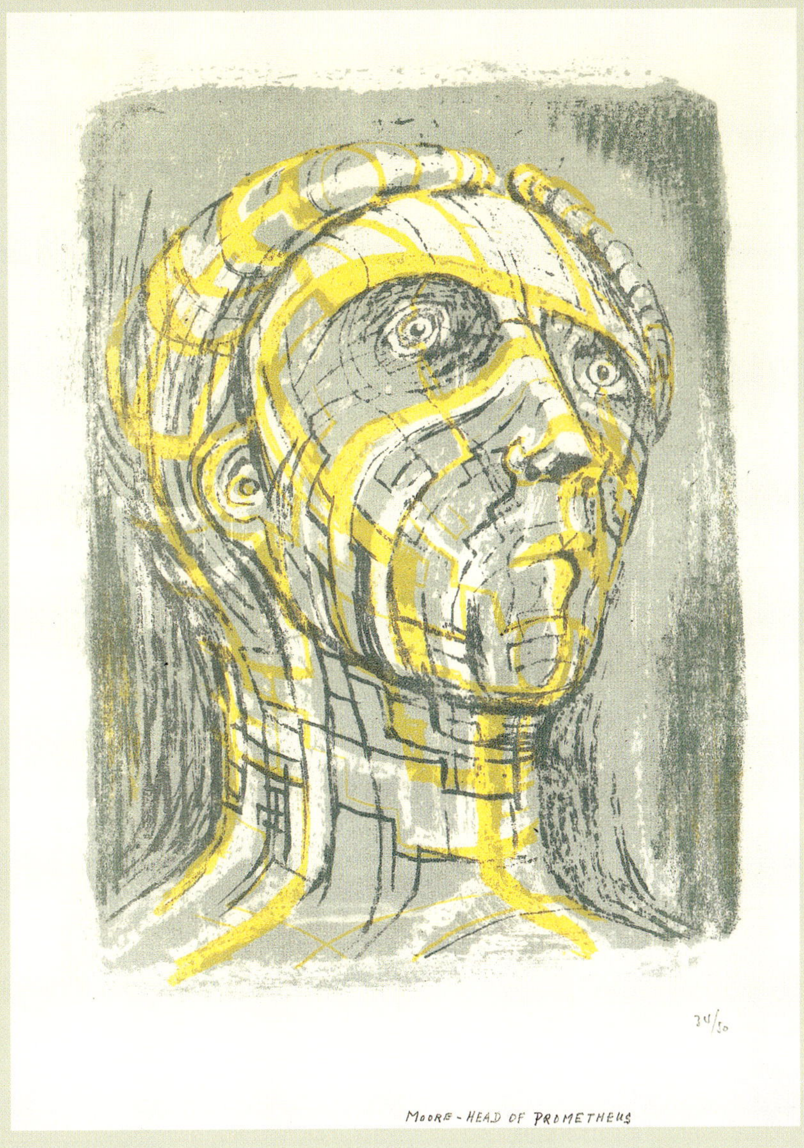

ראשו של פרומתאוס, 1950
Head of Prometheus, 1950

42

על צפייה ודמיון: האלבומים של מור

אוסף מוזיאון ישראל כולל יצירות מתוך 3 אלבומי הדפסים חשובים של הנרי מור: *פרומתאוס מ־1950, אלבום גולגולת הפיל מהשנים 70-1969 ושירי אודן/הדפסי־אבן מאת מור מ־1973*. הדפסי־אבן ותצריבים אלה משקפים את רגישותו ורב־גוניותו של מור כאמן גרפי וכן את הבנתו המעמיקה את הטכניקות ואת החומרים. כפסל רב־ניסיון העוסק בפרספקטיווה תלת־ממדית הוא העלה את הדו־ממדיות של דף הנייר למדרגה גבוהה יותר, המחיה ומעשירה את ההדפסים והרישומים שלו.

פרומתאוס

מור יצר 15 הדפסי־אבן לתרגום של אנדרה ז'יד ליצירתו של גתה *פרומתאוס*. זה היה הספר הראשון שכלל יצירות גרפיות של האמן, והוא התבסס על מחברת רישומים לפרומתאוס מהשנים 1949-50. ההדפס הראשון בספר, "ראשו של פרומתאוס" (מימין), מציג את האל היווני האמיץ כדמות מלנכולית בעלת עיניים עצובות ושפתיים קפוצות, כולה אומרת פגיעות. וכך כתב אריך נוימן על פרומתאוס של מור:

> הדמות הנשית אצל מור, חיובית ושלילית כאחד, מביעה תמיד עוצמה הרת־גורל, ואילו הדמות הגברית נשארת תקועה בשלב ה"התבגרות" ולעולם אינה משתחררת מכבלי האם הגדולה. כאן אנו חושבים על... "ראשו של פרומתאוס" הצעיר, שאיש אינו יכול לייחס לו יכולת לברוא את המין האנושי או לגנוב את סוד האש מן האלים.[1]

עם זה, מור מציג את הראש מלמטה, ובכך מעניק לדמות מבע של ניצחון הרואי. מבטו של פרומתאוס מופנה קדימה וכלפי מעלה, כאיש חזון. קווי הנפח שבציור מעניקים לדמות תלת־ממדיות כשל פסל וניתן לראות בהם מעין שריון, המגן, ובעת ובעונה אחת גם חדיר. חורי עיניו של פרומתאוס מתוארים בלבן ואפור דהויים, ואולם במקומות אחרים בדיוקן הוסיף האמן גוונים של צהוב לאפור הבהיר ולכחול האפרפר, ובכך העניק ליצירה עומק ועוצמה. באיור אחר מ־1950, "פנדורה והפסלים הכלואים", רוב הדמויות הביומורפיות חנוטות במעטפת דמוית־לֶבֶנים. זוהי מעין רמיזה מקדימה ליצירתו המאוחרת יותר של האמן, "צורה פנימית/חיצונית זקופה" (עמ' 36)[2] המצביעה על הזדהותו עם פרומתאוס, שהיה ה"פֶּסָל" הראשון של האדם.

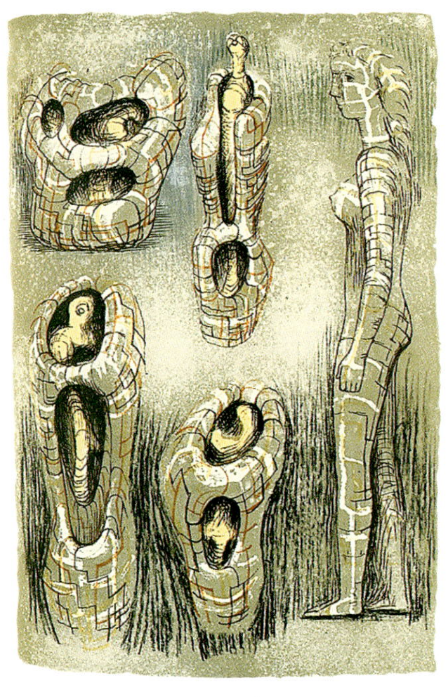

פנדורה והפסלים הכלואים, 1950
Pandora and the Imprisoned Statues, 1950

43

---

1   Neumann, *Archetypal World*, pp. 117–19. ברצוני להודות לשי דייוויס על עזרתו בהכנת מאמר זה.

2   Cramer et al., *Moore: Graphic Work*, vol. 1, p. 6

אלבום גולגולת הפיל

אלבום מרהיב זה שאב את השראתו מגולגולת של פיל
שהעניקו למור ידידיו ג'וליֵט וסר ג'וליאן האקסלי בשובם
מספארי בקנִיה בראשית שנות ה־60. מור אחסן את
הגולגולת בסטודיו שלו, והיא הפכה לאחר זמן – כהגדרתו
של מור – "לחפץ המרשים ביותר ב'ספרייה' שלי של
צורות טבעיות".[3] רעייתו של האמן, אירינה, הציעה לו
ליצור סדרת תצריבים של הגולגולת למדפיס ז'ראלד
קרמר מז'נווה. מור החל לחרוט על לוח הנחושת ומהר
מאוד נכבש במורכבותה של הגולגולת.

> כשאֲני מקרב את הגולגולת אליי ומצייר פרטים מסוימים
> בה, אני מוצא ניגודים כה רבים בצורתה ובעיצובה שאני
> יכול להעלות בדמיוני מדבריות ענק ונופים הרריים, או
> מערות גדולות במדרונות ההרים, אולי אף יצירות
> ארכיטקטוניות אדירות, עמודים או מחילות, כך שסדרת
> תצריבים זו איננה אלא שילוב של צפייה ודמיון.[4]

מור חקר את מתארי הגולגולת, את מחילותיה ונקיקיה,
ב־32 תצריבים. מגוון הצורות האינסופי בהם מדגיש את
התפעמותו מחללים ריקים, מן המסתורין ומגוף האדם.
כדי להשיג את האפקט של ממד העומק והמורכבות
שמוצאים ביצירות אלה, שינה מור את הזווית ואת הלחץ
שהפעיל על מחט החריטה ואת משך השרייתה של לוחית
התצריב בתמיסה חומצית. כתוצאה מכך נוצרו אפקטים
עדינים: "קו שנחרט במשך כדקה יכול להראות דקות
עדינה ושבירה ביותר, כפי שעשיתי כשניסיתי להמחיש
את דקיקותה של העצם, שעוביה אינו עולה על עוביו
של דף נייר".[5] האמן אף השתעשע בהבדלים בין הכהה
לבהיר כדי לתאר את הצללים והעומק הן בגולגולת עצמה
הן ברקע ובחללים השליליים.

בלוח 1 הרקע המתואר בקווים כלליים מדגיש את
הגולגולת בכל נועזותה. קווי הרקע אינם מסיטים ממנה
את תשומת־הלב אלא נותנים בה כוח. החזיתיות מציבה
את הצופה פנים אל פנים מול גולגולת הפיל. נדמה
שהניבים העצומים גולשים אל מחוץ לדף, ובכך מדגישים
את העצם העדינה שבצד שמאל. חורי העיניים מזכירים
מעט את אחת הדמויות השוכבות של מור. בלוח 8,
הרקע הכהה והמקווקקו מעמיק ומעצים את צורת העצם.
קווי הנפח הידועים של מור יוצרים גם כאן תלת־ממדיות,
והחלל השלילי המעוגל במרכז יכול להתפרש כדמות
אישה. על־פי טקסט נלווה שכתב מור, הוא ראה בלוח
זרוע של דמות שוכבת. כתיבת הטקסט היתה למור חוויה
חדשה, ובתבונתו הוא אפשר ליצירה בעיקר לדבר בעד
עצמה.

שירי אודן / הדפסי־אבן מאת מור

האלבום האחרון של מור הוא סדרת הדפסי־אבן המאיירים
את שירי המשורר ו"ה אודן; מור הכיר את אודן, שהיה
אף הוא יליד יורקשיר, מאז שנות ה־30 והתלהב
מהפרויקט המשותף. היה לו קשה להציב את פסליו מול
שיריו של אודן, אך בסופו של דבר החליט מור "לא לאייר,
כי אם להשלים או אולי אף לעמת"[6] את עבודותיו עם
יצירות עמיתו. מור גילה, כי עבודה על ספר "שונה לחלוטין
מרישומם או הדפס בודד ואף מעבודה על סדרה שאינה
מלווה בטקסט. צריך תמיד לחשוב על הספר כעל מכלול
ועל הדימויים בו לא כעומדים לעצמם, אלא על היחס
בינם לבין הכתוב ועל אופן ה'קריאה' בהם ברצף".[7]

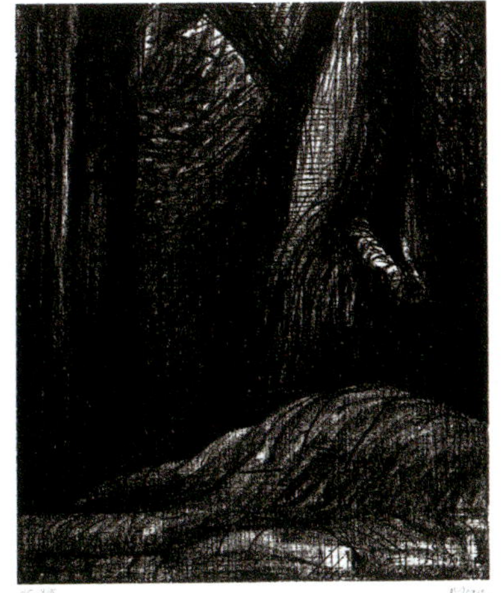

מערה, 1973
Cavern, 1973 | 76

"מערה" משקף את ייחודו של האלבום. הגוונים הכהים
של הדפס־האבן מזכירים את רישומי הפחם של ז'ורז'
סרה ומעוררים תחושה של מסתורין. על רקע עצים
מוסתרים למחצה, מבצבצים חמוקי פלג גופה התחתון
של דמות שוכבת, אף שהדימוי כולו עמום. מור יוצר
תמונת אווירה המזמינה אסוציאציות רבות ומגוונות. מור
הפסל איננו רואה בנייר מגבלה. להפך, הוא רותם את
פני השטח של הנייר, את המכחול, את העיפרון, ואת
מחט החריטה לבניית אשליה אפופת מסתורין.

---

3   מור, טקסט נלווה לאלבום *גולגולת הפיל*, לוח 23.
4   Cramer et al., *Moore: Graphic Work*, vol. 1, p. 5
5   Gilmour, *Graphics*, p. 13
6   Cramer et al., *Moore: Graphic Work*, vol. 1, p. 6
7   שם.

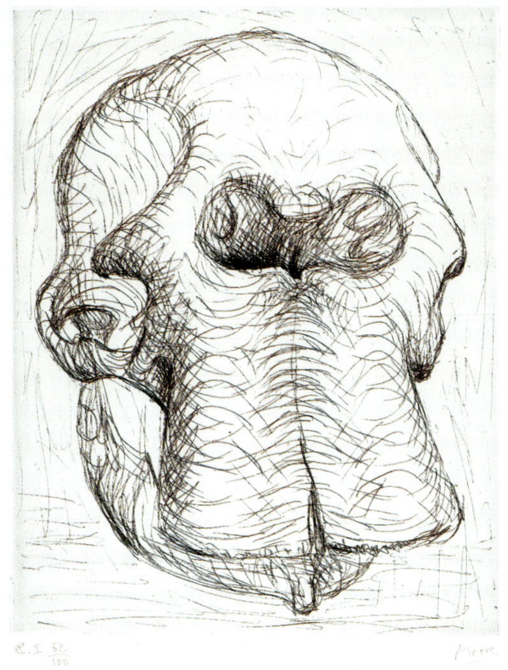

גולגולת פיל, לוח 1, 1969
Elephant Skull, Plate I, 1969 | **74**

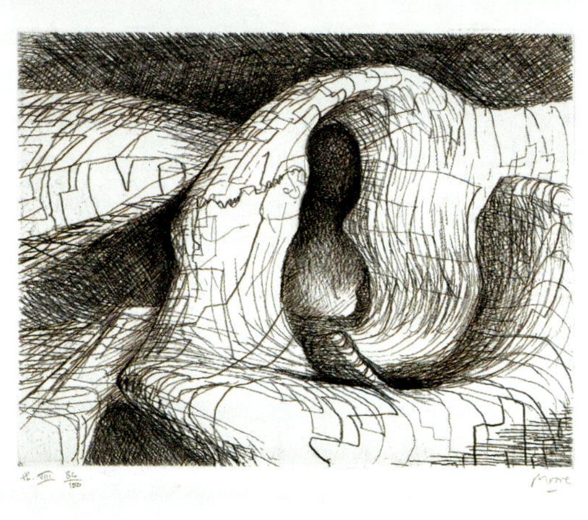

גולגולת פיל, לוח 8, 1969
Elephant Skull, Plate VIII, 1969 | **75**

רשימת העבודות באוסף*

1 **דמות אישה,** 1928
גבס, 12 x 6 x 4.5 ס"מ
מתנת הילדה גולדברג, ירושלים,
לזכר בעלה, הילרי גולדברג
B77.299; LH 130a
(עמ' 53 משמאל)

2 **עירומה יושבת,** 1929
עט ודיו, מכחול ודיו, גיר, מגוון,
430 x 320 מ"מ
מתנת שרלוט ברגמן, ירושלים,
לידידי מוזיאון ישראל בארה"ב
B85.525; HMF 704
(עמ' 54)

3 **שישה־עשר ראשים,** 1932 בקירוב
עיפרון, גיר, מגוון, עט ודיו,
381 x 318 מ"מ
HMF 935
(עמ' 66)

4 **מתווי ראשים,** 1932
גיר שמנוני, גיר, מגוון, עט ודיו,
413 x 330 מ"מ
HMF 934
(עמ' 64)

5 **חמש־עשרה דמויות עומדות,** 1933
עט ודיו, מגוון, 368 x 273 מ"מ
מתנת שרלוט ברגמן, ירושלים,
לידידי מוזיאון ישראל בארה"ב
B92.1103; HMF 1018

6 **חמש דמויות יושבות,** 1934
עט ודיו, מגוון, 380 x 275 מ"מ
מתנת שרלוט ברגמן, ירושלים,
לידידי מוזיאון ישראל בארה"ב
B85.526; HMF 1080
(עמ' 51)

7 **דמות,** 1935 בקירוב
ברונזה (מהדורה של 8(?)),
14.6 x 5.5 x 4.5 ס"מ
LH 157
(עמ' 58 מימין)

8 **דמות בהסבה,** 1938
ברונזה (מהדורה של 9),
8.3 x 12.7 x 7 ס"מ
LH 184
(עמ' 40 מימין)

9 **דמות שוכבת,** 1938
ברונזה מלוטשת (מהדורה של 9),
6.7 x 12.7 x 4 ס"מ
LH 193
(עמ' 43 למעלה)

10 **נשים וילדים בבניין שהופצץ,** 1940–41
עיפרון, גיר שעווה שמנוני, מגוון,
216 x 172 מ"מ
HMF 1753
(עמ' 75)

11 **ארבע דמויות,** 1941
גיר שעווה שמנוני, גיר, צבעי־מים, מגוון,
עט ודיו, 279 x 387 מ"מ
HMF 1548
(עמ' 60)

12 **תמונה מן המקלט,** 1941
עיפרון, גיר שעווה שמנוני,
גיר שמנוני צבעוני, גיר, מגוון, עט ודיו,
159 x 203 מ"מ
HMF 1803
(עמ' 73)

13 **רישום מן המקלט,** 1941
עיפרון, גיר שעווה שמנוני, מגוון, עט ודיו,
336 x 563 מ"מ
מתנת לורד ולוידי קלארק, סלטווד,
באמצעות הידידים הבריטים של
המוזיאונים לאמנות בישראל
B70.294; HMF 1850
(עמ' 74)

14 **תמונה מן המקלט: שתי דמויות שוכבות,** 1941
עיפרון, גיר שעווה שמנוני, מגוון,
330 x 305 מ"מ
HMF 1841
(עמ' 72)

15 **דמויות עטויות שוכבות,** 1942
עיפרון, גיר שעווה שמנוני, פחם, צבעי־מים
(מגוון), עט ודיו, 225 x 117 מ"מ
HMF 2042
(עמ' 49)

16 **מדונה וילד,** 1943
עיפרון, גיר שעווה שמנוני, גיר שמנוני
צבעוני, צבעי־מים (מגוון), עט ודיו,
250 x 175 מ"מ
מתנת שרלוט ברגמן, ירושלים,
לידידי מוזיאון ישראל בארה"ב
B85.523; HMF 2179
(עמ' 26 משמאל)

17 **מתווים למדונה וילד,** 1943
עיפרון, גיר שעווה שמנוני, גיר שמנוני
צבעוני, צבעי־מים (מגוון), עט ודיו,
175 x 159 מ"מ
HMF 2178
(עמ' 26 מימין)

18 **מתווים למדונה וילד,** 1943
עיפרון, גיר שעווה שמנוני, גיר שמנוני
צבעוני, צבעי־מים, עט ודיו,
215 x 175 מ"מ
מתנת שרלוט ברגמן, ירושלים,
לידידי מוזיאון ישראל בארה"ב
B85.524; HMF 2182
(עמ' 27 משמאל)

19 **מתווים למדונה וילד,** 1943
עיפרון, גיר שעווה שמנוני, גיר שמנוני
צבעוני, צבעי־מים (מגוון), עט ודיו,
200 x 165 מ"מ
מתנת שרלוט ברגמן, ירושלים,
לידידי מוזיאון ישראל בארה"ב
B85.522; HMF 2180
(עמ' 27 מימין)

20 **מתווים למדונה וילד,** 1943
עיפרון, גיר שעווה שמנוני, גיר שמנוני
צבעוני, צבעי־מים, עט ודיו, 222 x 172 מ"מ
HMF 2177
(עמ' 30 מימין)

---

* העבודות מושאלות מעיזבון שרלוט ברגמן,
אלא אם צוין אחרת

21 מתווים לאם וילד, 1943
עיפרון, גיר שעווה שמנוני,
צבעי־מים (מגוון), עט ודיו,
216 x 168 מ"מ
HMF 2186

22 שתי נשים וילדים, 1943–44
עיפרון, גיר שעווה שמנוני, גיר שמנוני
צבעוני, צבעי־מים (מגוון),
229 x 191 מ"מ
HMF 2201
(עמ' 28)

23 קבוצות משפחה ומדונה וילד,
1943–44 בקירוב
עיפרון, גיר שעווה שמנוני, גיר שמנוני
צבעוני, צבעי־מים (מגוון), עט ודיו,
229 x 165 מ"מ
HMF 2202
(עמ' 30 משמאל)

24 קבוצת משפחה, 1943–44 בקירוב
עיפרון, גיר שעווה שמנוני, גיר שמנוני
צבעוני, צבעי־מים (מגוון), עט ודיו,
165 x 178 מ"מ
HMF 2329
(עמ' 31 משמאל)

25 מתווים לקבוצות משפחה,
1943–44 בקירוב
עיפרון, גיר שעווה שמנוני, גיר שמנוני
צבעוני, צבעי־מים (מגוון), עט ודיו,
210 x 164 מ"מ
מתנת שרלוט ברגמן, ירושלים,
לידידי מוזיאון ישראל בארה"ב
HMF 2222 ;B80.2891

26 דמות שוכבת, 1945
ברונזה (מהדורה של 7),
7.2 x 19.8 x 6.4 ס"מ
LH 256
(עמ' 39)

27 דמות שוכבת (פסל־הכנה לדמות עץ
בוקיצה), 1945
ברונזה (מהדורה של 7),
8.7 x 17 x 7.5 ס"מ
LH 249
(עמ' 42 למעלה)

28 דמות שוכבת, 1945
ברונזה (מהדורה של 7), 8 x 15 x 7 ס"מ
LH 263
(עמ' 42 למטה)

29 דמות שוכבת, 1946–47
ברונזה (מהדורה של 8(?)),
8.2 x 16.8 x 8.5 ס"מ
LH 266
(עמ' 43 למטה)

30 מתווים לבת האמן, 1947 בקירוב
עיפרון, גיר שעווה שמנוני,
גיר שמנוני צבעוני, צבעי־מים (מגוון),
עט ודיו, 288.8 x 241.3 מ"מ
HMF 2399
(עמ' 32)

31 נשים עומדות, 1948
עיפרון, גיר שעווה שמנוני, עט ודיו, גואש,
711 x 546 מ"מ
HMF 2482
(עמ' 56)

32א חמישה מתווים לכיסאות נדנדה,
1949 בקירוב
עיפרון, גיר שמנוני צבעוני, מגוון פחם,
עט ודיו, 289 x 237 מ"מ
מתנת שרלוט ברגמן, ירושלים,
לידידי מוזיאון ישראל בארה"ב
HMF 2433 ;B79.951
(עמ' 37)

32ג צד ב
עיפרון, דיו, גיר שמנוני, צבעי־מים

33 קבוצות משפחה, 1949 בקירוב
עיפרון, גיר שעווה שמנוני, גיר שמנוני
צבעוני, צבעי־מים (מגוון), עט ודיו,
293 x 242 מ"מ
מתנת שרלוט ברגמן, ירושלים,
לידידי מוזיאון ישראל בארה"ב
HMF 2470 ;B92.1101
(עמ' 31 מימין)

34 דמות יושבת, 1949
ברונזה (מהדורה של 7),
24 x 11 x 10.5 ס"מ
LH 272
(עמ' 52 משמאל)

35 דמויות עומדות, יושבות ושוכבות,
1949 בקירוב
עיפרון, גיר שעווה שמנוני, גיר שמנוני
צבעוני, צבעי־מים (מגוון), עט ודיו,
230 x 290 מ"מ
מתנת שרלוט ברגמן, ירושלים,
לידידי מוזיאון ישראל בארה"ב
HMF 2459 ;B79.950
(עמ' 61)

36 קבוצת משפחה, 1950
הדפס־אבן, 43/50, 289 x 238 מ"מ
מתנת סינתיה פולסקי, ניו־יורק,
לידידי מוזיאון ישראל בארה"ב
CGM 12 ;B73.1044

37 מדונה וילד עטופים: יום, 1950
עיפרון, גיר שעווה שמנוני, גיר שמנוני
צבעוני, עט ודיו, גואש, 343 x 242 מ"מ
HMF 27150
(עמ' 16)

38 מדונה וילד עטופים: לילה, 1950
עיפרון, גיר שעווה שמנוני,
צבעי־מים (מגוון), עט ודיו,
342 x 242 מ"מ
HMF 2714
(עמ' 18)

39 שלוש אלות הגורל, 1950
גיר, גיר שמנוני צבעוני, צבעי־מים (מגוון),
גואש, 584 x 762 מ"מ
HMF 2618
(עמ' 23)

40 פסל־הכנה לדמות עומדת, 1950
ברונזה (מהדורה של 7),
26.8 x 6.4 x 4.5 ס"מ
LH 290a
(עמ' 20 משמאל)

41א ראשי קסדה, 1950
גואש, פחם, 292 x 244 מ"מ
מתנת שרלוט ברגמן, ירושלים,
לידידי מוזיאון ישראל בארה"ב
HMF 2641 ;B92.1102
(עמ' 68 מימין)

41ג צד ב
גואש, גיר שמנוני, פסטל
(עמ' 68 משמאל)

42 ראשו של פרומתאוס, 1950
הדפס־אבן, 34/50, 317 x 235 מ"מ
מתוך *פרומתאוס* מאת גתה,
תרגום: אנדרה ז'יד
מתנת לואס הנדלר, קליפורניה,
לידידי מוזיאון ישראל בארה"ב
B95.0844; CGM 22
(עמ' 76)

43 פנדורה והפסלים הכלואים, 1950
הדפס־אבן, 314 x 222 מ"מ
מתוך *פרומתאוס* מאת גתה,
תרגום: אנדרה ז'יד, ספר עם 14
הדפסי־אבן צבעוניים, 41/183,
הוצאת ניסז, פריז, 1951
אוסף ורה וארטורו שווארץ לאמנות
דאדא וסוראליזם במוזיאון ישראל
M00 76/SPE; CGM 31
(עמ' 77)

44א מתווים לפסל, 1950–51
גיר שעווה שמנוני, גיר שמנוני צבעוני,
צבעי־מים (מגוון), עט ודיו,
290 x 235 מ"מ
HMF 2637
(עמ' 34)

44ב צד ב
עיפרון

45א מתווים לפסל, 1950–51
עיפרון, גיר שעווה שמנוני, צבעי־מים
(מגוון), עט ודיו, גואש, 290 x 235 מ"מ
HMF 2638
(עמ' 35)

45ב צד ב
עיפרון, דיו, צבעי־מים
(עמ' 69)

**46 פסל־הכנה לצורה פנימית/חיצונית
זקופה, 1951**
ברונזה (מהדורה של 7),
21.2 x 8.4 x 6 ס"מ
LH 294
(עמ' 36)

47 שתי דמויות יושבות 1, 1951
תצריב, 22/50, 73 x 124 מ"מ
השאלה ארוכת־טווח מקרן פריץ נפתלי
B70.70; CGM 35

48 דמות עומדת מס' 1, 1952
ברונזה (מהדורה של 9),
23.8 x 6 x 5.5 ס"מ
LH 317
(עמ' 62 מימין)

49 דמות עומדת מס' 3, 1952
ברונזה (מהדורה של 9),
20.5 x 4.2 x 3.8 ס"מ
LH 319
(עמ' 62 משמאל)

50 אם וילד, 1952
קו פחם, 328 x 278 מ"מ
מתנת שרלוט ברגמן, ירושלים,
לידידי מוזיאון ישראל בארה"ב
B79.157; HMF 2738
(עמ' 33)

**51 פסל־הכנה לדמות עטויה שוכבת
(אישה שוכבת), 1952**
ברונזה (מהדורה של 10),
19 x 10 x 16 ס"מ
עיזבון לולה לסקר, ניו־יורק,
באמצעות קרן התרבות אמריקה־ישראל
B61.1039; LH 335
(עמ' 40 משמאל)

52 דמות שוכבת מס' 2, 1953
ברונזה (מהדורה של 7),
41 x 96 x 40 ס"מ
מתנת שרלוט ברגמן, ירושלים,
לידידי מוזיאון ישראל בארה"ב
B73.1166; LH 329
(עמ' 41)

53 ראש קטן, 1953
ברונזה (מהדורה של 10),
7 x 4.7 x 5.4 ס"מ
עיזבון לולה לסקר, ניו־יורק,
באמצעות קרן התרבות אמריקה־ישראל
B61.1040; LH 356
(עמ' 65)

54 דמות שוכבת: צורה חיצונית, 1953–54
ברונזה (מהדורה של 6),
105 x 215 x 85 ס"מ
מתנת סלסט וג'ואל סטרלס, שיקגו
B67.791; LH 299
(עמ' 38)

55 תבליט קיר: שלוש צורות, 1955
ברונזה (מהדורה של 12),
18.4 x 32.6 x 3.2 ס"מ
LH 374
(עמ' 70)

56 מוטיב ניצב מס' 7, 1955–56
ברונזה, 332 x 69 ס"מ
מתנת הידידים הבריטים של
המוזיאונים לאמנות בישראל
B69.199; LH 386
(עמ' 63)

**57 אם וילד מס' 1: מושיט יד לתפוח,
1956**
ברונזה, 72 x 45 x 50 ס"מ
מתנת אנדראה ברונפמן
וקפי פלנדרס, מונטראול,
לכבוד הוריהם דוריס וחיים מוריסון
B95.0137; LH 406
(עמ' 24)

58 ילדה יושבת, 1956
ברונזה, 21 x 18.5 x 12 ס"מ
אוסף סם שפיגל
B97.0511; LH 420
(עמ' 53 מימין)

**59 מתווים לפסל על רקע כחול-אפור,
1957**
הדפס־אבן, 38/60, 432 x 349 מ"מ
מתנת נורמן דייויס, סיאטל, וושינגטון,
באמצעות קרן התרבות אמריקה־ישראל
B66.684; CGM 39

60 אישה (טורסו ישוב), 1957–58
ברונזה (מהדורה של 8),
142.2 x 91.4 x 78.7 ס"מ
אוסף סם ואילה זקס
L-B04.002; LH 439
(עמ' 50)

**61 שער פנימי להנרי מור, ראשים,
דמויות ורעיונות**
הוצאת ג'ורג' רייגבו, לונדון וגריניץ', 1958
עיפרון על נייר, 238 x 287 מ"מ
אוסף ורה והנרי מוטק
בהשאלה מתמדת מן
האפוטרופוס הכללי של מדינת ישראל
L-B97.094

62 ראש מיתר, 1958
טרקוטה שרופה וחוט,
7.8 x 5.8 x 2.5 ס"מ
LH 186g
(עמ' 67 מימין)

63 תבליט מס' 1, 1959
ברונזה (מהדורה של 6),
224 x 12.5 x 48 ס"מ
מתנת האמן
LH 450 ;B73.1173
(עמ' 45)

64 פסל־הכנה לאישה יושבת:
צוואר דק, 1960
ברונזה (מהדורה של 11),
26.8 x 12 x 12 ס"מ
LH 471
(עמ' 52 מימין)

65 דמות שוכבת בשלושה חלקים:
פסל־הכנה מס' 1, 1961
ברונזה (מהדורה של 9),
11.4 x 20.4 x 9 ס"מ
LH 499
(עמ' 44 למטה)

66 שבע־עשרה דמויות שוכבות, 1963
הדפס־אבן, 585 x 800 ,40/50 מ"מ
מתוך אלבום בינלאומי, הוצאת פרד
א' פיקרד
רכישה בנדיבות ולטר ביק, אונטריו, קנדה
CGM 46 ;B74.689

67 דגם־הכנה לפסל בשלושה חלקים
מס' 2: קשת, 1964
ברונזה, 91.5 x 91.5 x 53.4 ,6/7 ס"מ
מתנת איזידור מ' כהן, ניו־יורק,
לידידי מוזיאון ישראל בארה"ב
LH 534 ;B73.105
(עמ' 48)

68 מחווה לרודן, 1966
הדפס־אבן, 295 x 235 מ"מ,
מתוך הפורטפוליו "מחווה לרודן", 1967
מתנת פרופ' איונל ז'יאנו, פריז
CGM 59 ;B68.446

69 שמונה דמויות שוכבות בצהוב,
באדום ובכחול, 1966
הדפס־אבן צבעוני, אבחנת האמן,
550 x 375 מ"מ
אוסף ורה והנרי מוטק
בהשאלה מתמדת מן
האפוטרופוס הכללי של מדינת ישראל
CGM 58 ;L-B97.092

70 דמות שחורה יושבת על רקע כתום,
1966
הדפס־אבן צבעוני, אבחנת האמן,
550 x 377 מ"מ
אוסף ורה והנרי מוטק
בהשאלה מתמדת מן
האפוטרופוס הכללי של מדינת ישראל
CGM 80 ;L-B97.091

71 מתווים לפסל: דמויות שוכבות בשניים
ובשלושה חלקים, 1967
תצריב ותחריט יבש, 110/125,
308 x 232 מ"מ
מתוך *30 שנות פעילות לז'ראלד קרמר*,
פורטפוליו עם 15 הדפסים מאת אמנים
שונים, 1967
מתנת ז'ראלד קרמר, ז'נווה
CGM 95 ;B72.1268
(עמ' 44 למעלה)

72 מתווים לפסל ראש וכתפיים, 1967
תצריב, 18/50, מצב ב', 308 x 238 מ"מ
השאלה ארוכת־טווח מקרן פריץ נפתלי
CGM 94 ;B71.70

73 פסל בשלושה חלקים: חוליות,
1968–69
ברונזה, 710 x 355 ס"מ (הבסיס)
מתנת האמן והידידים הבריטים של
המוזיאונים לאמנות בישראל
LH 580 ;B72.1277
(עמ' 46–47)

74 גולגולת פיל, לוח 1, 1969
תצריב, 254 x 200 מ"מ
מתוך אלבום גולגולת הפיל, 32 תצריבים
מאת הנרי מור, הוצאת ז'ראלד קרמר,
ז'נווה, 1970
רכישה בנדיבות פיליפ קלוצניק, שיקגו
CGM 114 ;B72.1256
(עמ' 79 למעלה)

75 גולגולת פיל, לוח 8, 1969
תצריב, 235 x 308 ,84/100 מ"מ
מתוך אלבום גולגולת הפיל, 1970
מתנת אדם מקלר, פסדינה, קליפורניה,
לידידי מוזיאון ישראל בארה"ב
CGM 121 ;B98.0651
(עמ' 79 למטה)

76 מערה, 1973
הדפס־אבן, 321 x 267 מ"מ
מתוך שירי אוזן/הדפסי־אבן מאת מור
מתנת סילביה גד, לונג בראנץ', ניו־ג'רזי,
לידידי מוזיאון ישראל בארה"ב
CGM 248 ;B88.14
(עמ' 80)

77 דמות שוכבת: רעיון לפסל, 1981
עט כדורי, עט לָבד, גיר שעווה שמנוני,
צבעי־מים (מגוון), עיפרון שחור,
140 x 275 מ"מ
מתנת קן מלמד, ניו־יורק,
לידידי מוזיאון ישראל בארה"ב,
לזכרה של שרה ר' בנינגסון
HMF 81 [317] ;B00.1102

78 טורסו אישה, 1984
ברונזה, 17.2 x 5.7 x 6 ,4/9 ס"מ
אוסף ורה וארטורו שוורץ לאמנות דאדא
וסוראליזם במוזיאון ישראל
LH 913 ;B98.0545
(עמ' 58 משמאל)

79 ראש מיתר, 1986
ברונזה וחוט, 2/5,
11.4 x 5 x 5 ס"מ
LH 186g
(עמ' 67 משמאל)

Moore, *Elephant Skull*

Moore, Henry. *Elephant Skull Album: Original Etchings by Henry Moore*. Geneva, 1970.

Moore, *Observer*

——. *Observer*, 30 April 1972. Quoted in Donald Hall, *Henry Moore*, London, 1966.

Moore: *Graphic Work*

Henry Moore: Graphic Work 1972–1974. London, 1974.

Moore: *Shelter Sketchbook*

The British Museum. *Henry Moore: A Shelter Sketchbook*. London, 1988.

Moore: *War and Utility*

Henry Moore: War and Utility. Much Hadham, England, 2001.

Neumann, *Archetypal World*

Neumann, Erich. *The Archetypal World of Henry Moore*. New York, 1959.

Penrose, *Scrap Book*

Penrose, Roland. *Scrap Book 1900–1981*. New York, 1981.

Pevsner, "Thoughts on Moore"

Pevsner, Nikolaus. "Thoughts on Henry Moore." *Burlington* 86 (1945). Quoted in Dorothy Kosinsky, *Henry Moore: Sculpting the 20th Century*, New Haven and London, 2001.

Read, *Moore: Life and Work*

Read, Herbert. *Henry Moore: A Study of His Life and Work*. London, 1965.

Roditi, *Dialogues*

Roditi, Edouard. *Dialogues on Art*. Santa Barbara, 1980.

Rose, *Greek Mythology*

Rose, H. J. *A Handbook of Greek Mythology*. London, 1960.

Russell, *Moore*

Russell, John. *Henry Moore*. New York, 1968.

Schneider, "Mother and Child"

Schneider, Laurie. "The Theme of Mother and Child in the Art of Henry Moore." *PPA* 1 (1985).

Stallabrass, "Mother and Child"

Stallabrass, Julian. "The Mother and Child Theme in the Work of Henry Moore." In *Henry Moore: Mother and Child*. The Henry Moore Foundation, Much Hadham, England, 1992.

Sylvester, *Moore*

Sylvester, David. *Henry Moore*. London, 1968.

Turner, *Dictionary*, s.v. "Henry Moore"

Turner, Jane, ed. *The Dictionary of Art*. New York and London, 1996.

Van Bruggen, *Nauman*

Van Bruggen, Coosje. *Bruce Nauman*. New York, 1988.

Wilkinson, *Drawings*

Wilkinson, Alan. *The Drawings of Henry Moore*. London, 1977.

Wilkinson, *Moore Collection*

Wilkinson, Alan G. *The Moore Collection in the Art Gallery of Ontario*. Art Gallery of Ontario, 1979.

Wilkinson, *Moore Remembered*

——. *Henry Moore Remembered: The Collection at the Art Gallery of Ontario in Toronto*. Ontario, 1987.

Wilkinson, *Writings and Conversations*

Wilkinson, Alan, ed. *Henry Moore: Writings and Conversations*. London, 2002.

Winter, "Iconography"

Winter, Irene J. "The King and the Cup: Iconography of the Royal Presentation Scene on Ur III Seals." *Bibliotheca Mesopotamia* 21 (1986).

Winter, "Royal Images"

——. "Idols of the King: Royal Images as Recipients of Ritual Action in Ancient Mesopotamia." *Journal of Ritual Studies* 6, no. 1 (1992).

References

Catalogue raisonné references have been abbreviated as follows:

קיצורי ההפניות לקטלוגים המקיפים:

CGM   *Henry Moore: Catalogue of Graphic Work*. Edited by Gérald Cramer, Alistair Grant, and David Mitchinson (vols. 1–2) and by Patrick Cramer, Grant, and Mitchinson (vols. 3–4). Geneva: Cramer, 1973, 1976, 1980, 1988.

HMF   *Henry Moore: Complete Drawings*. Edited by Ann Garrould. 6 vols. London: Henry Moore Foundation/Lund Humphries, 1996, 1998, 2001, 2003, 1994, 2003.

LH   *Henry Moore: Complete Sculpture*. Edited by David Sylvester (vol. 1) and Alan Bowness (vols. 2–6). London: Lund Humphries, 1988, 1985, 1986, 1991, 1994, 1999.

Auden Poems — Auden Poems, Moore Lithographs. London, 1974.

Berthoud, *Life of Moore* — Berthoud, Roger. The Life of Henry Moore. London and Boston, 1987.

Caro, "Master Sculptor" — Caro, Anthony. "The Master Sculptor." Observer, 27 November 1960. Quoted in Dorothy Kosinsky, Henry Moore: Sculpting the 20th Century, New Haven and London, 2001.

Clark, *Moore Drawings* — Clark, Kenneth. Henry Moore Drawings. London, 1974.

Cohen, "Who's Afraid of Moore?" — Cohen, David. "Who's Afraid of Henry Moore?" Quoted in Dorothy Kosinsky, Henry Moore: Sculpting the 20th Century, New Haven and London, 2001.

Compton, *Moore* — Compton, Susan. Henry Moore. London, 1988.

Cramer et al., *Moore: Graphic Work*, vol. 1 — Cramer, Gerald, Alistair Grant, and David Mitchinson, eds. Henry Moore: Catalogue of Graphic Work. Vol. 1, 1931–72. Geneva, 1973.

Deri, "Vicissitudes," in Schneider, "Mother and Child" — Deri, S. "Vicissitudes of Symbolization and Creativity." In Between Reality and Fantasy, edited by S. Grolnick and L. Barkin. New York, 1978. Quoted in

Laurie Schneider — "The Theme of Mother and Child in the Art of Henry Moore," PPA 1 (1985).

Feldman Bennet, "Drawings" — Feldman Bennet, Anita. "The Drawings of Henry Moore." In An Introduction to Henry Moore. Hertfordshire, England, 2002.

Fuller, "Mother-spaces" — Fuller, Peter. "Mother-spaces, Psychology and Henry Moore." The Age Monthly Review 5, no. 4 (August 1985).

Garlake, *New Art, New World* — Garlake, Margaret. New Art, New World: British Art in Postwar Society. New Haven and London, 1998.

Garrould, "Moore: Drawings" — Garrould, Ann. "Henry Moore: Drawings." In Mother and Child: The Art of Henry Moore, edited by Gail Gelburd. Hempstead, New York, 1987.

Garrould, *Moore: Complete Drawings*, vol. 3 — ——, ed. Henry Moore: Complete Drawings. Vol. 3, 1940–49. London, 2001.

Gilmour, *Graphics* — Gilmour, Pat. Henry Moore: Graphics in the Making. London, 1975.

Grohmann, *Art of Moore* — Grohmann, Will. The Art of Henry Moore. New York, 1960.

Hedgecoe, *Moore* — Hedgecoe, John, ed. Henry Moore. London, 1968.

James, *Moore on Sculpture* — James, Philip, ed. Henry Moore on Sculpture. London, 1966.

Melville, *Moore: Sculpture and Drawings* — Melville, Robert. Henry Moore: Sculpture and Drawings 1921–1969. New York, 1970.

Meshorer, *Archaeology* — Meshorer, Yaakov. Highlights of Archaeology. Jerusalem, 1984.

Moore, "Spatial and Pictorial Drawing" — Moore, Henry. "Spatial and Pictorial Drawing." Sec. 2 of Auden Poems, Moore Lithographs. London, 1974.